Great Books
for Cooks

Great Books for Cooks

Susan Wyler
and
Michael McLaughlin

Ballantine Books
New York

A Ballantine Book
Published by The Ballantine Publishing Group

www.randomhouse.com/BB/

LIBRARY OF CONGRESS CATALOGING-IN-PUBLICATION DATA
Wyler, Susan.
    Great books for cooks / by Susan Wyler and Michael McLaughlin.— 1st ed.
        p.   cm.
    ISBN 0-345-42149-3 (trade)
    1. Cookery—Bibliography.   I. McLaughlin, Michael.   II. Title.
Z5776.G2W95 1999
[TX714]
016.6415 — dc21   98-46798

Text design by Holly Johnson

Cover design by Jennifer Blanc
Cover illustration by Alison Seifer

Manufactured in the United States of America

First Edition: May 1999

10   9   8   7   6   5   4   3   2   1

Contents

CONTENTS

Acknowledgments

The authors would like to thank Chuck Kehoe and the staff of Cookworks, in Santa Fe, New Mexico, as well as the individual publishers for graciously providing many of the review copies used in preparing this book.

Introduction

So many books, so little time. If this project taught us one thing, it's that a lifetime is not long enough to enjoy all the marvelous books that have been written about food and cooking. Cookbook writers are a special breed. They write from a vantage point that encourages hedonism. It is a profession built upon sharing: sharing pleasure, sharing knowledge, sharing experience, and sharing love.

While it may seem as though there's nothing new under the sun, it is astonishing how writers discover new material, reinvent the traditional, synthesize disparate elements, and express it all in their own way. Every good writer has his or her story to tell. This is just as true with recipe books as it is with fiction.

Every reader uses a book differently. For many food lovers, a cookbook is a volume to curl up with at night, to read cover to cover as someone else might a mystery. Others plan their daily meals or menus for entertaining from cookbooks; they take the books right into the kitchen with them. Still others scan cookbooks for ideas—in the text, recipes, and photos—to inspire them, to keep them up on the latest ingredients and trends, and to energize their own cooking.

At present about 800 cookbooks are published each year. That's down from 1,000 two years ago, a number that held more or less steady for over fifteen years. It's hard work, even for a culinary professional, to wade through so much printed material. To judge at a glance good from bad, innovative from trite, usable from inherently flawed. They used to say if you gleaned one or two good recipes from a cookbook, you'd gotten your money's worth. With the price of books these days, we think the reader deserves more than that.

We like to think of this book as an advance force, plowing through the reams and reams of paper so that you don't have to. A good guide should show the way, and we hope we've done just that.

People often look at the shelves and shelves of recipe books in a store or in their own library and say, "Do we really need to publish another cookbook . . . ever?" The answer is a resounding yes! While new books in no way devalue what has gone before, styles in food change rapidly. New ingredients appear on supermarket shelves all the time. They filter down from chefs, gourmet food magazines, and foreign travels. Who knew what a sun-dried tomato was twenty years ago? And just try finding a recipe that used it as an ingredient in a cookbook before 1985. Waves of immigrants bring their food with them, setting up restaurants and building a familiarity with their cuisine. Different countries become tourist destinations. Nutritional standards change.

Sadly, it is the nature of the publishing business at present to remainder—that is, to remove from the warehouse and put out of print—any book that is not selling briskly. Consequently, many classics that have lasting value, longtime favorites of ours, are out of print. We wrote a number of them up anyway. There are ways to obtain out-of-print books, and at the end of this chapter we share our resources with you.

There are several ways to use this book. One is as a buying guide. *Great Books for Cooks* was designed to make the first cut for you. You can search for a particular type of book—baking, ethnic cooking, a good read—or you can browse through to see what's new. The latest trends show up in the most recent titles.

Many people who love cookbooks may enjoy just reading this book straight through. We've tried to bring the reviewed titles to life, to explain why each book made the cut, to give you an insider's view of some of the authors, and to add related information wherever possible. We also tried to bring forth the particular strengths of each cookbook. In some cases it might be the food; in others, the clarity of the instructions or the explanations of basic principles. Occasionally it's the writing.

Most of the reviews include a sampling of recipe titles from the cookbook. We included these for several reasons. Most of all, we wanted to engage the reader, to illustrate some of the "sexiness" of a food book, to entice with the good things to eat that each title had to offer. The way an author names a dish also tells you something about his or her sensibilities. For example, Coq au Vin would indicate a traditional recipe, while Chicken Braised in Wine with Wild Mushrooms might imply that the writer has updated the classic, perhaps simplified it, perhaps lightened it, perhaps added ingredients that weren't in the original.

Naming a recipe is an art that some practice better than others. Be sure to read a recipe through before you decide whether to make a dish. There may be ingredients you didn't expect—which could either delight or dismay you. Particularly these days, a dish may be more or less than what it sounds like from its title.

To help you find a particular cookbook or search for a subject, this book been divided into chapters, with subsections where appropriate within the chapters. For example, international and ethnic books make up one chapter. Within it, books are grouped by country—France, Italy, Mexico—or if there are only a few per country, within larger geographical divisions—Southeast Asian, for example, which covers Thai, Vietnamese, and Indonesian cookbooks. Within any section, all books are listed alphabetically by author. Order is no indication of preference.

Sometimes there is an overlap of criteria. Rick Bayless, for instance, is a professional chef who owns his own restaurants; so he could well be included in the chapter on cookbooks from chefs, restaurants, and TV personalities. But Bayless's books, written with his wife, Deann, are all about Mexican home cooking, and his mission is to educate American cooks about authentic Mexican food. So we put his two major titles in the Mexican section. All this is by way of saying, if you can't find a book in one place, look in another. Hopefully, it will be somewhere.

We both feel that the most important characteristic of a cookbook is that it be trustworthy. That is, at the very least you should be able to make a recipe with confidence and be assured it will turn out more or less as described in the text. Unfortunately, this is not always the case. Some fine-looking books were discarded if we saw a single recipe that we just knew wouldn't work. One beautiful vegetable book detailed an authentic Roman recipe for fried artichokes. After one initial bath in hot oil, the artichokes are dipped in cold water and then thrown back into the oil. It may be authentic, but it's not a tip we're going to pass along to our readers. The ensuing splatter could well be dangerous. So the book was left out.

Whose taste can you trust? In any listing, preferences are subjective. Between us we've written two dozen cookbooks, and one of us has been editing recipes for over twenty-five years. But as we said in the beginning, so many books, so little time. To help in our choice, we turned to the two most established cookbook awards in the business: the IACP (International Association of Culinary Professionals) Julia Child Awards and the James Beard Awards.

Panels for both these organizations, comprised of top culinary professionals, require sample recipe testing before a book is nominated. We felt confident including any of these nominees and award winners.

As we said earlier, one of the biggest problems with cookbook publishing today is the speed with which books are put out of print. On the happier side, some individuals are making a concerted effort to publish new editions of classic works they believe belong in print. Since this state can shift from moment to moment without warning, you may occasionally find the publishing information at the top of each title is no longer valid. Don't give up if you find a book that's listed has gone out of print. These days there are terrific resources for locating books that are not on conventional bookstore shelves.

If you love cookbooks and you like to collect, there are a couple of bookstores you should be aware of, devoted entirely to culinary titles. Kitchen Arts and Letters, owned by the extremely knowledgeable Nach Waxman, is one of a cook's best resources. While the large chains fill their shelves almost exclusively with the new and the popular—which is not necessarily the good—Waxman picks with discrimination, choosing titles for their quality and lasting value. Besides new books, he stocks many hard-to-find and out-of-print titles. If you are looking for a cookbook that's not in the store, he will search for it at no extra charge. (Kitchen Arts and Letters, 1435 Lexington Ave., New York, NY 10128. Phone: 212-876-5550; fax: 212-876-3584)

On the West Coast, Ellen Rose's The Cook's Library is devoted entirely to culinary books. Here every member of the staff is a cookbook groupie, and they are constantly cooking and testing from the different titles that come in. They are familiar with all the top authors and can steer you toward the best books for your particular needs. (The Cook's Library, 8373 West Third Street, Los Angeles, CA 90048. Phone: 323-655-3141; fax: 213-655-9530)

If you prefer cut-rate shopping, Jessica's Biscuit, a

cookbook-only catalog and mail-order firm, is a good way to go. The catalog is issued six times a year. It's packed with discounted books, some currently in print, others recently out of print. If you're looking for a book that's not in the catalog, be sure to call; they'll be happy to try and find it for you. With a sense of mission, this same firm under the name Biscuit Books is bringing back into print some culinary classics that they don't want to see disappear, including a couple of major Elizabeth David titles. (Jessica's Biscuit, Box 301, Newtonville, MA 02460. Phone: 800-878-4264; fax: 617-244-3376)

Anyone with a computer and an Internet connection has a great cookbook-finding source on the Internet: www.bibliofind.com is the best and the least expensive source for elusive titles. Their web page is a great place to come together with other cookbook collectors, and they frequently hold Internet "auctions," which afford a place where you can sell as well as buy.

Other Internet sources for cookbooks are, of course, www.amazon.com and Barnes & Noble on the Web— www.barnesandnoble.com. These sites sell practically every cookbook in print, often at a substantially reduced price. They also offer to look for out-of-print and hard-to-find titles, but they'll be more expensive here than at Bibliofind.

Of course, country auctions, garage sales, and used-book stores provide great opportunities to pick up cookbook treasures. And the process is more than half the fun. Antique stores that don't specialize in books are terrific sources for hidden bargains. Shelves of used-book stores occasionally hold treasures that are either overlooked or not popular in that neighborhood. You often come upon copies of the excellent Time-Life International series in these places.

Whether your interest in cookbooks is utilitarian or, as with us, an abiding passion, we hope *Great Books for Cooks* will serve you well. It was a labor of love and a chance to share favorite titles, which feel like old friends. A cookbook, whether just read for pleasure or put to the test in the kitchen, maintains a lasting value long after it is put down. It affects directly the way we cook and eat. We were happy for the opportunity to celebrate so much good food and so many fine writers.

Great Books
for Cooks

General Interest Cookbooks

General / Reference Cookbooks

Anderson, Jean, and Elaine Hanna. *The New Doubleday Cookbook.* **Hardcover: 965 pages with charts and technical drawings, over 4,500 recipes. Doubleday, 1985.**

Every household needs at least one basic cookbook as a foundation for its collection. It should be a resource that can reference how to cook almost anything, a place to look up culinary information (such as the temperature of the soft-ball stage of a sugar syrup), and a source for the latest nutritional information. It should offer boilerplate recipes for things such as fruit pies as well as an assortment of accessible, relatively easy-to-prepare recipes that bring new cooks in touch with food trends. In our opinion, this award-winner is the one to choose. Aside from extremely reliable facts and failproof recipes from prolific and dependable cookbook author Anderson (who was food editor of the *Ladies' Home Journal* for almost twenty years) and food editor and dietitian Hanna, the book boasts calorie, cholesterol, and sodium counts for almost all the dishes. It is American based but international in scope, and its traditional bent is lightened by an easy familiarity with contemporary ingredients like jicama and tomatillos. To make the volume even more helpful to use, descriptions of ingredients, how to do most anything in the kitchen, and troubleshooting tips abound.

Anderson, Pam. *The Perfect Recipe*. Hardcover: 372 pages with technical drawings, 150 recipes. Houghton Mifflin, 1998.

As the executive editor of *Cook's Illustrated* magazine, Anderson has over the past few years come to specialize in a particular kind of culinary investigation: Given the desire for some quintessential dish or other—prime rib, pancakes, cheesecake—what is the absolute best way to prepare said dish? Tireless at this (some recipes have been tested seventy-five different ways), she maintains an unflagging good humor. Now, many of those investigations have been gathered in one volume, and while the suspicion exists that she occasionally spends a lot of time reinventing the wheel (rice, pinto beans, and Grape-nuts all proved less successful as meatloaf binders than did good old bread crumbs), most of her insights are invaluable.

CONSIDER: Beef Noodle Soup; Simple Stir-Fry; The Best Macaroni and Cheese; Buttermilk Fried Chicken with Pan Gravy; Simple Chicken Pot Pie; Better Burgers; Oven-Roasted Turkey with Giblet Pan Sauce; Perfect Prime Rib; Strawberry Shortcake; An Even Better Apple Pie; Just-

Right Rolled Cookies; and A Fudgy, Chewy, Cakey Brownie.

Child, Julia. *The Way to Cook.* **Hardcover: 511 pages with over 600 color photographs of both finished food and how-to techniques, more than 800 recipes. Alfred A. Knopf, 1989.**

Feel intimidated in the kitchen? This is the book to inspire confidence. Nothing is taken for granted. For example, the most masterful cooking teacher of our time illustrates not only how to bone and serve a trout-shaped fish, but how to eat it. How to trim and truss a chicken as well as how to roast it and how to carve it. Master recipes are followed by variations and more complex uses of the basic preparation. Simple techniques are clearly explained as well as illustrated in photos. Child was TV's beloved French Chef for years, but here she wears her American hat, with recipes that encompass French cooking but extend to traditional and contemporary American dishes—many of them dramatically simple.

Child's typical humor—"Don't Murder the Yeast and Other Random Notes," for example—and her detailed directions lead you through the recipes while holding your hand. If you want to learn how to cook, this is the place. Even ten years out, this book remains a standard.

CONSIDER: Santa Barbara Fish Stew; Country Buttermilk Rye Bread; Whole Salmon Braised in Wine; Deviled Chicken; Cranberry Chutney; Roast Prime Ribs of Beef; Granny's Ham and Potato Gratin for a Crowd; Puree of Parsnips Mellowed with Cream; Flaming Apple Crepes; Holiday Roulade.

Claiborne, Craig. *The New York Times Cook Book,* revised edition. Hardcover: 799 pages, 1,500 recipes. HarperCollins, 1990.

In the updating of this classic, which took into account the recent revolution in the food scene, about 40 percent of the original 1962 edition was replaced. As with the way of things, some critics felt not enough modernizing had been done, while others thought too many alterations had been made. The result, now that hindsight softens the picture, is that this large and reliable cooking resource remains a desirable addition to any basic cookbook shelf. Written with the editorial restraint of the *Times* itself, this can't be called a personal work, and Claiborne rarely inserts himself into the picture. The point with this kind of book is not the author, after all, but the recipes, and they remain impeccably clear, well-balanced, and nonrevolutionary.

CONSIDER: Old House Chiles Rellenos; Tuna Carpaccio with Lime Mayonnaise; Cream of Carrot Soup; Kung Pao Chicken; Baked Red Snapper with Shrimp Stuffing; Steak au Poivre; Fettuccine Alfredo; Banana–Sour Cream Pie; One-Bowl Chocolate Cake; Scotch Shortbread; Brandy Snaps; and Peach Melba.

Conran, Caroline, Terence Conran, and Simon Hopkinson. *The Essential Cook Book.* Hardcover: 432 pages with color photographs, 450 recipes. Stewart, Tabori, and Chang, 1997.

Written (or at least overseen) by British style magnate Sir Terence Conran and his wife, Caroline, this work is an updated and revised version of one originally published in

1980. Even for those who own dozens (maybe hundreds) of cookbooks, the desire for the one book that includes it all is hard to suppress. This one makes that attempt, and on many fronts succeeds. Ingredients, equipment, and recipes are the three main sections, all heavily illustrated with photographs that seem a mixture of the old edition and the new. The seafood section, with handy technique photos, is as thorough as many books devoted to the subject, but elsewhere the coverage seems excessive: What can one learn by comparing photos of salted and unsalted butter? Along the margins of the recipes run cross-references to needed information elsewhere in the book—a brilliant touch. The recipes are mostly clean and classic and have been Americanized by the food writer Rick Rodgers.

CONSIDER: Sausage and Beer Gumbo; Mussels with Coconut Milk and Chiles; Sautéed Duck Breasts with Gingered Pears; Jamaican Baked Bananas; and Crème Brûlée.

Corriher, Shirley O. *Cookwise: The Hows and Whys of Successful Cooking*. Hardcover: 524 pages with color photographs and many helpful diagrams and charts and information, over 230 recipes. William Morrow, 1997.

A must-have for the serious cook! For years, cooking teacher and food scientist Corriher has been a generous secret resource for many professional cooks. In this book she shares her extensive knowledge with home cooks. All technical aspects of cooking, from how to form an emulsion—i.e., how to make mayonnaise thicken—to how baking powder makes cakes rise—are clearly explained in a friendly, entertaining fashion. Each recipe illustrates some technique or process. Truly helpful tips and notes are scattered throughout the book. Extensive charts list information like the burning temperatures of different oils and the gluten content of different flours. Corriher teaches how to make perfect flaky pastry, how to make strawberries their brightest red; best of all, she covers how to cook with confidence, because you understand what's going on.

CONSIDER: Lemon Burst Shrimp with Caviar; Poached Pears with Walnut–Blue Cheese Rounds; Seven-Bone Steak Gumbo; Chocolate Soufflé with White Chocolate Chunks; Bourbon Pecan Pie; Honey-Walnut Sticky Buns; and Raspberry and Cream Cake.

Fobel, Jim. *Jim Fobel's Big Flavors*. Paperback: 404 pages, 400 recipes. Clarkson Potter, 1995.

This is a personal book about the author's love of "taste-intensive" food, and yet it is so technically well founded and so well written that it was voted best general cookbook by the Beard Foundation. Not content to just lavish a lot of chiles or other extraneous seasonings on a dish to develop those intense flavors, he also takes into account texture and aroma. Crucial ingredients are listed in the Big Flavor Pantry, and sidebars throughout the book explain tastemakers like olive oil, mustard, chiles, herbs, and spices, or give bonus recipes and variations. This is a generously overstuffed work, exactly what one would expect from a man who cooks with such gusto.

CONSIDER: Mesquite-Grilled Stuffed Jalapeños; Fragrant Vietnamese Chicken Noodle Soup; Pesto Lasagna;

Deep-Dish Spinach Pie; Scalloped Potatoes with Ham and Cheese; Browned and Braised Belgian Endive with Lime Butter; Crunchy-Spicy Fried Chicken; Yangchow Meaty Fried Rice; Mango Macadamia Muffins; Georgia Peach Freeze; Berry-Berry Shortcake; Strawberry-Chocolate Cream Pie; and Blueberry-Cassis Cobbler.

Kamman, Madeleine. *The New Making of a Cook: The Art, Techniques, and Science of Good Cooking*. Hardcover: 1,228 pages, black-and-white line drawings, over 400 recipes. William Morrow, 1997.

Fiercely passionate about what she does and dedicated to passing along as much knowledge as is humanly possible, Kamman has educated thousands of today's culinary professionals. At the 1998 James Beard Awards, this blockbuster walked away with all the top honors: best general cookbook, best cookbook of the year.

The first *Making of a Cook* was published in 1971. Then Kamman was one of the early visionaries, teaching Americans how they could transform their native ingredients using classical French cooking techniques. Not a woman to remain mired in the past, she honed the techniques and skills essential to good cooking and then took them a step further. She was an early exponent of reduction sauces and lighter, more flavorful cooking, which is reflected in this volume in the many flavored oils and essences.

With its comprehensive glossary, illustrative line drawings, informative and encouraging copy, and "state-of-the art" Kamman recipes, this book is like an advanced degree in cooking bound into a single volume. It also tells you everything you need to know about equipment, technique, ingredients, recipes, nutrition, and the art of cooking. A must-have for every serious cook.

CONSIDER: Chilean Sea Bass Steaks on Black Bean Salsa; Shoulder of Lamb Braised in Zinfandel; Mango-Apricot Chutney; Timbale of Carrots with Chervil Oil Vinaigrette; Sauternes and Roquefort Bavarian Cream with Baked Figs; Cappuccino and Walnut Crunch Pudding; Amaretto Soufflé.

Lewis, Edna. *In Pursuit of Flavor*. Hardcover: 323 pages, 200 recipes. Alfred A. Knopf, 1988.

Lewis, descended from slaves, grew up on a Virginia farm and has worked in New York as a restaurant chef, caterer, and cooking teacher. Graceful and quiet, she seems genuinely surprised that anyone would be interested in her style of cookery, one that blends down-home wisdom with touches of big-city style, always in pursuit of flavor. Much in this book comes from her childhood memories of good things to eat, but Lewis also gives us more "evolved" fare, including a rabbit pâté, red snapper served with a dollop of trendy black olive mayonnaise, and a sauté of mixed wild mushrooms. Slices of country ham are topped with poached eggs and served with glazed apples and grits; beef tenderloin is napped with classic sauce béarnaise. Uptown or down, she always has a sense of respect for seasons, ingredients, and preparations that bring out the best in the food.

CONSIDER: Roast Chicken with Stuffing; Deviled Crab; Long-Cooked Green Beans; Vidalia Onion Pickles;

Crispy Corn Sticks; Coconut Layer Cake with Lemon Filling; and Raspberry Pie.

Lukins, Sheila. *Sheila Lukins' All Around the World Cookbook.* **Hardcover and paperback: 591 pages with beer and wine information by Barbara Ensrud, 450 recipes. Workman, 1994.**

Lukins visited thirty-three countries in two years, immersing herself in the local cuisines before returning to New York to put her unique spin on a nearly overwhelming number of food ideas. Like an overstuffed and slightly disorganized scrapbook of history's longest summer vacation, the results are mixed. Making no claims for authenticity, Lukins distills each cuisine to a "palette" of essential flavors, then applies her improvisatory skills to produce something usually delicious, occasionally odd. No explanation is made for the use of the fruit-studded Italian holiday bread panettone in what is billed as "Mexican" bread pudding. What is not in doubt is her enthusiasm for what must have been an exhausting quest to taste it all.

CONSIDER: Swedish Pancakes with Cherry Compote; Sunday Farmhouse Roast Pork; Homestyle Jamaican Chicken; and Rum Raisin Ice Cream.

Morgan, Pamela, and Michael McLaughlin. *Pamela Morgan's Flavors.* **Hardcover: 239 pages with color photographs, 190 recipes. Viking, 1998.**

Morgan and McLaughlin met while working at the famed Silver Palate gourmet shop in the early 1980s. He went on to write cookbooks full-time while she founded

Flavors, a popular Manhattan carryout shop and catering business. Born in Texas and trained in Provence, Morgan likes big bold flavors and applies spices, herbs, and garlic with a generous but thoughtful hand. The stylish food in this book is geared for the home cook, with easy, downscale dishes mixed with more celebratory fare suitable for entertaining. Sidebars give ingredient information, serving tips, and food history, and the eclectic recipes, which span the globe, are often quite low in fat. (Others, say the authors, "exist for the sheer pleasure of eating.")

CONSIDER: Baja Beach Clams Steamed in Beer; BBQ Chicken Breast Sandwiches with Mustardy Slaw; Crisp Unfried Chicken; Thai Red Seafood Curry; Whiskey-Glazed Scotch Shortbreads; and Blushing Pear Granita.

Pepin, Jacques. *La Technique*. Paperback: over 150 recipes with 1,500 step-by-step black-and-white photographs. Times Books, 1978.

Pepin, Jacques. *La Méthode*. Paperback: 390 pages, 141 recipes with step-by-step black-and-white photographs and 15 pages of color. Times Books, 1979.

These two books are covered together because they are companion volumes, both subtitled *An Illustrated Guide to the Fundamental Techniques of Cooking*. Together they comprise an entire cooking course, made completely accessible by the photos of Pepin preparing the dishes himself. A handsome wunderkind, Pepin, who was chef to three French presidents before he arrived in this country, holds advanced degrees from Columbia University in philosophy and French literature. He is also an accomplished artist and produced these books himself. While they are utilitarian rather than ornamental, the two titles are as appropriate for the advanced cook as they are for beginners. You couldn't find a better, or simpler, Apple Tart than the one in *La Technique*. Pepin illustrates how to dice, mince, truss a chicken, make a perfect omelet, whip up Crèpes Suzettes, fold egg whites into a soufflé. Advanced cooks will enjoy the elaborate decorations, tricks for boning different birds and meats, ways of working with puff pastry, and fine recipes (many ahead of their time) for such specialties as Home-Smoked Salmon and Jambon en Gelée.

There is very little that is dated about these works. Happily, both were recently inducted into the James Beard Hall of Fame. We hope that confers upon them a certain degree of immortality. Look for the hardcover version in used-book stores and on the Internet.

Rombauer, Irma S., and Marion Rombauer and Ethan Becker. *Joy of Cooking*. Hardcover: 1,136 pages with black-and-white illustrations, over 1,800 recipes. Scribner, 1997.

While many cookbooks these days claim to be the bible, this one really is: old and new testaments combined. This first revision of the classic American cookbook in more than twenty years is half traditional, half heretical. Rather than possessing a single focus, this edition reflects the vision of about seventy apostles. It is new American cooking we see here, multicultural to a fault. While the baking and dessert chapters feel familiar and tempting, others are spare. The only listings for salmon, for example—at present the country's most popular fish—besides plain grilled or broiled salmon steaks, include Teriyaki Grilled Salmon, which calls for mirin and sake, and Broiled Salmon with Tomatoes, Basil, and Mint.

More important, the facts contained in this chunky volume are staggering. Anything you want to know about ingredients and technique are covered in depth. And the names associated with the book read like a who's who of the food world. It's a great reference. But for those old boilerplate recipes, we're glad we kept our 1975 edition, whose marvelous chapters on jellies and preserves and pickles and relishes were dropped this time round. The two editions combined would make the best American basic we can imagine.

Rosso, Julee, and Sheila Lukins, with Michael McLaughlin. *The Silver Palate Cookbook*. Hardcover and paperback: 362 pages, 350 recipes, illustrations by Lukins. Workman, 1982.

It's rare for a cookbook to define an era, but this one, based upon the foods of a noted Manhattan catering company, inspired a whole generation of cooks and was recently inducted into the James Beard Cookbook Hall of Fame. French classics and homey American fare alike get transformed by the authors' zeal for then-unfamiliar ingredients (pink peppercorns, wild mushrooms), unusual combinations (bluefish with apples), and creative presentations. Everything from chocolate chip cookies to roast suckling pig gets the Silver Palate treatment, while a wealth of sidebars holds shopping information, entertaining tips, and culinary quotes.

CONSIDER: Chicken Marbella; Cracked Wheat Salad; Salmon Mousse; Chocolate Glazed Pears; Campari-Orange Ice; and Chunky Apple Walnut Cake with Apple Cider Glaze.

Rosso, Julee, and Sheila Lukins. *The New Basics*. Hardcover and paperback: 848 pages, 900 recipes. Workman, 1989.

A massive work, the apparent final collaboration between the two writers famed for *The Silver Palate* series, this bestseller may be *the* cookbook for the nineties, a kind of upscale *Joy of Cooking*, combining technique and ingredient information, entertaining advice, and enough dazzling recipes for virtually everyone to find something in it that he or she craves right now. If much of it is not very basic at all, well, is that really what we turn to Julee and Sheila for? Desserts are particularly strong, and reason enough to head for the kitchen.

CONSIDER: Pasta with Fresh Fennel and Sardines; a brunch pizza topped with hash browns and goat cheese; fresh chanterelle mushrooms braised with dried apricots; Baked Fresh Ham with Applejack Gravy; Triple Chocolate Terrine; Wild Huckleberry Shortcake; and Persimmon Spice Sorbet.

Schmidt, Stephen. *Master Recipes—The Art of Cooking Made Simple*. Hardcover: 941 pages with charts and

technical drawings, 1,000 recipes. Clear Light Publishers, 1998.

This large and useful book, long out of print and somewhat of a legend among cookbook lovers, is again available, thanks to the efforts of one of its editors and a small New Mexico publisher. Subtitled "A Complete Cooking Course" and built around the concept of master recipes and variations, the book is based upon the connections between dishes. Understanding that the egg-based dessert sauce known as crème anglaise can also be churned and frozen to produce vanilla ice cream or sipped uncooked as eggnog empowers the cook in a way that three unrelated recipes, however good, cannot. Once the basic fruit pie is mastered, a chart lists thirteen variations, with sugar, thickener, and spice choices spelled out in detail. Techniques (roasting, deep-frying, stewing) get master recipes, too, and Schmidt serves up advice with a calm and reassuring voice.

CONSIDER: Cheddar and Jalapeño Quiche; Broiler-Grilled Bluefish Teriyaki; Creamed Chicken with Olives and Toasted Almonds; Chinese-Style Spinach Sauté; Crème Brûlée; Chocolate Brownie Cake; Lemon Chiffon Pie; and Macaroons.

Schneider, Elizabeth. *Uncommon Fruits and Vegetables: A Commonsense Guide*. Hardcover: 546 pages, black-and-white illustrations throughout, over 400 recipes. William Morrow, 1998.

Every now and then someone writes a book that is so good and so reliable that it instantly becomes a standard reference in the field. That's what food writer and specialty produce consultant Elizabeth Schneider has done here. In clear and cogent fashion, she explains the names of these less-than-ordinary fruits and vegetables. Schneider describes what these exotics look like, how to buy them, and how to store them; she surveys general uses and details how to prepare them. She even provides nutritional highlights. All this information is followed by recipes, which illustrate the different ways to use an ingredient. For example, under *quince*, you'll find Honey Baked Quince Slices, Chicken Baked with Quince, Stew of Quinces and Lamb with Saffron and Split Peas, Quince Conserve with Vanilla, and Quince Marmalade with Lemon and Ginger. What makes this updated edition so timely is that many of these once-rare fruits and vegetables are being carried in the exotic and tropical produce sections of supermarkets, and many old-fashioned varieties are enjoying a culinary renaissance.

Trotter, Charlie, with Judi Carle and Sari Zernich. *Gourmet Cooking for Dummies*. Paperback: 390 pages with cartoons, charts, and color photographs, 200 recipes. IDG Books, 1997.

Designed for that awkward transitional zone when one's cooking "crosses from 'normal' to 'gourmet,' " this book is not for actual kitchen idiots but for good cooks ready to take the next step. A passionate perfectionist, Trotter, his flights of fancy filtered through the Dummies populist format, was probably the right man for the job. A gourmet is committed to fresh ingredients, contrasting flavors and textures, and taking extra care in preparing and in plating attractively, says Trotter, who defines terms, explains techniques, and describes exotic ingredients with democratic patience while insisting that only fresh herbs will do.

CONSIDER: Grilled Brats on Sourdough Buns with Hot and Spicy Zucchini, Napa Cabbage, and Mustard Relish; Yukon Gold Potato Soup with Braised Leeks; Sautéed Pork Chops with Fig, Raisin, and Thyme Chutney; and Open-Faced Basil-Studded Strawberry and Peach Pie.

Willan, Anne. *Anne Willan's Cook It Right: Achieve Perfection with Every Dish You Cook*. Hardcover: 320 pages with color photographs, 150 recipes. Reader's Digest Books, 1998.

This big, handsome book features something you'll rarely see anywhere else—graphic photographs of failures. In the interest of letting us know what's right, Willan doesn't hesitate to show us something gone wrong. Pale, under-browned roast chicken, soggy steamed rice, and lumpy béchamel sauce show up in living color, alongside their successful counterparts. Sound and simple technical information of all kinds accompanies dishes that many beginners will consider too tough to tackle, despite all the illustrated help. It's nevertheless a book seasoned cooks will want to use.

CONSIDER: Seafood Trio in Beer Batter; Spaghetti with Red Mussel Sauce; Lemon Roast Duck with Olives and Capers; Roast Beef Tenderloin with Coffee Pan Gravy; Spicy Lamb Stew with Almond and Coconut; Broiled Peach and Strawberry Kebabs; Italian Iced Praline Mousse; and Belgian Apple Crepes.

Willan, Anne. *La Varenne Pratique*. Hardcover: 528 pages with 2,500 color photographs, 300 recipes. Crown, 1989.

With heavy emphasis on ingredients and slightly less focus on techniques and tools, this book's strengths lie in the many photographs, which truly do provide a sense of how any given dish looks at crucial moments. Unfortunately, there are organizational problems, probably inevitable in any book purporting to be "complete." Novices may be stymied and even advanced cooks annoyed to find, for example, that the only recipe for risotto appears accompanying the entry on saffron in the herbs and spice chapter, rather than in the grains chapter, while turning up nowhere at all in the index. For browsing, daydreaming, basic recipes, and fundamental culinary information delivered in factoid-like snippets, however, this is a book that will give hours of reading pleasure to many, and nuggets of sound cooking know-how to those persistent enough to unlock its secrets.

Williams, Chuck. *Celebrating the Pleasures of Cooking*. Hardcover: 176 pages with color and black-and-white photographs, 150 recipes. Time-Life, 1997.

For forty years Williams-Sonoma founder Chuck Williams has been at the forefront of American cookery. Part observer of trends, part trendsetter, from his first influential shop in San Francisco in 1958 to a chain of 150 stores and an unstoppable glut of catalogs today, he has helped transform how we cook and what we eat. With this book, Williams looks back decade by decade at the people, cookbooks, and multiple kitchen innovations that have brought us to where we are today. From Elizabeth David and James Beard to Joyce Goldstein and John Sedlar, chefs are quoted, equipment recommended, and recipes given. The latter run heavily to the Francocentric, but then, until recently, so did much of America's serious food.

CONSIDER: Deviled Crab; Blanquette de Veau; Quiche Lorraine; Fettuccine Alfredo; Chicken Breasts with Raspberry Vinegar; Fajitas; Walnut Bread; Caramel Crunch Cake; Tarte Tatin; Petit Pots de Crème au Chocolat; and Frozen Coffee Mousse.

Cooking for Beginners

Corn, Elaine. *Now You're Cooking—Everything a Beginner Needs to Know to Start Cooking Today.* **Hardcover: 320 pages, 120 recipes. Harlow and Ratner, 1994.**

Chatty, funny, and confidence-inspiring, this book is truly written for the utter novice in the kitchen. In the style of a self-help bestseller (with apparent tongue in cheek), Corn sets out the "eight steps to achieving your cooking potential" (#3: Believe You Can Do It; #5: Set the Table Before You Begin), followed by the Eight Immortal Chores (how to mince garlic, clean lettuce, peel potatoes, etc.). Sidebars give tips, variations, and assurance in equal measure. The success of such a book is in how much it assumes people don't know. Solely on the basis of the (admittedly) short paragraph titled "How to Melt Butter," this book is a hit.

CONSIDER: Egg Salad; Macaroni and Real Stringy

Cheese; Boiled Shrimp with Cocktail Sauce; Pasta Primavera; and Chocolate Birthday Cake with Chocolate Frosting.

Cunningham, Marion. *Cooking with Children*. Hardcover: 171 pages with color photographs and cartoon-like technical drawings, 35 recipes. Alfred A. Knopf, 1995.

Who better to teach children to cook than the grandmotherly Cunningham, famed for revising *The Fannie Farmer Cookbook?* Organized into fifteen cooking lessons, on such subjects as vegetable soup, pasta, and shortcake, this book is thoughtfully and sensibly produced and positioned. "Cooking and eating together," says Cunningham, "is a satisfaction that is rapidly disappearing." Working with small groups, she developed these lessons for children seven and up "who really want to cook"—motivated children, in other words. No electrical appliances are used, since the author wants her cooks to stay in contact with the ingredients, and sensible safety recommendations for knives and such are given. Some fare, such as a green salad dressed with vinaigrette or broccoli sautéed with garlic and olive oil, may be too sophisticated for many children, but most of the food is exactly what kids want to eat.

CONSIDER: Knothole Eggs; Pancakes; Baked Potatoes; Macaroni and Cheese; Roast Chicken; Meatloaf; Chewy Oatmeal Raisin Cookies; and Chocolate Birthday Cake.

Kirsch, Abigail, with Susan M. Greenberg. *The Bride and Groom's First Cookbook—Recipes and Menus for Cooking Together in the 90's*. Hardcover: 310 pages, 120 recipes. Doubleday, 1996.

Written by a famed New York caterer and off-premise party planner, this book aims to help newlyweds turn out sophisticated fare to be proud of. Kirsch obviously understands that a new generation of Americans knows about good food from restaurants and certainly wants to make such food part of their lives, but lacks the basic kitchen know-how. Packed with lively recipes, with sound technical points interspersed, the book also has menus, pantry-stocking advice, timetables, and more. A little breathless (rarely have so many exclamation points appeared in one book), this is also a pragmatic work. Two major pieces of advice: "Always wear an apron" and "Register! Register! Register!"

CONSIDER: Apricot-Glazed Chicken Wings; Sweet Potato and Green Apple Soup; Lemon Chicken with Capers; Leg of Lamb with Mustard Crust; Garlicky Mashed Potatoes with Frizzled Onions; Fail-Safe Meatloaf; Double-Dipped Challah French Toast; Whisky-Pecan Pie; and Strawberry Shortcake Cream Puffs.

Miller, Bryan, and Marie Rama. *Cooking for Dummies*. Paperback: 402 pages with charts, technical drawings, and cartoons, 150 recipes. IDG Books, 1996.

Despite the nonculinary look of the book (most of the extensive Dummies series is, after all, not about food, and there's presumably something reassuring about the generic night-school textbook design), this is a good start for the inexperienced cook. Lighthearted and often funny, the book takes its teaching in small bites, often in lists such as "Common Blunders Explained and Fixed" and "The 10 Commandments of Cooking." Sidebars cover such fundamentals as tools, kitchen setup, proper lighting (bravo!), and a lesson on how to measure. Perhaps it is Miller's former job as restaurant critic for *The New York Times*, but the recipes have a little more panache than those in the typical beginning book. It is a little sparse in the dessert department.

CONSIDER: Salsa; Carrot Soup with Dill; Watercress, Endive, and Orange Salad; Sea Scallops Provençal; Sautéed Peppered Filet of Beef; Braised Lamb with White Beans; Garlic Grilled Mushrooms; and Spaghetti with Clam Sauce.

Sax, Richard, with David Ricketts. *Get in There and Cook*. Hardcover: 240 pages with how-to drawings, over 140 recipes. Clarkson Potter, 1997.

One of Richard Sax's most endearing qualities was the generosity with which he shared his extensive culinary knowledge with both his professional colleagues and his students. In this, his last book before his untimely death at the age of forty-six, Sax puts forth everything he believed a beginning cook needs. He also includes a collection of recipes any cook would be happy to have in his or her repertoire.

Sax explains it all: how to shop for, prepare, and serve the dishes. He takes nothing for granted. He explains "How to Read an Ingredient List as Well as the Recipe," describes how to prepare any number of basic ingredients, defines many culinary terms and techniques, and lets you know what every kitchen needs in the way of equipment and gadgets. Sax's self-proclaimed goal in writing this book was to

"take the fear out of cooking." We'd say he not only succeeded in that, he made it a joy.

CONSIDER: Pasta with Marinated Tomatoes and Four
Cheeses; Fresh Salsa with Avocado; Soy and Ginger-Glazed
Salmon; Braised Lamb Shanks with White Beans and Gre-
molata; Warm Apple Crumble Cake; Crisp, Juicy Roast
Chicken; and Beer-Steamed Shrimp with Romesco Sauce.

Waters, Alice, with Bob Carrau and Patricia Curtan.
Fanny at Chez Panisse. **Paperback: 133 pages, 46
recipes. HarperCollins, 1998.**

What an odd creature this book is. Told in the voice of
a character named Fanny whose mother owns a restaurant
(Waters's daughter is indeed named Fanny), it gets filed in
the children's cooking department in most stores, but it
really is more of a commercial for the philosophy of Chez
Panisse than it is a children's book. Still, very sophisticated
kids already interested in food and cooking can take away
some lessons about restaurant life and choosing premium
seasonal ingredients from the text, and others, also sophisticated, may want to try cooking some of the dishes. (But
does anyone actually know children who crave Cucumber
Raita, Garlic Mayonnaise, or Halibut Baked on a Fig Leaf?)
Adults, on the other hand, will be inspired to take their
own cooking and eating more seriously, and, if they have
kids, may decide to take more responsibility for their culinary educations. Waters seems to be working on a trickle-
down theory here, and given the lively color illustrations by
Ann Arnold and the admirable intent, further carping
seems churlish.

CONSIDER: Carrot and Parsley Salad; Quesadillas; Cherry Tomato Pasta; Colored Peppers Pizza; Peach Crisp; and Blackberry Ice Cream.

Wright, Jeni, and Eric Treuille. *Le Cordon Bleu Complete Cooking Techniques*. 351 pages with color photographs, 200 recipes. William Morrow, 1996.

Developed in conjunction with chefs from the famed Le Cordon Bleu Cooking School, this book is packed with clear and attractive photographs illustrating precisely those techniques that give cooks (beginning and otherwise) difficulty. From dispatching and cutting up a lobster to forming and baking brioches to trimming artichokes properly, the information is concise (even compact) but thorough and classically reliable. Though there are recipes, most are fairly simple, even sketchy; true novices may find this a little disconcerting. At least once in each section, though, comes the sort of complex dish (escargot ravioli in an herbed butter sauce, for example) that one expects to learn at a cooking school.

CONSIDER: Creole Bouillabaisse; Szechuan Fish; Coq au Vin; Roast Pheasant with Wine Gravy; Fajitas; Thai Beef Salad; Meatloaf; Chiles Rellenos; Seafood Risotto; Spring Rolls; Hollandaise Sauce; Baked Vanilla Soufflés; Crème Caramel; Apple Strudel; and Raspberry Cheesecake.

Quick Cooking Cookbooks

Carpenter, Hugh, and Teri Sandison. *Quick Cooking with Pacific Flavors.* **Hardcover: 191 pages with color photographs, 110 recipes. Stewart, Tabori, and Chang, 1997.**

This beautiful book is a fairly thoroughly revised version of *Chopstix*, one of Carpenter and Sandison's early works. Taking into account increased availability of Pacific Rim ingredients, the authors have completely replaced about half the original recipes; all are said to be simpler and easier to prepare. This is fusion food that works, despite some hybridizations that just sound silly—Sichuan Veal Meat Loaf, for example. The book has lots of photography (by Sandison), much of it shot on one-of-a-kind ceramics with custom-painted backgrounds.

CONSIDER: Thai Salmon Satay; Chile Shrimp with Basil; Tex-Mex Wontons with New Age Guacamole; Chilled Avocado Soup with Ancho Chile Jam; Chicken Salad with Spicy Peanut Glaze; Smoked Baby Back Ribs with Pacific Flavors Barbecue Sauce; Mango Ice Cream; Orange Ginger Brownies; Caramel Fudge Tart with Crumble Crust; and Warm Chocolate Crème Brûlée.

Gassenheimer, Linda. *Dinner in Minutes—Memorable Meals for Busy Cooks*. **Paperback: 320 pages, 270 recipes. Chapters Publishing, 1995.**

Gassenheimer, author of a popular syndicated newspaper column on quick cooking, comes by her knack of preparing speedy, filling, interesting, affordable, and nutritionally sound from-scratch meals naturally. A working mother of three athletic—and hungry—sons, she daily answers the question "What should I cook?" With more than eighty menus designed to feed four in forty-five minutes or less, this book provides many admirable answers. Organizational advice is followed by a pantry-stocking plan. How-to-shop tips are included, and equipment is recommended. As in Gassenheimer's column, helpful shopping lists are given, and brief nutritional counts are included as well; there are even wine suggestions. A repertoire of quick desserts lets the cook turn these same menus into fare fit for a dinner party.

CONSIDER: Italian Stuffed Shells served with Colorful Greens and Beans Salad; Devil's Chicken and Sautéed Garlic Potatoes followed by Watercress and Endive Salad; Whiskey Pork paired with Rosemary Lentils.

Gold, Rozanne. *Little Meals: A Great New Way to Eat and Cook*. **Hardcover: 253 pages, 135 recipes. Villard, 1993.**

Little meals are, according to Gold, single dishes that by virtue of their comfort quotient can be almost as satisfying as a multicourse meal. Such enlarged snacks also fit nicely into our modern lives, which often don't allow time for full-fledged menus and yet are grueling enough to have us desperately needing a treat. This is high-concept food (particularly if your idea of a small meal is a tuna sandwich), and it helps to know that Gold is a restaurant consultant and menu designer used to taking things to the creative max. The author also gives a list of sixty-second, almost-no-work little meal suggestions (apple cider and doughnuts, a good ham sandwich, omelet and a glass of wine) that won't tax anyone's energy.

CONSIDER: Red Bean Hash with Poached Egg and Salsa; Scallops Provençal on Olive Toast; Spicy Thai Chicken with Red Peppers and Peanuts; Succotash Chowder; Barbecued Salmon Brochettes on Pineapple Rice; Ultra-Light Chocolate Cake; Watermelon and Bitter Chocolate Salad; Sticky Pears with Maple Nut Sauce; and Drunken Fruit Compote.

Hamilton, Paula. *The 5 in 10 Cookbook: 5 Ingredients in 10 Minutes or Less*. Hardcover: Wire-O binding, 180 pages, 170 recipes. Hearst Books, 1993.

This is the book for people who *must* put dinner on the table night after night and are not natural cooks. The dishes are almost all made from scratch, but with only five ingredients, not counting salt and pepper. With so few ingredients, there's less to buy and less to do. Not only are many of these recipes great for every day, there are plenty of choices that will allow the culinarily overwhelmed to entertain with aplomb.

CONSIDER: Ravioli in Walnut Cream Sauce; Broiled Tuna with an Orange Sesame Glaze; Pork Medallions with Apricot Glaze; Caribbean Chicken Curry; Avocado and Crabmeat with Watercress Mayonnaise; and Glazed Bananas over Coffee Ice Cream.

Schloss, Andrew, with Ken Bookman. *Fifty Ways to Cook Most Everything: 2,500 Creative Solutions to the Daily Dilemma of What to Cook.* Hardcover: 477 pages, 2,500 recipes. Simon & Schuster, 1992.

Among the 2,500 recipes, tips, and techniques that make up this book, there is surely something for everyone. Grouped into fifty occasionally wacky chapters ("Fifty Ways to Sauce the Spaghetti"; "Fifty Ways to Clean Out the Refrigerator"; "Fifty Berried Treasures"), the recipes are crammed into a necessarily tight format that nevertheless manages to include most of the information needed for happy cooking.

CONSIDER: Stir-Fried Red Curry Chicken; Roasted Eggplant and Feta Pizza; Lamb Chili Mole; Tabbouleh with Lentils; Veal Shanks with Apples and Cream; Turkey Waldorf Salad; Poppyseed Buttermilk Scones; Girl Scout Thin Mint Cookie Ice Cream Log; Grand Marnier White Chocolate Truffles; and Chewy-Gooey Lemon Pecan Bars.

Simmons, Marie. *Fresh and Fast: Inspired Cooking for Every Season and Every Day.* Hardcover: 352 pages with color photographs, 200 recipes. Chapters Publishing, 1996.

For Simmons, a prolific writer, fresh food can be quicker—and is certainly better—than processed. That is the premise of this book as well as of Simmons's nationally syndicated newspaper column of the same name. Most recipes can be prepared in under an hour; a few, labeled "When You Have More Time," take longer but don't necessarily involve active preparation (cold soups must chill, for example). Each recipe comes with an estimate of prep and cooking times, while occasional sidebars give pertinent ingredient information. Aside from the obvious (frozen limas and canned beans, tomatoes, and chicken broth), there simply are no convenience foods in this book. Familiar recipes go even faster, of course, and more than a few of these attractive dishes are worthy of an encore mealtime appearance.

CONSIDER: Chilled Fresh Corn and Buttermilk Chowder with Shrimp; Penne with White Beans, Tomatoes, and Basil; Pork Tenderloin Marinated in Soy and Orange; Rough-Mashed Potatoes with Garlic; Grandpa's Peaches in Red Wine; Fresh Pear Compote; Summer Fruits in Lime Syrup; and Rich Chocolate Pudding.

Urvater, Michele. *Monday to Friday Cookbook*. Paperback: 357 pages, 300 recipes. Workman, 1995.

Urvater, a longtime corporate chef, host of a weekly TVFN cooking show, and a wife and working mother, wrote this thoroughly organized book, she says, for people with complicated lives who don't have time to cook but care about what they eat. Weekends may or may not be for gourmet hobby cookery, but during the workweek, when delivery pizza and speedy Chinese pall, fresh and speedy strategies are required. The Monday to Friday System includes advice on setting up the pantry. Plans for a variety of typical weeks follow, ranging from those with time to stock the refrigerator from a Sunday's worth of cooking, to a last-minute dash through the cupboard to get anything on the table right now. Of the latter, a recipe combining jarred pimientos, canned chickpeas, and tinned smoked oysters over greens can only be considered desperation dining.

CONSIDER: Chunky Peasant Vegetable Soup; New-fangled Macaroni and Cheese; Crackling Fish Fillets; Wine-Braised Pears; Brown Betty Peaches; and Chocolate-Walnut Pudding.

Willan, Anne. *In and Out of the Kitchen—in Fifteen Minutes or Less*. Hardcover: 128 pages with color photographs, 70 recipes. Rizzoli International Publications, 1995.

Among quick-food books, this classy production stands out. Looking not at all like a home-economics manual (it is nicely produced, with spare, elegant photographs throughout) and relying on market-fresh ingredients, not convenience products, the book is thoughtfully organized and packed with interesting, tasty food. Following a get-organized section (the well-stocked pantry is a must, says Willan, noted food writer and founder of the French cooking school La Varenne), five fast chapters spell out dishes—many of them standing alone as a meal—that are stylish enough for company. A traditional recipe format is followed by the recipe at a glance, in which the kitchen work is reduced to a concise timetable. The book concludes with a selection of one-hour menus, showing how the various fifteen-minute recipes can be combined into an artful whole.

CONSIDER: Salmon Carpaccio; Chicken in Chili Coconut Sauce; Sicilian Spaghetti; Quick Ratatouille; Cherry Strudel; and Marmalade Soufflé.

Entertaining

Bailey, Lee. *Lee Bailey's The Way I Cook.* **Hardcover: 531 pages with black-and-white photographs, 1,300 recipes. Clarkson Potter, 1996.**

It is a measure of the durability of Bailey's career that this compendium of recipes collected from all his works is so weighty. Having all his fairly easy, often imaginative, frequently (but not always) southern-influenced fare in one book is a resource his fans should welcome. Some fresh material has been added and some new menus created. It's interesting to watch favorite ideas from individual books (cornbread or chopped salads or poultry sausage) solidify into trends here.

CONSIDER: Creamed Corn and Red Bell Pepper Soup; Crab Gazpacho; Fettuccine with Spicy Tomato and Bacon Sauce; Skillet Potatoes and Eggs with Chili and Ham; Chicken Pancakes with Papaya Salsa; Grilled Teriyaki Snapper; Roast Tenderloin of Pork with Mustard Wine

Sauce; Almond Tart with Apricot Ice Cream; Berry Dumplings; Chocolate Chunk Cookies; and Natchez Lemon Cake.

Bailey, Lee. *Lee Bailey's Portable Food: Great-Tasting Food for Entertaining Away from Home.* **Hardcover: 95 pages with color photographs, 80 recipes. Clarkson Potter, 1996.**

From the beginning, Bailey was a cook who had a knack for picnics and other portable food, so this collection, however slim, seems a natural and will surely please his legions of fans. Here the theme is take-along food of all kinds, not just picnic fare. Much of the food is good cold, but then plenty of it can be reheated as well. Aside from a brief bit of advice on saving and using various containers (a lot of the food is photographed in plastic), there's no science of portability given here, just easy, flavorful Bailey-style recipes that won't tip over and make a mess in the car.

CONSIDER: Smoked Trout Spread; Potato and Red Pepper Soup; Southern-Fried Pecan Chicken; Oriental Beef Salad; Chicken Enchiladas with Andouille Sausage; Little Savory Pies with Ham and Chicken Filling; Fresh Tuna Salad; Onion-Parmesan Bread Sticks; Dried Strawberry-Cherry Muffins; Mashed Pear Cake; and Espresso Chocolate Loaf with Walnuts.

Bailey, Lee. *Lee Bailey's Long Weekends: Recipes for Good Food and Easy Living.* **Hardcover: 175 pages with color photographs, 120 recipes. Clarkson Potter, 1994.**

Spotting a change in vacation planning, Bailey suggests

that we are taking fewer traditional getaways but more long weekends; thus he organizes this book's twenty laid-back menus around the proposition that the best time for entertaining falls between the first cocktail on Friday and the last bite of Sunday supper dessert. (It can be argued, of course, that in Lee Bailey's perfect world, it's always the weekend.) Visiting stylish hosts from South Carolina to Santa Fe to Orcas Island, Washington, he uses their always gorgeous houses as the settings (photographed by Langdon Clay) for his signature parties.

CONSIDER: Gulf Shrimp, Crab, and Oyster Stew; Best Yankee Meatloaf with Oven-Cured Tomatoes; Country-Style Spare Ribs; Blue Corn Enchiladas; Pork Medallions with Prunes and Port; Grilled Chicken Breasts with Dried Cranberry Relish; Sweet Red Pepper Aspic with Celery Root Rémoulade; White Chocolate Chocolate Brownies; Raspberry Tiramisù; Rum Cherry Ice Cream; and Fig Pudding Cake.

Burros, Marian, and Lois Levine. *The New Elegant but Easy Cookbook*. Hardcover: 342 pages, 200 recipes. Simon & Schuster, 1998.

Nearly forty years after it was published, Burros's and Levine's classic book on easy entertaining has been updated. Fifty recipes from the early version remain (though many of them have been modernized), while the authors' reliance on such now-retro products as canned soup and Jell-O has given way to an emphasis on fresh ingredients. Less butter and other fats are used, and popular dishes from the intervening culinary revolution have replaced some dated warhorses. All dishes can still be completed in advance and refrigerated or frozen, helping the reader produce a festive party with relative ease.

CONSIDER: Brie and Pesto; Chinese Chicken Wings; Chafing Dish Meatballs; Cold Poached Salmon with Dill Mayonnaise; Breezy Barbecued Chicken; Grilled Pork with Lime-Ginger Marinade; Shrimp Fra Diavolo; Lemon Angel Trifle; Strawberry "Icebox" Cake; Ginger Crème Brûlée; Baked Peaches and Almonds; and Chocolate Pecan Pie.

Cowie, Colin, with Maureen Clancy. *Effortless Elegance with Colin Cowie.* **Hardcover: 260 pages with color photographs, 200 recipes. HarperStyle, 1996.**

Despite Cowie's reputation as the ultimate party planner for Hollywood's elite, much in this book is surprisingly approachable. Though some of the real events depicted (and some of the menus suggested) are well beyond the capabilities of those of us who must entertain without a staff, others are simple but stylish and can indeed be pulled off with minimal—if not zero—effort. Some of the more fantastic parties, on the other hand, suggest not all of Cowie's clients have gotten the less-is-more message.

CONSIDER: Chèvre Mousse on Artichoke Hearts with Roasted Tomatoes; Salad with Grilled Salmon, Mango, and Crispy Leeks; Asparagus with Chopped Egg in a Walnut Vinaigrette; Yellowtail Tartar in Cucumber Parcels; Pappardelle with Grilled Chicken and Mushrooms in a Light Broth; Blueberry Cobbler with Vanilla Ice Cream; Classic Pear Tart; and Baked Bananas with Rum-Spiked Crème Fraîche.

Kafka, Barbara. *Party Food: Small and Savory.* **Hardcover: 323 pages with color photographs, 450 recipes. William Morrow, 1992.**

With well over four hundred zesty and impeccably tested recipes, plus enough levelheaded party-planning advice to calm the most jittery of hosts, this book is simply the bible of party fare. Kafka's palate is renowned and experienced—if it tastes good and it can be eaten standing up, it's in here. From the simplest of dunks, spreads, dips, and salsas, to caviar, canapés, tartlets, mini-sandwiches, country hams, skewered bits, and pâtés and terrines of all kinds, this book runs the gamut. Loads of seductive color photos get the juices flowing and show creative ways to present your party fare.

CONSIDER: Fragrant Mango Salsa; Lacy Cheese Cookies; Sesame Curried Almonds; Miniature Anchovy Basil Cheesecakes; Smoked Fish Mousse; Pigs in Blankets; Grilled Chicken Satés; and mustardy little ham sandwiches on Buttermilk Biscuits.

Maggipinto, Donata. *Real-Life Entertaining—Great Food and Simple Style for Hectic Lives.* **Hardcover: 239 pages with color photographs, 175 recipes. Clarkson Potter, 1998.**

Whether this book achieves its stated goal of helping create memorable affairs with minimal stress remains to be seen. What is clear is that Maggipinto, Food and Entertaining Director for Williams-Sonoma, has great contemporary style and a sure way with food that seems festive enough for company but simple enough to let the cook have as good a time as the guests. This is a menu book, but in the current way of things, food—even good food—is no longer enough. Alongside the recipes for events like Casual Suppers, Big-Deal Meals, and a July Fourth Bring-a-Dish Party, there appear "Style Notes" on forcing bulbs, enjoying tassels, using vintage silverware, and setting an outdoor table. Sometimes soup is served in hollowed-out pumpkins, while eggs are scrambled and then presented spooned back into their shells and topped with caviar. On the other hand, barbecued ribs are eaten with the fingers, and lobster rolls are quite properly served in hotdog buns. One very useful section at the end of the book gives great ideas for embellishing and personalizing take-out food. It's all tasteful, doable, and very pretty.

CONSIDER: Scallop and Corn Chowder; Steamed Clams with Lemongrass-Ginger Broth; Pasta with Zucchini, Basil, and Ricotta; Beef Stroganoff with Chanterelle Mushrooms; Moroccan Chicken Tagine; Shirred Eggs with Asparagus and Country Ham; Old-Fashioned Buttermilk Doughnuts; and Three-Apple Pie with Calvados Whipped Cream.

O'Neill, Molly. *The Pleasure of Your Company: How to Give a Dinner Party Without Losing Your Mind.* Hardcover: 288 pages, 150 recipes. Viking, 1997.

As the dust jacket says, this is "part novel, part cookbook, part self-help, and part social satire." It arose out of O'Neill's observation that modern hosts and hostesses were struggling to reconcile their "Martha Stewart impulses with the reality of the time pressure in their daily lives." Apparently based on a focus group of people frustrated by their inability to entertain, the book uses the stories of five fictionalized characters to pose and solve various dilemmas on the way to becoming successful hosts. These are amusing and may be of some help in encouraging the helpless to cook for a crowd, but it is probably O'Neill's interesting menus and progressive but not difficult recipes that will really do the trick.

CONSIDER: Roasted Tomato Soup with a Savory Froth; Pepper-Chive Popovers; Steamed Spring Vegetables in Warm Leek Vinaigrette; Light Tomato and Seafood Stew with Lemongrass and Jalapeños; Oven-Braised Salmon and Fennel; Mustard and Curry Roast Pork; Blueberry Crumb Cake; Almond Shortbread Rounds; and Fallen Angel Cake with Lemon Curd and Raspberries.

Peck, Carole, with Carolyn Hart Bryant. *The Buffet Book*. Hardcover: 298 pages with color photographs, 175 recipes. Viking, 1997.

This welcome book is from a noted Connecticut caterer and restaurant owner. Filled with buffet-style menus for a variety of occasions from brunches to soup suppers to weddings, this book also includes sound but too-brief advice on setting up and covering tables; assembling or renting serving pieces, china, and flatware; and other bits of wisdom on feeding a crowd. The various parties, typically designed for sixteen to twenty guests, are photographed, apparently as they happened, in some very attractive homes, while the "new-style" food (all in recipes with plenty of do-ahead advice) runs to the kind of near-gimmicky dishes that earn caterers their reputations—and may do the same for you.

CONSIDER: Chilled Cherry Soup; Fresh and Light Crab Cakes; Halibut Topped with Olive Tapenade and Zucchini "Scales"; Seasoned Lamb Stew with Tomatoes and Green Olives; Roasted Pork Loin with Ginger Mustard Rub; Strawberry-Rhubarb Torte; Rose Geranium Cakes with Black Currant Sauce; and "Queen of Hearts" Chocolate Buttermilk Wedding Cake.

Rose, Ellen, and Jessica Strand. *Intimate Gatherings: Great Food for Good Friends*. Hardcover: 132 pages with color photographs, 50 recipes. Chronicle Books, 1998.

After years as operator of one of the country's best cookbook stores, Rose has finally written her own cookbook. Modest but imaginative, and attractively produced, it features twelve menus, three for each season, designed to serve two, four, and six diners respectively. The dishes are mostly classic American fare with French, Italian, or Mediterranean influences, and all sound delicious and look doable. Menu Managers and prep countdowns help with the organizational details, while lots of colorful photographs serve as inspiration and setup guides. A good small book for both entertaining beginners and seasoned hosts.

CONSIDER: Barbecued Mussels in the Shell; Grilled Tuna with Summer Nectarine Salsa; Roasted Corn Salad with Avocado Vinaigrette; Homemade Yogurt Cheese with Marinated Cherries; Braised Roman-Style Artichokes; Lamb Marinated in Lemon and Garlic with Mint Pesto;

Mixed Florentine Bean Salad; and Chocolate Pots de Crème.

Smith, Barbara, with Kathleen Cromwell. *B. Smith's Entertaining and Cooking for Friends*. Hardcover: 176 pages with color photographs, 100 recipes. Artisan, 1995.

Smith, a fashion-model-turned-restaurateur, brings a sense of doable high style to this book of entertaining tips and recipes. Beginning with five themed parties, Smith shares an attractive "relax and enjoy your own party" philosophy. Each begins with a fairly long how-to section, spelling out planning tips and advice on candles, flowers, plates, silver, wines, and so on, followed by the specific recipes in question. At midpoint the book switches gears and becomes a straight recipe collection, with a southern accent.

CONSIDER: Pan-Fried Crab Cakes with Chili Mayonnaise; Gingery Chicken Kabobs with Honey Mustard Sauce; Black-Eyed Pea Soup with Smoked Turkey; Jerk Duckling with Banana Hash; Old-Fashioned Baked Macaroni and Cheese; Cornbread Chicken Pot Pie; Smothered Pork Chops; Profiteroles with Ice Cream, Crème Anglaise, and Chocolate Sauce; Sweet Potato Pie with Praline Pecan Sauce; and Peach Cobbler.

Sorosky, Marlene. *Entertaining on the Run: Easy Menus for Faster Lives*. Hardcover: 312 pages with color photographs, 200 recipes. William Morrow, 1994.

This book supplies twenty-eight complete menus for

entertaining. Ranging from the casual ("Sandwiches for Super Sports"; "On-the-Run Cocktail Party") to the important ("Ceremonial Passover Seder"; "Thanksgiving Feast"), each comes with a do-ahead game plan and an estimate of prep time, as well as sidebar information on optional table decorations, centerpieces, party favors, mood music, and even lighting. Nutritional information is given for each recipe. Ingredients are easy to find, techniques unfussy, and dishes usually light and appealing. Though the themes occasionally cross over into the cute zone (one menu is dubbed "Mucho Feisty Fiesta"), this is a book that will provide as little or as much help as necessary.

CONSIDER: Paella with Grilled Chicken and Shrimp; Pasta with Roasted Garlic Sauce; Red-Spangled Slaw with Dried Cranberries; Light and Lush Lemon Cake; Fresh Summer Fruit in Jack Daniel's Caramel-Mint Sauce; Espresso Fudge Cups; and Lemon-Pineapple Trifle.

Wyler, Susan. *Cooking for a Crowd*. Hardcover: 159 pages with color photographs, 150 recipes. Harmony Books, 1988.

Though long out of print, this work remains one of the few—and one of the best—resources for menus, strategies, and recipes suitable for feeding a crowd; it's well worth hunting for. At the time the book was published, Wyler was an editor at *Food & Wine Magazine* and had access to the culinary leading edge. Fortunately, time has not staled the book's sense of style, and the do-ahead advice and logistical tips remain invaluable. Twenty-two themed parties feeding from ten to fifty fall into categories many will relate to, and the very doable food is just flashy enough to earn kudos without causing a breakdown.

CONSIDER: Grilled Stuffed Grape Leaves; Shrimp, Avocado, and Papaya Salad with Coconut-Lime Dressing; Three-Mushroom Lasagne with Gorgonzola Sauce; Mediterranean Seafood Casserole with Garlic Croutons; Oven-Baked Deviled Chicken; Gratin of Sweet Potatoes Flambéed with Bourbon; Strawberry–Chocolate Chip Bread Pudding; Apricot-Apple Crisp; and Marbled Sour Cream Coffee Cake.

Regional American Cooking

General American Cooking

Anderson, Jean. *The American Century Cookbook: The Most Popular Recipes of the 20th Century.* Hardcover: 547 pages with two-color photographs and illustrations, over 500 recipes. Clarkson Potter, 1997.

If we were to choose one book about mainstream American cooking over the past century to put in a time capsule, this would be it. Chockful of history, food lore, old advertisements, culinary knowledge, and all manner of juicy tidbits, it is wildly entertaining. You'll find almost any traditional American recipe you're looking for here as well as modern dishes that illustrate a point: the advent of the food processor or the microwave, for example, or the introduction of a new ingredient, such as the kiwi fruit. Many of the recipes come from previously published sources, and Anderson's commentary makes a terrific read.

CONSIDER: Mamie Eisenhower's Million-Dollar Fudge; Lindy's New York–Style Cheesecake; Roasted Eggplant

Soup; Barbara Kafka's Fabulous Microwave Risotto and Grilled Beef Fajitas; Marshmallow-Topped Sweet Potato Casserole; Union Square Café's Mashed Sweet Potatoes with Balsamic Vinegar.

Chase, Sarah Leah. *Sarah Leah Chase's Cold-Weather Cooking.* **Paperback: 418 pages, 300 recipes. Workman, 1990.**

From the waning days of summer to the first teasing approach of spring, Chase, author of the summery *Nantucket Open House* (as well as *The Silver Palate Goodtimes Cookbook*), clearly knows what to do when the weather turns cold and the island tourists go home. This is hearty food, though still with fresh touches of the kind to earn the cook kudos. There is a good bit of fruit in the savory dishes and some of the recipes are rich, indeed. Neither of these caveats should bother Silver Palate fans or cold, hungry people. This is real food that takes real kitchen time, not the improvised, no-cook meals of July.

CONSIDER: Shrimp and Orange Potstickers; Lamb and Lentil Soup; Spaghetti with Meatballs; Seafood Potpie; Crown Roast of Pork; Slow-Cooked Beef Stew; Wild Rice and Cider Pilaf; Raised Waffles; Chocolate-Chestnut Cake; Christmas Truffle Tart; Pineapple Upside-Down Cake; and Rhubarb Custard Pie.

James, Michael. *Slow Food: Flavors and Memories of America's Hometowns.* **Hardcover: 338 pages with black-and-white photographs, 100 recipes. Warner Books, 1992.**

The late Michael James was a cooking teacher, restaurant consultant, and coauthor of Simone Beck's *New Menus from Simca's Cuisine*. Here he takes a leisurely journey through the kitchens of some of America's best cooks, who range from Avis DeVoto (a friend of and collaborator with Julia Child) and the Duchess of Windsor to actress and Indian cooking expert Madhur Jaffrey. These profiles are tied together by the thread of good food, cooked in its own time and "worth waiting for." This kind of personal odyssey cookbook rarely gets published these days, so even as a read, this is a treasure.

CONSIDER: Fresh Morels in Cracker Crumbs and Butter; Wedges of Iceberg with White Cheddar Cheese and Chive Dressing; Long Island Lobster Potpie with Corn and Cabernet; Garlic Chicken and Dumplings with Long Gravy; Cold Passion Fruit Soufflé with Passion Fruit and Fresh Mint Sauce; Blackberry Cream Cobbler; and Shenandoah Valley Apple Gingerbread.

Kimball, Christopher. *The Cook's Bible: The Best of American Home Cooking*. Hardcover: 443 pages with technical illustrations, 450 recipes. Little, Brown, 1996.

It says a lot about these times that a book purporting to contain the best of American home cooking can include recipes for both fried chicken and homemade ravioli. Kimball—founder, publisher, and editor of *Cook's Illustrated* magazine—wants this book to be a "marriage of real home cooking with the culinary knowledge and skills necessary to produce honest, from-scratch food, quickly and well." From basic equipment-buying information (which will soon be outdated) to essential techniques, shopping and storage advice, and sound knife skills, the fundamentals as they will appeal to the modern American home cook are here, along with master recipes and many variations.

CONSIDER: Avocado Salsa with Corn and Red Pepper; Chicken Caesar Salad; Pork Stew with Anchovies and Peppers; Braised Salmon Puttanesca; Vermont Baked Beans; No-Knead American Bread; Best Bran Muffins; Creamy Pecan Pie; The Best Oatmeal Cookie; and Rich Chocolate Soufflé.

Lukins, Sheila. *Sheila Lukins's U.S.A. Cookbook.* Hardcover: 605 pages, 600 recipes. Workman, 1997.

In reaction to the exotic fare she sampled while writing her *All Around the World Cookbook*, Lukins stuck closer to home with this work, traveling the food highways and byways of her native land. It's a big, loving, people- and information-packed book (recipe-packed, too), and the food, on occasion at least, is simpler than we've come to expect from this Silver Palate cofounder. From the annual Lima Bean Festival in Cape May, New Jersey, to the Garlic Festival in Gilroy, California, Lukins crisscrossed the land, brought home recipes, and gave them her unique Manhattan culinary spin. Nice essays on ingredients and the people who grow, catch, or harvest them, but way too much fruit where it doesn't belong (grapes in the shrimp rémoulade, etc.).

CONSIDER: Savannah Cocktail Crab Bites; Panhandle Pickled Shrimp; Lancaster Apple Butter; Banana Buttermilk Waffles; Raisin Pumpernickel Bread; Bacon, Lettuce, and Fried Green Tomato Sandwiches; California Shellfish Stew; Brisket BBQ with Goode's Mop; Country Meatloaf with Mushroom Gravy; South Beach Red Snapper; Dixie Banana Pudding; Blueberry Cornmeal Cake; Sweet Cherry Pie; and Blushing Peach Crunch.

Pierce, Charles (editor), and The Settlement Cookbook Company. *The New Settlement Cookbook.* **Hardcover: 814 pages with technical drawings, 1,000 recipes. Simon & Schuster, 1991.**

Beginning as a slim volume published in Milwaukee in 1901, this book was intended to help immigrant girls adapt to American life and was the first to include "ethnic" recipes. This most recent updating, supervised by food writer and editor Pierce, is the most thorough to date. The recipes are a wild mix, but reflect the way Americans eat these days: Pasta Primavera and Chinese Egg Noodles with Spicy Peanut Sauce exist happily (if startlingly) alongside Gefilte Fish and Wiener Schnitzel. There is a lot of solid basic information, with most recipes following modern nutritional guidelines. High-fat "heirloom" dishes from earlier editions have not been much altered.

CONSIDER: Deviled Eggs; Hot German Potato Salad; Oysters Rockefeller; Medallions of Veal in Sorrel Sauce; Mocha Icebox Cake; Peppermint Stick Ice Cream; Cherry Strudel; Matzo Cookies; Classic Jelly Roll; and Peanut Brittle.

Editors of *Saveur* Magazine. *Saveur Cooks Authentic American*. Hardcover: 320 pages with color photographs, 400 recipes. Chronicle Books, 1998.

From its launch, *Saveur* (Sa-VURR) was clearly a risk-taking magazine, abandoning controlled studio photography for more richly atmospheric location shoots, and giving the same seriousness to American ingredients, dishes, and cooks as it did to those from Europe and Asia. Even the unpronounceable name seemed chancy. Several years (and a number of magazine awards) later, however, *Saveur* endures and continues to break the mold. For this book, the editors (chiefly Dorothy Kalins, Coleman Andrews, and Christopher Hersheimer) have collected the magazine's best writing on and recipes for American cooking. With stunning photos, many by Hersheimer, and writing derived from pieces by such contributors as Marion Cunningham, Schuyler Ingle, and Elizabeth Schneider, the book is a stylish and mouthwatering tribute to the United States.

CONSIDER: Lobster and Corn Chowder; Iceberg Wedge with Blue Cheese Dressing; Smoked Trout Hash; Morel Omelettes; Mrs. Garrett's Chicken Pies; Sweet and Sour Pork; Chiles Rellenos; Blueberry Pie; Very Moist Chocolate Layer Cake; and Christmas Cookies.

Schulz, Phillip Stephen. *As American As Apple Pie*. Hardcover: 400 pages, 240 recipes. Wings, 1996.

This book, by Bert Greene's longtime collaborator, has a simple premise: take twenty best-loved American dishes (meatloaves, baked beans, potpies, stews, chocolate cakes, waffles, etc.) and create a dozen different and very creative variations on each theme. The result is a chatty, quote-filled book, packed with familiar food presented in versions that may not be the ones your mom made, but cook from this book a time or two, and you'll be feeling very well taken care of and very well fed indeed.

CONSIDER: Seattle Salmon Chowder; Texas Border-Town Meatloaf; Ultimate Chicken Hash; Honey and Bacon Fried Chicken with Lemon Gravy; Smothered Pot Roast with Sausages and Salami; Mom's Rhubarb-Apple Pie; Old-Fashioned Layer Cake with Fudge Frosting; Omaha Grandmotherly Brownies; and Florida Keys Bread Pudding with Rum Sauce.

Worthington, Diane Rossen. *American Bistro.* **Hardcover: 207 pages with color photographs, 125 recipes. Chronicle Books, 1997.**

These recipes come from the creative mind of the author, who normally concentrates on California food, not from the menus of actual bistros, but it's very much in the style of the kind of laid-back white-tablecloth restaurants that we love. This means that while the food may be on the casual side, it's not everyday fare (and it's not exclusively French). Instead, serve these imaginative, internationally influenced dishes to friends at small dinner parties (there's also a breakfast and brunch chapter) and you'll earn bravos.

CONSIDER: Tuna Tartare with Cucumber-Avocado Relish; Bistro Pâté with Cornichons, Olives, and Assorted

Mustards; Lima Bean Soup with Sun-Dried Tomato Cream; Lemon-Rosemary Roasted Chicken; Braised Lamb Shanks with Merlot and Prunes; Garden Vegetable Stew with Couscous; Perfect Mashed Potatoes; Mixed Berry Bread Pudding; Winter Apple Crisp with Dried Fruits; Warm Chocolate Pudding Cakes; and Pumpkin Caramel Flan.

California Cooking

Ash, John, with Sid Goldstein. *From the Earth to the Table*. Hardcover: 429 pages with color photographs, 300 recipes. Dutton, 1995.

Here is a book so packed with terrific recipes and food information, it's no wonder it was voted Book of the Year by the IACP. Ash takes all the multicultural influences of modern California, mixes them up with a lot of laid-back wine-country style, and produces a cuisine that is simultaneously casual, elegant, and richly flavored. All the recipes come with wine suggestions, enabling you to enjoy this same good life at home. This is an altogether rewarding book, filled with many notions that will inspire immediate kitchen activity.

CONSIDER: Warm Red Cabbage Salad with Pancetta and California Goat Cheese; Lavender-Blueberry Soup; Lobster and Fennel Lasagne with Shiitake Cream Sauce; Smoked Chicken Burritos with Roasted White Corn Salsa;

Spicy Lamb Stew with Cracked Green Olives and Orange Rice; Applejack Tart with Ginger Custard Sauce; Espresso Brownie Tart; Fresh Corn Ice Cream; and Meyer Lemon Sorbet.

Bailey, Lee. *Lee Bailey's California Wine Country Cooking.* **Hardcover: 176 pages with color photographs, 160 recipes. Clarkson Potter, 1991.**

For this book, Bailey headed to the wine country of Northern California. Traveling through Napa and Sonoma, he visited many of the region's best winegrowers, discovering a passion for stylish, seasonal food that perfectly matched their dedication to producing fine wine. Vineyards and winegrowers' homes are natural settings for these sun-dappled menus, twenty-three in all, stunningly photographed by one of the author's longtime collaborators, Tom Eckerle. Since many of these recipes were contributed by the winegrowers or their chefs, there is less of the southern sensibility here. But Bailey is still the boss, and ease in the kitchen paired with natural but attractive presentation remain, as always, of chief importance. Flexible wine suggestions accompany each menu.

CONSIDER: White Corn and Oyster Chowder with Ancho Chile Cream; Chicken with Chardonnay; Grilled Pork Tenderloin with Cabernet Mustard Sauce; Mushroom, Fennel, and Artichoke Ragout; Lemon Walnut Bars; Strawberry Amaretto Custard Tart; Cabernet and Honey-Poached Figs; Triple Chocolate Terrine; and Boysenberry Cobbler with Cream.

Brown, Helen. *Helen Brown's West Coast Cookbook.* **Hardcover: 423 pages, 400 recipes. Alfred A. Knopf, 1991.**

The late Helen Evans Brown, extolled by James Beard as one of the great ladies of the American kitchen, was the first writer to bring the vast culinary melting pot of the West Coast into some kind of order understandable to the rest of the country. This handsomely designed book, part of the Knopf Cooks American Series, is a reprinting of her 1952 masterwork, annotated by her husband and collaborator, Phillip Brown. From the oysters of Seattle to the tacos of Ensenada, in home recipes and restaurant classics, the book encompasses the region as well as any ever has. The ethnic dishes are necessarily very fifties, limited by what could be found in stores, and the format is eccentric. But the food is extraordinary.

CONSIDER: Rumaki; Tomato Aspic; Sourdough Biscuits; Crab Louis; Chicken Liver Spaghetti Sauce; Sand Dabs Meunière; Green Goddess Dressing; Abalone Chowder; and Los Angeles Lemon Pie.

Jordan, Michele Anna. *California Home Cooking.* **Hardcover and paperback: 501 pages, 400 recipes. Harvard Common Press, 1997.**

In introducing this award-winning work, the author admits that in these times, and in California especially, the line between restaurant and home cooking has blurred. The recipe mix that results is wildly eclectic, taking full advantage of California's twin reputations as market basket and melting pot. Lots of sidebars provide information on people, history, geography, and ingredients, while the sheer number of recipes almost guarantees you'll find something you want to make.

CONSIDER: Spicy Grilled Oysters; Thai Meatballs with Coconut-Peanut Sauce; Melon Gazpacho; Avocado-Grapefruit Salad with Pomegranate Seeds; Huevos Rancheros; Linguine with Dungeness Crab; Cioppino; Olive Harvest Lamb; Bing Cherry Compote; Medjhool Date Mousse; Brie with Strawberries, Chocolate, and Garlic; Ginger-Chèvre Tart; and Walnut–Black Pepper Biscotti.

Mondavi, Robert, Margrit Biever Mondavi, and Carolyn Dille. *Seasons of the Vineyard: Celebrations and Recipes from the Robert Mondavi Winery.* **Hardcover: 224 pages with color photographs and illustrations, 100 recipes. Simon & Schuster, 1996.**

One of California's largest working vineyards, Mondavi is also home to the family as well as a destination, serving fine meals in its dining room and hosting concerts, exhibits, and cultural events throughout the year. Born into the European tradition (his parents came from Italy, she is Swiss), the couple believe that food and wine are partners, contributing to one's well-being and happiness. Certainly the lovely, casual, wine-compatible menus with which this beautiful book is overstuffed will engender a lot of delight.

CONSIDER: Fresh Avocado Soup; Seared Sea Scallops with Citrus-Ginger Vinaigrette; Dungeness Crab Cakes with Jalapeño Mayonnaise; Lamb Shanks with Red Wine and White Beans; and Apple Tart with Almond Crust.

Southwestern Cooking

Atkinson, Leland. *¡Cocina! A Hands-On Guide to the Techniques of Southwestern Cooking*. Paperback: 135 pages with color photographs, 55 recipes. Ten Speed Press, 1996.

This award-winning book does what no other has yet attempted, illustrating through color photography the techniques necessary for cooking great southwestern food at home. Atkinson is a chef who has worked for Mark Miller, and a "new" southwestern restaurant sensibility is at work here. One illustrated "technique," for example, is that of decoratively squirting sauces from squeeze bottles onto presentation plates. Still, the information on ingredients and fundamental methods, such as roasting and peeling fresh chiles, are ones that cooks interested in this popular cuisine will use over and over again. The book stops short of being complete by staying away from most entrées and side dishes, but tortilla- and other corn-based preparations get deserved attention. Less usual topics include dry rubs for grilling, jerky (one is of venison with pureed blackberries), and the easy pickled dishes known as escabeches.

CONSIDER: Papaya and Black Bean Salsa; Barbecued Duck Empanadas; Smoked Salmon and Spinach Tamale Tarts; Wild Mushroom and Goat Cheese Flautas (corn tortilla "flutes"); Chocolate and Banana Flan.

Dent, Huntley. *The Feast of Santa Fe*. Paperback: 397 pages, 150 recipes. Fireside, 1993.

Since feasting is what occupies much of one's time in Santa Fe, it's only natural that this book has entered classic status and remains a steady seller. Natives complain that a lot of the fare is not authentic, but Dent's sense of history and place is so sure that even his creative flights of fancy are well rooted in Northern New Mexico's red earth. If these dishes are not authentic, well, perhaps they should be. The many wonderful recipes aside, the book is also a fine cook's read. The ingredient and technique information, personal asides, and detailed observations of the actual processes give the impression of a wise and seasoned friend in the kitchen.

CONSIDER: Sage-and-Cumin Bread with a Cheese Filling; creamy Cheddar Soup with Green Chiles; fiery Pork Spareribs with Chipotle-and-Peanut Sauce; Spanish-derived Chicken Braised with Rice, Tomatoes, Saffron, and Peas; Chocolate-Piñon Torte; Flan with Pineapple and Lime; and the traditional anise-scented Christmas cookies, Bizcochitos.

Jamison, Cheryl Alters, and Bill Jamison. *The Border Cookbook*. Hardcover and paperback: 500 pages, 300 recipes. Harvard Common Press, 1995.

From the Gulf of Mexico on the east to the Pacific Ocean on the west, the border between the United States and Mexico defines a region of powerful political, cultural, and culinary influences. Seasoned travelers and dedicated researchers, the award-winning Jamisons were the ideal authors for this largest and most complete work of southwestern cooking yet assembled. Many sidebars cover everything from historical events to mail-order sources; vintage cookbooks are often cited. With Houston, Texas, as one terminal city and Monterrey, California, as the other, the sweep of the recipes is huge but approachable.

CONSIDER: Rio Bravo Brisket Hash; Piñon Pancakes with Apple Cider Syrup; Chilled Avocado-Tomatillo Soup; Grilled Fish Tacos; Texas Truckstop Enchiladas; Mango Chimichangas; Baja Date Cake; Sweet Tamales with brown sugar and pineapple; and the odd but good caramelized raisin, cheese, and bread pudding known as Capirotada.

Jamison, Cheryl Alters, and Bill Jamison. *Texas Home Cooking*. Hardcover and paperback: 584 pages, 400 recipes. Harvard Common Press, 1993.

"Big state, big food, big book" sums up *Texas Home Cooking*, but doesn't begin to indicate the pleasures of this chatty, informative, and recipe-packed work. The Jamisons are ardent fans of Lone Star cooking (he's a native), believing that any state with the cultural diversity and innate hospitality of Texas just naturally has to be a hotbed of great home cooking. The emphasis here, by the way, is on "home"; while acknowledging the many great restaurants of Texas, the Jamisons wrote this book for real people, not chefs. From barbecue, chili, and Tex-Mex classics, to game cookery, home canning, football food, and "heart-thumping" breakfasts, all the good Texas things to eat are here.

CONSIDER: Drunk and Dirty Tenderloin; Old Buffalo Breath Chili; King Ranch Chicken Casserole; Grilled Pork Tenderloin with Peach Sauce; Catfish Salad; Huevos Rancheros; Sweet Potato Hash Browns; Peanut Butter Pie; Big Thicket Coconut Cake; and Triple Chocolate Toffee Brownies.

Peyton, James W. *La Cocina de la Frontera: Mexican-American Cooking from the Southwest*. Paperback: 349 pages with color and black-and-white photographs, 200 recipes. Red Crane Books, 1994.

This is the best book yet written on the cooking of the American Southwest. Peyton spent nearly twenty years crisscrossing the region, collecting recipes from restaurants and home cooks. Clear, simple, and well-written, with modest suggestions for making some modern nutritional modifications, the recipes are nevertheless not as important as the introductory material, which puts the Mexican origins of this food, both pre- and post-Hispanic conquest, in a context that makes it comprehensible. Peyton also explains in a fascinating and completely believable way why the southwestern foods of the four U.S. states that make up the region—Texas, New Mexico, Arizona, and California—

developed so differently from each other. There is also a terrific chapter on red and green chile "master" sauces, which form the heart of this cuisine.

CONSIDER: Sonoran Cheese Soup; El Chaparral's Soft Creole Tacos; New Mexico Stacked Enchiladas; Shrimp in Garlic Sauce; Panocha (a sprouted wheat pudding); Sweet Tamales (with strawberry jam); classic caramel Flan; and Empanaditas (fried pumpkin-filled turnovers).

Southern Cooking

Bailey, Lee, and the Pilgrimage Garden Club. *Lee Bailey's Southern Food and Plantation Houses*. Hardcover: 176 pages with color photographs, 125 recipes. Clarkson Potter, 1990.

This lovely, oversized book consists of nineteen menus, each set in one of Natchez, Mississippi's finest pre–Civil War houses. Bailey, a frequent visitor to Natchez over the years, here enlists the help of the Pilgrimage Garden Club to set the stately antebellum scene. With overblown flower arrangements, antique silver, glass, and china, and lush interior and food photography by the inimitable Tom Eckerle, the look of this book is a far cry from Bailey's usual tailored but casual elegance. The food, on the other hand, will seem wonderfully familiar to the author's legions of fans.

CONSIDER: Natchez Sloe Gin Rickey; Tomato Aspic with Mayonnaise; Spicy Milk Fried Chicken with Pan Gravy; Gumbo Potpie; Smothered Crawfish with Ham

Stuffing; Smothered Quail; Skillet Cornbread; Bourbon-Mint Ice Cream; Deep-Dish Dewberry Pie; Peach Sherbet; Chocolate Pots de Crème; and Pineapple-Lemon Mousse.

Glenn, Camille. *The Heritage of Southern Cooking*. **Paperback: 480 pages with black-and-white photographs and illustrations throughout, 550 recipes. Workman, 1986.**

Born into a Kentucky family that ran a country inn, educated in classic French cuisine, trained as a journalist, and experienced as a food writer, caterer, and cooking teacher, Camille Glenn has written what is probably the definitive traditional southern cookbook. Nothing like a warm, generous personality and over fifty years of hard work to build such a collection. Chapters on pickles and preserves, desserts and candies, and "Brunches, Punches, Coffees, and Teas"—not to mention a wealth of game recipes—offer dishes not seen everywhere else.

CONSIDER: Colonel Hambry's Barbecued Haunch of Venison; Kentucky Burgoo; Carolina Silk Snapper Soup; Sour Cream Corn Muffins; Vidalia Onion Pie; Deep South Red Beans and Rice; and New Orleans Oysters and Artichokes.

The Picayune Creole Cookbook. **Paperback: 456 pages, 1,200 recipes. Dover Publications, 1971.**

This is an unabridged facsimile of the second edition of the legendary book of Creole recipes, collected by the New Orleans newspaper *The Picayune* in 1901. Intended for home use and motivated by the passing of the "faithful old Negro cooks," this book is a snapshot of the Crescent City, both socially and culinarily, not all that long after the end of the Civil War. While some of its messages are badly dated, others—"People are the better, the happier and the longer lived for the good, wholesome, well cooked daily meal," for example—seem startlingly modern. These recipes were compiled before fat and calories were concerns, so they are richer than we are now used to. The quirky format (the first chapter is "Creole Coffee," while the second is "Soups") is more suited to browsing than to looking up a specific dish.

CONSIDER: Crab Soup; Turkey Gumbo; Baked Red Snapper; Oysters en Brochettes; Chicken with Dumplings; Shrimp Jambalaya; Red Beans and Rice; Sweet Potato Biscuits; Beignets; Pralines; and Bread Pudding.

Raichlen, Steven. *Miami Spice*. Paperback: 348 pages, 200 recipes. Workman, 1993.

Just when it seems there are no fresh corners of American cooking to investigate, along comes a book singing the praises of a cuisine so fresh and interesting it seems brand-new. Lower Florida, it has been suggested, is not part of the Deep South, but instead is a Caribbean island or a Latin American country, attached by accident to the United States. Nowhere is that message louder than in this lively, zesty idea- and information-packed work. What has happened, says Raichlen, is that after years of serving Continental and California cuisine, the chefs of Miami have gone back to their regional roots, celebrating the incredible tropical larder available to them. Wondrous seafood, exotic fruits and vegetables, and the influences of half a dozen cultures are blended in a lively and appealing ragout.

CONSIDER: West Indian Pumpkin Soup, topped with a cumin-scented cream; Media Noche, the classic griddled Cuban sandwich; Macadamia-Crusted Pompano; Turkey Picadillo; Baby Back Ribs with Guava Barbecue Sauce; Maida Heatter's Key Lime Cake; Mango Napoleons with Rachel's Hot Fudge Sauce; and Ginger-Molasses Flan.

Taylor, John Martin. *The New Southern Cook.* Hardcover: 322 pages, over 200 recipes. Bantam Books, 1995.

If Camille Glenn documents the heritage of southern cooking, Taylor brings to life southern cooking as it is today and as it promises to be tomorrow. This time he journeys beyond his home base of Charleston to offer what appears to be a very personal collection of recipes. The author takes his marvelous southern ingredients and pairs them with cosmopolitan concepts he's picked up on his extensive European travels and through exposure to other southern food writers and chefs. Taylor has a very individual and appealing food sensibility, and this collection in particular feels fresh and new. Wine suggestions, by his friend Debbie Marlowe, are interesting.

CONSIDER: Smoked Tomato Soup with Basil Sorbet; Duck Soup with Turnips and Parsnips; Duck and Oyster Jambalaya; Grilled Lamb Chops with Fresh Mint Pesto; Black Walnut Brownies; Goat Cheese Biscuits; and Sweet Potatoes with Horseradish.

Taylor, John Martin. *Hoppin' John's Lowcountry Cooking: Recipes and Ruminations from Charleston and the Carolina Coastal Plain.* **Hardcover: 345 pages, 230 recipes. Bantam Books, 1992.**

Many people have never heard of the "lowcountry," which stretches across the bottom triangle of South Carolina, from just below Pawley's Island to just above Savannah. Given its climate and history, it is an area rich in both raw materials and history, which gave rise to a particular flavor of southern cuisine. Settled in the late seventeenth century, the fecund coastal plain was subject to many foreign influences: English, French, African, and West Indian, among others. As Taylor notes, "Mediterranean traditions, such as sun-drying tomatoes and making pasta, appear in early Charleston cookbooks." Taylor has a colorful, masterly way with the English language. This book is a great read.

CONSIDER: Cheese Pigs (a.k.a. straws); Corn Oysters; Shrimp Pilau; Deviled Crabs; Crawfish Gumbo; and Huguenot Torte, Charleston's signature dessert, a butterless nut and apple sponge cake, topped with whipped cream and sugared pecans.

Voltz, Jeanne, and Caroline Stuart. *The Florida Cookbook.* **Hardcover: 393 pages, 200 recipes. Alfred A. Knopf, 1993.**

Voltz, a prizewinning newspaper editor and cookbook author, and Stuart, a third-generation Floridian who is a trustee of the James Beard Foundation, confidently label Florida "the cradle of American cooking as we know it now, the place where European foods were first blended with the foodways of Native Americans." With its richly assorted influences of Spanish, African, Minorcan, Greek, Jewish, Native American, and Cuban cuisines; its tropical climate; and its long coastline, many say Florida is poised to be the next California. The roots of that revolution, when it comes, will be found here, part of the excellent Knopf Cooks American Series. Sometimes exotic, sometimes homey, always a fine read, this book conjures up a Florida that is both uniquely American and yet firmly foreign.

CONSIDER: Tallahassee Chicken Salad, in a mustardy chowchow dressing; tangy Barbecued Shrimp, always served with garlic bread for the mopping-up operation; Cuban-Style Okra and Pork, spooned over rice with fried plantains on the side; Key Lime Pie; Miss Etta's Fresh Coconut Cake; and strawberry-glazed Miami Beach Cheesecake.

Other American Regional Cooking

Adams, Marcia. *Cooking from Quilt Country: Hearty Recipes from Amish and Mennonite Kitchens.* Hardcover: 202 pages with color photographs, 180 recipes. Clarkson Potter, 1989.

This is the best of several books that Adams, a food columnist and television cooking show host, has written about the pastoral life and hearty food of Amish and Mennonite sects. Most of these recipes—and the wonderful photos that illustrate the book—come from Adams's home turf of Indiana, though the origins of both groups hark back to Germany and Switzerland. Most of the dishes are what we now think of as midwestern or American heartland food. If your family originates from western Pennsylvania, Indiana, Ohio, or Iowa, you will recognize this as comfort food. If you have always wondered what midwestern cooking was all about, this book is your key to the mystery.

CONSIDER: Sausage Gravy on Biscuits; Baked Ham

Slices in Milk and Brown Sugar; Sauerkraut Soup; Swiss Meatloaf; New Lettuce with Sour Cream Dressing; Noodles with Buttered Crumbs; Lemonade in a Crock; Butterscotch Tapioca; Apple Cake with Hot Caramel Sauce; Deep-Dish Cherry Pie; Rhubarb Dumplings; and Shoo-Fly Cookies.

Barr, Nancy Verde. *We Called It Macaroni: An American Heritage of Southern Italian Cooking.* **Paperback: 344 pages with black-and-white photographs, 250 recipes. Alfred A. Knopf, 1990.**

This book explores the indelible impact America had on the food of immigrants to this country from Southern Italy. Seen through the eyes of several generations of Barr's family and friends, these transformations are inevitable and bittersweet. Family traditions began to change as immigrants from different places intermarried. The American practice of serving meat with every meal soon turned a relatively lean peasant cuisine into the hearty Italian red sauce dishes we know today. Barr clears away the clutter, and the recipes are lusty, tasty, and often simple to prepare.

CONSIDER: Marinated Shrimp and Fennel; Farmer's Fresh Tomato Soup; Spaghetti with Tuna Fish and Swiss Chard; Chicken with Green Olives; Spicy Cabbage with Beans; Frozen Zabaglione; Peaches in White Wine; and Easter Pie.

Cox, Beverly, and Martin Jacobs. *Spirit of the West: Cooking from Ranch House and Range.* **Hardcover: 224 pages with color photographs, 100 recipes. Artisan, 1996.**

This prizewinning collaboration, a lush and evocative re-creation of the western culinary heritage, is beautifully illustrated by Jacobs and authoritatively written by Cox, who lives on a vast cattle ranch in Wyoming. The format nicely divides up the various influences that led to what, even today, is a clearly definable (and enjoyable) cuisine. From hearty ranch-house breakfasts to big feeds for a crowd, the book is packed with what can only be called vittles.

CONSIDER: Sourdough Hotcakes; Butterscotch Rolls; Trail Drive and Bunkhouse Milk Gravy; Biscuits on a Stick; Muleskinner's Chili; Skyline Ranch Baby Back Ribs with Chipotle Barbecue Sauce; Dakota Golden Pheasant Fricassee; Marie Ketchum's Molded Lime Salad; Fried Apricot Pies; Dried Peach Cobbler with Sourdough Crust; Mrs. Swan's White Cake with Coconut Frosting; Texas Apple Cake; and Grandma's Molasses Taffy.

Fertig, Judith M. *Prairie Home Cooking*. Hardcover and paperback: 528 pages, 400 recipes. Harvard Common Press, 1999.

The Midwest, even now, generations after the rich prairie soil first felt the bite of the plow, is the heartland of America. Wide-open space tamed and turned into a rich breadbasket, it was and is a melting pot of simple good food. In the modern Midwest, innovation has joined with tradition to create a cuisine, says Fertig, as ample and exciting as anywhere in the world. A native of the Midwest and a Kansas resident, she has studied at London's Le Cordon Bleu and Paris's La Varenne, and brings the appreciative eye of a world traveler returned home to this oversized work. As generous as a midwestern welcome, the book takes inspiration from European settlers and native Americans, from home cooks and restaurant chefs, from farmers and hunters and fishermen, from barbecue pitmasters and state fair blue-ribbon winners. Start cooking now, if you ever want to finish making every great-sounding recipe in this big-hearted wonder of a book.

CONSIDER: Smoked Whitefish Appetizer; Sauerkraut Balls; Kansas City–Style Barbecued Brisket Dip; Polish Wild Mushroom and Potato Soup; Baked Walleye Pike; Comfort Food Chicken and Noodles; Wisconsin Dilly Beer Brats; Maytag Blue Cheese Mashed Potatoes; Mennonite Oatmeal–Whole Wheat Bread; German Cheese Tart; Hoosier Sugar Cream Pie; County Fair Caramel Apple Tarts; Lemon Curd Bread Pudding; and Old-Fashioned Chocolate Cake with Boiled Dressing.

Hibler, Janie. *Dungeness Crabs and Blackberry Cobblers: The Northwest Heritage Cookbook.* **Paperback: 329 pages with archival black-and-white photographs, 210 recipes. Alfred A. Knopf, 1991.**

Since the Pacific Northwest was the last region of the United States to be settled, it has had less influence on this country's cuisine than, say, New England, which is a pity. As this book amply illustrates, when it comes to food, at least, the Northwest is rich in both resources and cultural heritage. Stewed together with the ingenuity typical of both the American home cook and the chefs of the new generation, this bounty results in some breathtaking food, as Hibler, a cooking teacher and editor, shows.

CONSIDER: Cream of Cauliflower Soup with Hazelnut Butter; Sourdough English Muffins; Lentils with Bratwurst and Beer; Vietnamese Ginger Chicken; Broiled Petrale Sole in Cornmeal; Cracked Dungeness Crab with Herb Mayonnaise; Venison Stew with Ham Hocks and Black Beans; Fresh Morels Simmered in Cream; Blueberry-Raspberry Upside-Down Cake; Elderberry Dumplings; Individual Cherry Cobblers; and McIntosh Apple Tart.

Hom, Ken. *Easy Family Recipes from a Chinese-American Childhood*. Hardcover: 319 pages with black-and-white archival photographs and technique drawings, 150 recipes. Alfred A. Knopf, 1997.

Thanks to Asian chef/educators such as Hom, Americans have a greater appreciation for authentic Chinese cooking (still the nation's most popular ethnic cuisine) than ever before. This food is still not much cooked at home, however, an omission Hom intends to correct with this book. Part memoir, part recipe collection, it deals with the life—and by extension the food—of Hom and his widowed mother, in the Chicago Chinatown of the fifties and sixties. If she, working in a factory six days a week, could prepare fresh and delicious Chinese meals at the end of the day, so can you. The autobiographical details are never less than moving and informative, and the recipes are a tasty revelation. Much of what is here is from Canton (Hom's mother's home region), and often includes authentic versions of familiarly tacky restaurant dishes.

CONSIDER: Chinese Mustard Greens Soup; Savory Black Bean Clams; Stir-Fried Chicken with Glazed Walnuts; Minced Squab in Lettuce Leaves; and Traditional Chow Mein.

Laudan, Rachel. *The Food of Paradise: Exploring Hawaii's Culinary Heritage*. Hardcover and paperback: 296 pages with black-and-white photographs, 150 recipes. University of Hawaii Press, 1996.

Before beginning her investigation into what Hawaiians call "local food," Laudan had the common misperception that it consisted of either Trader Vic–style "slop" or the inventive fine dining of Hawaii's new superchefs. The truth, she learned, is far more interesting. Expounding on the curious cultural fusion that has created this combination of East-West and Pacific cuisines, in which Polynesian, Japanese, Portuguese, and American (among other) influences have resulted in dishes such as Saimin, in which a Japanese-style fish broth is served thickly afloat with rice noodles and Spam, she manages to be funny and erudite while never condescending to unique food that is polyglot, comforting, and curiously attractive.

CONSIDER: Chicken Simmered in Soy Sauce; Kim Chee (Korean spicy pickled cabbage); Poke (diced raw fish); Plate Lunch (rice with meat and gravy); Char Sui (Chinese Roast Pork); Dim Sum; Crack Seed (sweet-salty dried fruit snacks); and Shave Ice (similar to snow cones).

Malouf, Waldy, with Molly Finn. *The Hudson River Valley Cookbook*. Paperback: 336 pages, 200 recipes. Harvard Common Press, 1998.

This book celebrates one of this country's richest and

most beautiful river valleys. Stretching from New York harbor to Albany (and beyond), the valley of the Hudson is fertile, and remains, despite its proximity to Manhattan, relatively rural. Some farmers, gardeners, fishermen, cheesemakers, and other food producers and purveyors have never disappeared, while others are part of a recent renaissance, spurred, at least in part, by the demands of the excellent city farmers' markets and by restaurant chefs like Malouf, who have entered, at one level or another, into partnership with the food producers to make this happen. Celebrating the products of the valley while taking his inspiration from them and the region's long and varied history, Malouf, chef at the Rainbow Room, has written a book of richly seductive recipes that will have cooks itching to head for the kitchen. Mail-order sources will provide the premium raw ingredients for those who want to replicate Malouf's dishes exactly, but such long-distance shopping isn't essential for cooking these recipes.

CONSIDER: Foie Gras Terrine with Ice Wine Jelly; Pumpkin Apple Soup with Cinnamon Croutons; Baked Shad Fillets with Sorrel Sauce; Mallard Duck Breasts with Wild Rice Custard; Rabbit Pot Pies; Home-Style Roast Chicken with Garlic and Fingerling Potatoes; Stone Ridge Succotash; Warm Apple Stacks with Clabbered Cream; Wild Huckleberry Custard Pie; and Indian Pudding with Butterscotch Sauce.

O'Neill, Molly. *New York Cookbook*. Hardcover: 443 pages with black-and-white photographs, 400 recipes. Workman, 1992.

Eight million people, three meals a day—you do the math. Any book purporting to truly represent the food of New York City will necessarily be a big one (this is) and will necessarily strain at the seams to contain all the culinary possibilities of this genuine melting pot of a city (this does). O'Neill succeeds by heading for the streets and talking to the people. From gourmet shops to street vendors, from fine restaurants to fire stations, from famous food writers to winners of cooking contests, from the Bronx to the Battery, every edible bit of New York is between these covers.

CONSIDER: Horn & Hardart's Baked Beans; Zabar's Scallion Cream Cheese Spread; Bleecker Street Green Minestrone; Raisin Pumpernickel Bread; Le Cirque's Spaghetti Primavera; Ebinger's Blackout Cake; and the Pink Teacup's Sweet Potato Pie.

Schiavelli, Vincent. *Bruculinu, America.* Hardcover: 336 pages, 70 recipes. Houghton Mifflin, 1998.

Schiavelli, a noted character actor in films and on television, here tells the story of his Sicilian-American family as they make the occasionally awkward transition from life in Italy to life in Bruculinu (Brooklyn). It's a colorful and well-written tale, funny, poignant, and often mouthwatering, thanks to the importance good cooking and eating played for the family and thanks to Schiavelli's way with a story and a recipe. Close-knit and dedicated to preserving as much of their Sicilian way of life as possible, Schiavelli's family often used food as their method of reinforcing their ties to Italy. From family folk remedies to street gangs to the all-important celebration of "Easta," this book is a literary and culinary feast.

CONSIDER: Andrea's Veal Cutlets; Calamari Fritti; Christmas Eve Salt Cod; Sicilian-Style Meat Loaf; Roasted Leg of Lamb with Pecorino and Bread Crumbs; Cherry Ice; and Sfinci'i San Giuseppi, the sweet ricotta-filled cream puffs traditionally enjoyed on the feast day of St. Joseph.

Stallworth, Lyn, and Rod Kennedy, Jr. *The Brooklyn Cookbook.* **Hardcover: 415 pages with black-and-white photographs, 250 recipes. Alfred A. Knopf, 1991.**

Pluck Brooklyn away from the other boroughs that form New York City and it would still be the fourth-largest city in the country. But is there such a thing as Brooklyn food? Yes, say the authors, but rather than being a group of distinct dishes, it is defined by memory and attitude. This is a melting pot cuisine, each ethnic neighborhood—the book pinpoints at least seventeen—cooking up tasty memories of home and serving them up with in-your-face Brooklyn pride. Replete with history, nostalgia, interviews, and photos, this handsome book (from the Knopf Cooks American Series) is a treasure trove of great food.

CONSIDER: Chicken Kiev; Genoese Sauce with Pot Roast; Kasha Varnitchkas; Swedish Pea Soup; Sauerbraten; Puerto Rican Codfish Stew; Irish Soda Bread; Couscous Salad; Lobster Thermidor; Curried Goat; Cassata Siciliana; and Junior's Cheesecake.

Ethnic
and
International
Cookbooks

Asian, Indian, and Southeast Asian Cooking

Andoh, Elizabeth. *An American Taste of Japan.* Hardcover: 334 pages with color photographs and illustrations throughout, 8-page color insert, over 120 recipes. William Morrow, 1985.

Out of print but still available, this is an eminently usable cookbook by a meticulous cooking teacher and writer who has a unique perspective on Japanese cooking and its place in the American kitchen. Andoh is married to a Japanese man, splits her time between New York and Tokyo, and lived and worked in Japan for over twenty years. She earned her stripes by studying at the Yanagihara School of Classical Japanese Cooking for six years and subsequently started her own culinary school in Tokyo. Chapters are organized according to Western fashion—soups, appetizers, main dishes, etc.—and menu suggestions follow each recipe. Some recipes are pure Japanese; others are Japanese treatments of Western ingredients, such as leg of lamb.

Andoh was well ahead of her time in this East-West approach, and she has a way of making food sound exceptionally enticing.

CONSIDER: Cold Noodle Salad with Smoky Sesame-Citron Sauce; Glazed Beef and Asparagus Rolls; Sliced Fresh Tuna with Lime and Soy; and Lamb Chops with Fresh Wild Japanese Mushrooms.

Bhumichitr, Varacharin. *The Essential Thai Cookbook.* Hardcover: 192 pages with color photographs, 100 recipes. Clarkson Potter, 1994.

Among leading books on Thai cooking, this one stands out by virtue of its photography, which evokes exotic Thailand, illustrates essential ingredients, and reveals finished dishes in all their fiery and colorful splendor. The author, "Europe's leading expert" on the subject, also operates London's most highly regarded Thai restaurant. Organized by region, the book is then further broken down by the ingredients that make each region's fare distinctive. Recipes are simple, at least by Asian standards, and appear not to be compromised. There is a rather cumbersome marking system to help the cook combine these dishes along traditional Thai menu-making lines. Vegetarian dishes are also marked.

CONSIDER: Crispy Rice with Pork, Prawns, and Coconut Sauce; Roast Chicken Wings with Black Bean Sauce; Hot and Sour Dried Shrimp and Mango Salad; Beef with Garlic and Green Peppercorns; and Duck with Lime Pickle.

Brennan, Jennifer. *The Original Thai Cookbook*. Paperback: 318 pages, 140 recipes. Perigee Books, 1981.

That this first complete book of Thai cooking published in the United States remains in print nearly twenty years later is a testament to how useful and readable it is. Although the recipes are many and fine, this book's real strength is in its chapters on Thai history, ingredients, and menu planning: With food as the core, the complete Thai culture is presented in short form. Hot, sweet, herbal, and salty—often all at once—this is vivid food that the modern American palate finds easy to enjoy. With the essential ingredients now available even at the supermarket level, cooking up a Thai feast at home is relatively easy.

CONSIDER: Pork and Shrimp Toast; Chicken and Coconut Milk Soup; Green Curry of Duck; Papaya and Shrimp Salad; Mangos and Sticky Rice; Bananas and Corn in Coconut Cream; and Chilled Lychees in Custard.

Carpenter, Hugh, and Terry Sandison. *Fusion Food*. Hardcover: 232 pages with color photographs, 150 recipes. Artisan, 1994.

The eclectic blending of two or more separate but compatible cuisines is a popular chef's conceit these days. Though dubbed fusion cooking, *confusion* is the likelier result, at least in the hands of lesser artists. Carpenter, a restaurateur and noted cooking teacher, displays a surer hand at mingling influences than most who try, and this handsome volume gives new life to a concept that at its best can lead to some terrific food. Though the strengths are in the Asian area, particularly Thailand and China, Carpenter confidently stirs elements of the American Southwest, the Caribbean, and the Mediterranean into his simmering pot, and the results are frequently dazzling. The dumpling chapter alone makes this book worth owning.

CONSIDER: Scallop and Avocado Tostadas; Thai Meatballs with Green Curry Sauce; Creole Osso Bucco; Garlic Mashed Potatoes with Mascarpone; Fantastic Raspberry Ice Cream with Velvet Chocolate Sauce; Black and White Bread Pudding; and Valrhona Chocolate Truffles.

Downer, Lesley. *At the Japanese Table: New and Traditional Recipes*. Paperback: 224 pages with color photographs and technical drawings, 90 recipes. Chronicle Books, 1993.

Add to our general unfamiliarity with Japanese cooking a sense that it takes hard-to-find ingredients, uses unfamiliar techniques, and somehow requires years of ritualistic training, and it's no wonder so few of us prepare it at home. Those who like to delve into a culture by way of its food will find the process particularly rewarding when it comes to Japan, however, and this compact but thorough book makes a fine first step. Downer is a British journalist and noted cooking teacher specializing in Japan whose book will clear up much of the mystery and send those looking for adventure eagerly to the kitchen. Good ingredient and technique information follows a solid general introduction to food in Japanese life.

CONSIDER: Various sushi and sashimi; Classic Miso Soup; Grilled Chicken Kebabs (Yakitori); Salmon Teriyaki; Sake-Steamed Chicken with a Lemony Sauce; Mixed Tempura; Chilled Somen Noodles; Sukiyaki; Five-Thing Rice; and Crab and Cucumber Salad.

Gelle, Gerry G. *Filipino Cuisine*. Hardcover: 280 pages with color photographs, 200 recipes. Red Crane Books, 1997.

The island nation of the Philippines has been swept by various indelible influences over the centuries, resulting in food that is predominantly Spanish while showing touches of the Chinese and Malaysian cuisines. Since World War II, American ingredients and restaurants have also had an effect. In recent years, Japanese and German tourists have added their touches as well. Written by a second-generation Filipino-American chef, the book has brief but good discussions of Filipino geography, eating customs, and ingredients.

CONSIDER: Crabs in Coconut Milk; Chicken Adobo (marinated and simmered); Steamed Pork Dumplings; Empanadas (Spanish meat turnovers); Sautéed Chinese Noodles with Mushrooms; Paella; Cashew Tarts; Filipino Fruit Sundaes; Mocha and Coconut Roll; and Purple Yam Pudding.

Greeley, Alexandra. *Asian Soups, Stews, and Curries*. Hardcover: 318 pages, 200 recipes. Macmillan, 1998.

Culinary nirvana, says the author, is most likely achieved while eating Asian food, which "has it all." Concentrate your Asian eating on this book's big, bold, and comforting one-dish meals and the bliss is even closer to hand. From morning to night, and incorporating dishes from an Asia that includes India and Tibet as well as

Indonesia and the Philippines, the food in this book is off-beat but enticing (it can also be quite labor-intensive). Ingredient information is thorough and essays that delineate the various regional culinary patterns are informative. A number of recipes, including Seaweed Cucumber Soup and Green Curry with Tofu, are meatless.

CONSIDER: Burmese Coconut Noodles; Lao Chicken Soup with Galangal; Portuguese Saucepan Soup; Crispy Roast Duck Sour Soup; Singaporean-Malay Chicken Curry; Vietnamese Vinegar Beef; Cambodian Pork, Peanut, and Coconut Milk Soup.

Jaffrey, Madhur. *An Invitation to Indian Cooking*. Paperback: 285 pages with illustrations by the author, 150 recipes. Vintage Books, 1973.

This first noncondescending, noncompromised look at Indian cuisine covered the bases and let us begin to cook without intimidation. Jaffrey, a noted film actress, has gone on to write larger books and host television cooking programs, but her greatest legacy might well be this modest introductory paperback, which was originally published back when cilantro was still called Chinese parsley. Barely scratching the surface of an admittedly vast and complicated cuisine, it's still as good a start for the new India hand as any we know of.

CONSIDER: Cold Yogurt Soup; Vegetable Fritters (Pakoris); Sikh Kebabs; Lamb Korma with Almonds, Pecans, and Sour Cream; Pork Chops Cooked with Spices and Tamarind Juice; Roast Chicken Stuffed with Spiced Rice;

Sea Bass in Green Chutney; Crisp Fried Okra; Chapati; Puri; and Kulfi—cardamom-pistachio ice cream.

Lo, Eileen Lin-Fei. *The Dim Sum Dumpling Book.* **Paperback: 199 pages with technical drawings, 75 recipes. Macmillan, 1995.**

Certain foods are so entwined with the social process of going somewhere else to eat them, one rarely thinks to cook them at home. Dim sum—the wondrous array of dumplings and other savory morsels so beloved of the Cantonese—are public foods, the clattering conversation, the endless pots of tea, and the servers passing with cart after cart of tempting little bites as much a part of the pleasure as the food itself. Nevertheless, dim sum can be prepared at home, as this book, by one of the best writers on Chinese cooking, shows. There is no mystery to a new cuisine, says Lo, only learning. Good sections on the dim sum tradition, on teamaking, and on essential ingredients, precede the nice array of doughs, dipping sauces, and dim sum.

CONSIDER: Shrimp Dumplings, or Har Gau; Steamed Pork Buns, or Char Sui Bau; Pot Stickers, or Wor Tip—and Steamed Vegetable Buns.

MacMillan, Maya Kaimal. *Curried Flavors.* **Hardcover: 180 pages with color photographs, 100 recipes. Abbeville Press, 1996.**

Writers are only just beginning to explore the vast culinary differences in India's regional cooking, which boasts more culinary divisions than Italy's. This award-winning book focuses on the cuisine of Kerala, on the Malabar Coast of India's southwestern tip. Colonized by the Portuguese, who sought Kerala's rich spices, the state today is more Christian than much of India (the slaughter of cattle is allowed there). A veritable rain forest during the monsoon season, Kerala is known for seafood cookery, much of it seasoned with black pepper, cinnamon, ginger, turmeric, and mustard, with tropical notes of coconut and tamarind.

CONSIDER: Rava Dosa (spicy griddle cakes) with Coconut Chutney; Pakora (chickpea fritters) with Cilantro and Mint Chutney; Fish Baked in Coconut; Shrimp Vindaloo; Lamb Kebabs; Stir-Fried Okra; Dhal (lentils) with Spinach; Fried Bananas; Gulab Jamun (tender fried cakes in cardamom syrup); and Sooji Halva (farina candy with raisins and cashews).

Marks, Copeland, and Mintari Soeharjo. *The Indonesian Kitchen*. Hardcover: 278 pages, 180 recipes. Atheneum, 1981.

Marks's first cookbook (written with Soeharjo, an Indonesian friend) is now out of print but worth seeking out. For people who like highly seasoned food, the cuisine is eminently appealing, full of sweet-hot-sour tastes, loaded with fresh ginger, garlic, coconut milk, peanut butter, chiles, and aromatic spices. A simple glossary explains all unusual ingredients. Marks has a keen talent for tailoring exotic foods to an American kitchen while retaining their authenticity, and many of the ingredients used are familiar, making the excellent recipes very approachable.

CONSIDER: Corn and Shrimp Fritters; Beef Stew with

Sweet Soy Sauce; Chicken in Aromatic Nut Sauce; and Gado, the main course salad with creamy sweet-hot peanut dressing that is the signature national dish.

Marks, Copeland. *The Exotic Kitchens of Indonesia: Recipes from the Outer Islands*. Paperback: 314 pages, 247 recipes. M. Evans and Company, Inc., 1993.

Eight years and three cookbooks after Marks's first Indonesian cookbook, he has clearly come into his own with this vibrant, exotic book. Suggesting an awareness of the increasing sophistication of the American palate and the availability of many more Southeast Asian ingredients—such as fresh lemongrass, chiles, long beans, and palm sugar—he offers recipes a bit more adventuresome, with flavors reaching even closer to their ethnic origins. This food, Marks informs us, is deeply influenced by the Arabs and Indians who invaded the northern end of Sumatra centuries ago, and can be mixed for a completely authentic Indonesian meal or paired with complementary Western food.

CONSIDER: Asinan, a refreshing salad that pairs cool cucumber, crisp jicama, and tart watercress with creamy bean curd and sweet pineapple in a spicy hot peanut sauce; and Duck in Anise Sauce (Gulai Pliek), grilled lightly, then braised in coconut milk thickened with nuts and enlivened with sweet spices and tamarind.

Marks, Copeland. *The Korean Kitchen: Classic Recipes from the Land of the Morning Calm*. Paperback: 236 pages, over 125 recipes. Chronicle Books, 1999.

This attractive, redesigned edition of the volume written

by Marks in 1993 is one of the few and by far the best of the books of Korean cooking available in English. It is valuable both as a guide in the kitchen, for those who want to explore yet another Asian cuisine, and as a guidebook to the unfamiliar savory foods available in the Korean restaurants mushrooming up in urban centers around the United States. Besides an introduction to Korean culture and culinary philosophy, the book offers a glossary of ethnic ingredients and an assortment of recipes at once accessible and uncompromising in authenticity. Marks's charming, evocative text is full of interesting tidbits of information. One entire chapter is devoted to Kimchi, or pickles, another to Pancakes, Fritters, and Dumplings.

CONSIDER: Young Bachelor Radish Pickle; Fried Spiced Bean Curd; Sweet Potato Vine and Mushroom Stir-Fry; Eggplant Salad with Red Chili; Oyster and Scallion Pancake; Cold Noodle Soup; Vegetable, Noodle, and Steak Stir-Fry; Braised Short Ribs with Chestnuts and Mushrooms; and Persimmon Punch.

Marks, Copeland. *Indian and Chinese Cooking from the Himalayan Rim.* Hardcover: 304 pages, over 170 recipes. Donald I. Fine Books, 1996.

While trying to master the general cuisines of a distant part of the world—China, India, the Himalayan Rim—we sometimes forget that these vast tracts of land are inhabited by myriad ethnic and tribal groups, all with their own unique art, customs, and, of course, cooking. Marks, a culinary anthropologist of the most adventurous kind, travels to these places and documents the food of a particular region, sometimes even a specific neighborhood. Wherever possible, he cooks with local inhabitants in their homes. The destinations outlined in the title of this book may seem disparate—until you look at a map. Here are chile-laden dishes of Bhutan and Sikkim, the lush Persian-influenced cooking of Kashmir, and food from the Baghdadi Jews of Calcutta, the Marwaris (strict Hindu vegetarians), the Eurasians and Anglo-Indians, Armenians living in India, and a Hakka Chinese community that migrated to Calcutta several centuries ago.

CONSIDER: Fried Fresh Lotus Snacks made of lotus root, potato, green banana, chickpea flour, pomegranate concentrate, chile, and salt, served with Mint and Coriander Chutney; intricately spiced fish barbecue; and Royal Lamb in Nut Sauce—a Moghul curry of lamb flavored with poppy seeds, almonds, cashews, rosebuds, and cardamom.

McDermott, Nancie. *The Curry Book*. Paperback: 271 pages, 110 recipes. Chapters Publishing, 1997.

McDermott has a "passion for curries, spices, and fragrant herbs, for intense and memorable flavors and for recipes that bring a taste of faraway places to the home kitchen." First developed when she lived in Thailand (about whose cooking she has written two books), this passion has now been extended to India, Africa, and, along with plenty of Thai flavors, informs this book with a genuinely spicy sense of adventure. There is good general information on equipment and techniques and many recipes for chile pastes and powders—infinitely preferable to store-bought, says the author. There are also plenty of raitas, chutneys, and other curry coolers, as well as a chapter on the necessarily bland and absorbent grains and breads these assertive dishes require. (Desserts, however, are up to you.) McDermott's enthusiasm is infectious, her techniques reliable, and her recipes, for all their complexity of flavor, easy to prepare.

CONSIDER: Crispy Lamb Wontons with Ginger Pear Chutney; Spicy Peanut Chicken Soup West African Style; Curried Broccoli Slaw with Cashews and Bacon; Tandoori Chicken Homestyle; Malay-Style Rice Noodles with Shrimp in Coconut Curry Sauce; Sweet and Sour Cucumber Salad; and Mango Yogurt Smoothie.

McDermott, Nancie. *Real Thai: The Best of Thailand's Regional Cooking.* Paperback: 218 pages, over 100 recipes. Chronicle Books, 1992.

Don't let the Irish name fool you. McDermott was a Peace Corps volunteer who lived in Thailand for three years, and these recipes are authentic. Beautifully written, in a way that gives even a total outsider a colorful glimpse into the markets, menus, cultural mores, even the climate of the country—the book is divided into sections based on region. McDermott also explains the strong Chinese and Indian influences on Thai cooking. Full of exuberance and dosed with explanations of words as well as ingredients, cooking techniques, and folklore, the text offers immersion in Thai culture.

CONSIDER: Spicy Shrimp Soup with Lemongrass and

Lime; Chicken with Crispy Shallots in Yellow Rice; Crab Cakes with Cilantro Pesto; Fiery Grilled Beef Salad; and Bananas Stewed in Coconut Milk.

McDermott, Nancie. *Real Thai Vegetarian*. Paperback: 256 pages, 100 recipes. Chronicle Books, 1997.

Though there are certain religious groups in Thailand who do not eat meat, there is not a great vegetarian tradition. Rather, much classic Thai cookery is meatless by default, mainly because of the cost of meat or seafood. The recipes in this collection, then, are a mixture of vegetable dishes and authentic meat dishes without the meat. As with McDermott's first work, information is solid and the recipes are fully reflective of the explosively tasty and fragrant Thai cuisine. Vegetarians (and others) will find plenty here to experience.

CONSIDER: Curried Corncakes with Sweet and Hot Garlic Sauce; Satay Peanut Sauce with Grilled Vegetables, Fried Tofu, and Toast; Jasmine Rice Soup with Mushrooms, Green Onions, and Crispy Garlic; Eggplant and Red Sweet Peppers in Roasted Chili Paste; the popular sweet-and-hot noodle dish called Paht Thai (without the chicken or shrimp); Sticky Rice with Mangoes; Thai Coffee Ice Cream; Lemongrass-Ginger Sorbet; and Thai Ice Cream Sandwiches (served on white bread!).

Miller, Gloria Bley. *The Thousand-Recipe Chinese Cookbook*. Paperback: 926 pages, 1,000 recipes. Simon & Schuster, 1994.

Originally published in 1966, this weighty tome filled a cookbook need that to some degree still exists. Frustrated by the lack of information on and recipes for Chinese food, Bley set out to learn all she could about this very large subject, and then turned it into a very large book. Despite the abundance, plenty of newer works go into Chinese cooking in greater depth and with more regional authenticity and preparation subtlety. For a certain type of cook, though, who wants lots of recipe choices and not too much cultural information, this seminal work continues to serve as the single necessary Chinese cookbook on the shelf.

CONSIDER: Shrimp Toast; Chicken Velvet and Corn Soup; Stir-Fried Pork and Lily Buds; Red-Simmered Spiced Beef with Turnips; Steamed Tangerine Duck; Stir-Fried Chicken and Peanuts; Crabmeat Lo Mein; Yangchow Fried Rice; Pork-and-Shrimp Eggrolls; Honeyed Crab Apples; Sugared Chestnut Balls; and Sesame Seed Cookies.

Pham, Mai. *The Best of Vietnamese and Thai Cooking.* Paperback: 274 pages with color and black-and-white photographs, 130 recipes. Prima Publishing, 1996.

Vietnamese cuisine, light and cool, and bold and spicy Thai food are brought into harmony by the enthusiasm of Pham (who owns two popular Sacramento, California, restaurants) and our own desire to cook these delicious foods at home. With good sections on equipment and ingredients (many shared by both cuisines), as well as nice memoir-type essays from Pham, who is of both Vietnamese and Thai descent, this is a good beginning book on both cuisines. Some may find this the only book they ever need on either.

CONSIDER: Spicy Thai Cucumber Salad; Vietnamese Beef Carpaccio; Spicy Crab Cake Delights; Five-Spice Quail; Grilled Prawns with Spicy Peanut Sauce; Caramelized Pork in Claypot; Grilled Lemongrass Chicken; Bananas Flambé; and Peach Scones with Passion Fruit Glaze.

Routhier, Nicole. *The Foods of Vietnam*. Hardcover: 239 pages with color photographs, 150 recipes. Stewart, Tabori, and Chang, 1989.

Still the best single book on the elegant, complex, and fascinating food of Vietnam, this prizewinning volume belongs in the kitchen of any cook seriously interested in the cuisines of Asia. Routhier was born in Saigon of Vietnamese and French parentage, and the book is a loving tribute to the food of her native land. Modified by a succession of conquering nations, including China, Mongolia, and France, and heavily influenced by neighboring Thailand, the food of Vietnam combines traditional Asian elements like fish sauce, lemongrass, and chiles with European touches such as dairy products, French bread, and dark-roasted coffee. The result is food that is lighter than Chinese, less fiery than Thai, and to many palates as refined as that of France.

CONSIDER: Fresh Spring Rolls; Green Papaya Salad; Shrimp and Sweet Potato Cakes; Chicken with Pineapple and Cashews; Grilled Beef with Lemon Grass; Pork Simmered in Coconut Water; the legendary Hanoi beef and noodle soup/stew known as Pho; Coconut Tartlets; and Sweet Rice Dumplings with Ginger Syrup.

Simonds, Nina. *China Express*. Hardcover: 416 pages, 200 recipes. William Morrow, 1993.

Wanting to enjoy the flavors of fine Chinese cooking, but not always able to find time for an authentic meal, Simonds developed a series of lighter, fresher, faster, and easier workday dishes that nevertheless pack the same rich flavors as traditional Chinese cuisine. Quicker than carry-out (cheaper and less fattening, too), these remodeled recipes are touted as "Chinese cooking for the rest of us." For experienced Asia hands, the recipes will be a great convenience; for beginners, they can serve as an introduction to basic ingredients and streamlined techniques.

CONSIDER: Sweet Corn Soup; Skewered Tangerine-Peel Beef; Spicy Lamb in Lettuce Packets; peanut-sprinkled Peking Chicken Salad; Pan-Fried Sweet-and-Sour Fish; curry-scented Singapore Fried Rice Noodles; Poached Peaches in Cinnamon Ginger Syrup; and Steamed Lemon Cake.

Simonds, Nina. *Classic Chinese Cuisine*. Paperback: 399 pages with color photographs, 250 recipes. Chapters Publishing, 1994.

This oversized paperback cookbook is the revised edition of an important work originally published in 1982, with thirty new recipes. The changes can only improve a work that remains one of the best and most comprehensive books on the large and complex subject of Chinese cooking. It may not be, as one critic has written, the only Chinese cookbook you'll need, but it surely will be the one you reach for the most often. Information on Chinese ingredients, techniques, equipment, and culture, as well as darkly lustrous photographs, make it a rewarding browse.

CONSIDER: Saucy Shrimp Noodles; Eight-Treasure Stir-Fried Dumplings with Meat; Hunan-Style Smoked Chicken; Crispy-Skin Duck; Stir-Fried Squid with Hot Red Peppers; Steamed Spareribs in Black Bean Sauce; Ginger Lamb in Dipping Sauce; Drunken Clams; Steamed Pears in Honey; Almond Cookies; and Custard Tartlets.

Tropp, Barbara. *The Modern Art of Chinese Cooking*. Paperback: 613 pages, 330 recipes. Hearst Books, 1982.

This big, serious, thorough cookbook for the dedicated lover of Chinese food preceded Tropp's *China Moon Cookbook* (a more personal, revisionist, and California-modified work) and represents her self-conducted study of Chinese cooking as it's practiced today. Though written with a spirit of rigorous authenticity, it's nevertheless a lively read, with recipes that entice, ingredient and technique information that encourages, and practical observations that ring true.

CONSIDER: Mongolian Fried Peanuts; Hot and Sour Hunan Chicken; Cold Duck Salad with Two Sauces; Stir-Fried Tangy Beef; Deep-Fried Shrimp Balls; Brussels Sprouts with Black Sesame Seeds; Stir-Fried Noodles with Chicken and Mushrooms; Moslem-Style Pot Stickers; Chinese Steamed Buns; Mendocino Lemon Tart; Pear and Jasmine Tea Sorbet; and Glacéed Orange Slices.

Tsuji, Shizuo, with Mary Sutherland. *Japanese Cooking: A Simple Art*. Hardcover: 517 pages with black-and-white

illustrations throughout and 16 pages color, 130 recipes. Kodansha, 1980.

With an introduction by M. F. K. Fisher and a simple, gorgeous design, this substantial volume is probably the best introduction to Japanese food you can find. The Japanese meal is explained in depth down to its seasonal changes. Every detail is attended to, even the garnish. Though this book was published almost twenty years ago, there was no stinting on authentic ingredients, which are much more available now than they were then. Shizuo Tsuji is described by Fisher as a wunderkind, a master of both classic Japanese and haute French cuisine. In Osaka, he runs one of the top culinary academies in Japan, turning out chefs for the very best restaurants. It was Tsuji's wish to produce a cookbook that would teach Western cooks the simplicity and beauty of Japanese cuisine. His success is evident.

CONSIDER: Salt-Grilled Sea Bass; Tempura; Spinach with Sesame Dressing; Nigiri Sushi; Grilled Chicken Rolls; Spicy Eggplant; Nagasaki-Style Braised Pork; Candied Chestnuts.

European, Central European, and Russian Cooking

Allen, Darina. *The Complete Book of Irish Cooking*. Hardcover: 287 pages with color photographs, 300 recipes. Penguin Studio, 1995.

Allen is the founder of the Ballymaloe Cooking School and has done more than any other single person to promote the cause of fine Irish cooking. This book deals with the authentic and historical roots of today's modern Irish culinary revolution, exploring and preserving the dishes of an isolated, agrarian, and often poor country. If you have even a passing knowledge of Irish food, many of the ingredients (oats, dairy products, farm and game meats, bacon, potatoes, honey, ale) will seem familiar, while others (sea kale and nettles) may take some explaining—as will dishes with names such as boxty, fadge, colcannon, and black pudding.

CONSIDER: Potato, Onion, and Lovage Soup; Potted Crab; Baked Cod with Cream and Bay Leaves; Venison Stew; Beef and Guinness Stew; Corned Beef with Cabbage;

Potato and Caraway Seed Cakes; Blackcurrant Summer Pudding; Apple Custard Pie; Brown Soda Bread; and Traditional Irish Sherry Trifle.

Anderson, Jean, and Hedy Würz. *The New German Cookbook.* **Hardcover: 416 pages, over 230 recipes. Harper-Collins, 1993.**

Given the dearth of German cookbooks, this is a fine addition to the library of anyone who wants an international collection, offering a good mix of contemporary German dishes as well as all the traditional recipes you'd expect, many of them appropriately lightened for a modern audience. After much travel throughout Germany, Anderson and Würz collected recipes from both home cooks and cutting-edge chefs. The book also boasts an excellent glossary, which is truly helpful, because many German foods and culinary terms are not as familiar to us as French or even Spanish ones.

CONSIDER: Pulled Leg of Pork on a Bed of Potatoes; Sauerkraut and Onions; Calf's Liver in Horseradish Mustard Cream Sauce; Puree of Potatoes and Apples; Black Forest Cherry Pudding; and Bavarian Apple Strudel.

Goldstein, Darra. *The Georgian Feast.* **Hardcover: 229 pages with black-and-white photographs, 100 recipes. HarperCollins, 1993.**

The first recipe in this book appears on page 61, an indication of the importance its scholarly author places on the history, culture, and geography of this vibrant former Soviet republic. Georgians are a lively, proud, and feast-prone lot, who cook up a cuisine variously influenced by Turkey, Persia, and Northern India. The result is nothing much like the food of anyplace else, says Goldstein, who clearly holds her subject in the highest regard. Home cooks, too, will appreciate the hearty fare, much of it based upon vegetables and fruits, and all of it easily replicated at home.

CONSIDER: Tomato Soup with Walnuts and Vermicelli; Braised Lamb Chops (in a sauce flavored with tart plums); Garlic Fried Chicken; Cold Fish in Cilantro Sauce; Eggplant with Cheese and Yogurt; Beets with Cherry Sauce; Walnut-Raisin Torte; Lemon Tea Cake; and Wheat Berries with Honey.

Lang, George. *The Cuisine of Hungary*. Hardcover: 495 pages with black-and-white illustrations and photographs, over 300 recipes. Wings Books, 1994.

Given George Lang's breadth of knowledge and erudition, perhaps it's not surprising that a full third of the book he wrote about his culinary heritage contains text: history, culture, geography, memoir. Sprinkled with songs, poetry, literary references, along with lots of recipes, it makes delightful and informative reading. Here he explains the regional variations of Hungary and their varied culinary traditions. The recipes are classic, both simple and complex. An entire chapter is devoted to cabbage "Pickled or Otherwise." Another presents dumplings; yet another, pancakes. In many cases, it's worth reading the recipes through to catch their appeal, since the many Hungarian titles and words won't mean much to most readers.

CONSIDER: Cream of Chestnut Soup; Goose Drumstick

with Barley and Beans; Veal Fricassee with Early Peas; Paprika Chicken; Potato Dumplings with Sheep's Milk Cheese; Dobos Torte; the classic intensely chocolate Rigo Janci; a 200-year-old recipe for Water-Dragging Butter Crescents; and Roasted Hazelnut Torte.

van Waerebeek, Ruth, with Maria Robbins. *Everybody Eats Well in Belgium Cookbook.* **Hardcover and paperback: 336 pages, two-color with illustrations, over 215 recipes. Workman, 1996.**

It's easy to believe they're eating well in Belgium, assuming they're cooking from this book. While among the many extremely appealing recipes are plenty of summery dishes, a preponderance of the food sounds just perfect to warm up the kitchen on a chilly winter day. True to its country of origin, the book features an entire chapter about cooking with beer, and other beer-based recipes are scattered throughout. Intriguingly, the recipe titles are listed in English, Flemish, and French.

CONSIDER: Flemish Potato Buttermilk Soup; Mussels Grilled en Brochette; Gratin of Belgian Endives (with ham and Gruyère cheese sauce); Loin of Pork with Turnips; Venison Steaks with Gin and Juniper Berries; Smoked Herring with Apple-Onion Cream; and White Peaches in Red Currant Syrup.

von Bremzen, Anya, and John Welchman. *Please to the Table: The Russian Cookbook.* **Hardcover and paperback: 659 pages, 400 recipes. Workman, 1990.**

This James Beard Award winner might better be subtitled "The *Definitive* Russian Cookbook." Former Moscow native von Bremzen and travel writer Welchman teamed up to produce an authentic and extremely enticing collection of recipes from all fifteen regions of the former Soviet Republic, stretching from the Baltics to Central Asia. Creative chapter breakdowns include, besides the usual, "Dumplings and Noodles," "Brunch and Tea Dishes," and "From the Pantry," which includes pickles and preserves. A helpful list of mail-order sources for specialty ingredients is provided. Tidbits of culinary information, food quotes from great Russian writers, and suggested menus round out this delightful book.

CONSIDER: Latvian Pork Chops with Apples Braised in Beer; Lamb Stew with Chestnuts and Pomegranate from Azerbaijan; Veal and Quince Stew from Moldavia; Georgian Cold Tuna in Walnut Sauce; Cherry Sour Cream Cake; and Almond and Pistachio Paklava (Baklava), from Armenia.

French Cooking

Beck, Simone (Simca). *Simca's Cuisine.* **Hardcover: 346 pages with black-and-white decorative illustrations throughout, over 100 recipes. Alfred A. Knopf, 1972.**

This first solo book by one of Julia Child's two collaborators on *Mastering the Art of French Cooking* contains thirty-one menus tailored for a variety of occasions. Menus from this book formed the framework for many a dinner party during its decade, and a number of the recipes are now classics. The short essays before each menu are a delight to read. They tell something about Simca, much about the food and entertaining, and a lot about French home cooking. Since it was recently inducted into the James Beard Cookbook Hall of Fame, we're hoping the title will be reissued. In the meantime, it's well worth seeking out in used-book stores.

CONSIDER: Le Diablo, an early, almost flourless chocolate cake; Potatoes Sautéed with Unpeeled Garlic (another dish ahead of its time); Pork Braised with Bourbon and Prunes; and Paul Child's Banana Soufflé with Apricot Rum Sauce.

Beck, Simone, with Suzanne Patterson. *Food and Friends: Recipes and Memories from Simca's Cuisine*. Hardcover: 528 pages with vintage black-and-white photographs, 200 recipes. Viking, 1991.

Though not as well known as her friend and colleague, Julia Child, Simone "Simca" Beck was a beloved culinary figure. This work—part memoir, part cookbook—details the extraordinary life of a true pioneer. Sections of personal history are interspersed with appropriate menus; a lengthy recipe-only section follows. A child of privilege who had to finagle cooking lessons, Beck eventually began to put together *Mastering the Art of French Cooking*. A lanky American named Julia Child was added to the team, and the book became an enduring classic. Beck's life with husband Jules, much of it spent at her beloved Provençal home, Bramafam; the droppings in of various culinary figures; trips to America to promote subsequent books; even the lives of family pets are detailed with affection.

CONSIDER: Fish Pâté in a Crust with Hollandaise Sauce; Succulent Ham Slices with Tomato Cream Sauce; Chicken Fricassee with Curry; Fork-Tender Leg of Lamb; Green Fennel Puree with Sweet Peas; Chocolate Soufflé; Pineapple Timbale with Red Currant Sauce; and Brazilian Mocha Ice Cream.

Blanc, Georges. *The French Vineyard Table.* **Hardcover: 254 pages with color and black-and-white photographs, 170 recipes. Clarkson Potter, 1997.**

For this book, Blanc, legendary chef of La Mère Blanc, celebrates France's great wine regions, commenting on their output and then using the best wines of each region in his brilliant neoclassic cuisine. Tradition gets its due as well, with one quintessential recipe for a favorite warhorse dish from each region. Add the stunning photography of Christopher Baker and you have a work that lovers of great food and of great wines alike will want to own.

CONSIDER: Snail Ratatouille Chablisienne; Oyster Gratin with Champagne; Chicken "Oysters" with Lemon and Macon Wine; Circle of Frog's Legs with Tomatoes and Curry; Salmon with Asparagus; Wild Duck with Cherries and Red Wine; Marinated Lamb Filets in Tapenade with Bandol Sauce; A Trio of Pineapple Desserts with Late-Harvest Riesling and Rosemary-Scented Ice Cream; and Frozen Bombe with Marc de Bourgogne and Strawberry Compote.

Brennan, Georgeanne. *Aperitif: Recipes for Simple Pleasures in the French Style.* **Hardcover: 344 pages with color photographs, 50 recipes. Chronicle Books, 1997.**

This remarkable, beautiful book celebrates the unique French custom and ritual of the pre-meal drink. Brennan gives formulas for homemade fortified aperitifs such as sour-cherry-flavored guignolet. She describes classics like Campari and sherry and recommends the best ways to serve them, includes versions of juice-based refreshers like citron pressé, then concludes with a chapter of recipes for the kind of intense snacks that are aperitifs' best partners. Kathryn Kleinman's softly luminous photographs reinforce the ineffable Frenchness of it all.

CONSIDER: Vin de Noix (green walnut wine); Vin de Pêche (fortified peach aperitif); Sangría; Vin Chaud (warm spiced wine); Strawberry Lemonade; Tomato Juice with Basil; Green Olives with Lemon and Bay; Dried Figs with Bacon and Fresh Goat Cheese; Anchovy Puffs; and Rosemary-Walnut Biscotti.

Brennan, Georgeanne. *The Food and Flavors of Haute Provence*. Hardcover: 319 pages, 125 recipes. Chronicle Books, 1997.

Brennan amazes in this loving tribute to the real Provence of fields and farms, evoking the vivid sights, fragrant smells, and intense flavors of Haute Provence with her skilled descriptions. This book is free of photos but rich with word images that will linger, and is cleverly organized by essential ingredients, such as wild herbs, lavender, mushrooms, truffles, olives, cheeses, game, lamb, and more. Brennan, who lives part of the year in California, nicely balances authentic and evocative French recipes with those that can find a place in modern American life.

CONSIDER: Peppered Citrus Olives; Fennel-Flavored Cream of Summer Squash Soup; Cherry Tomato Pasta with Fresh Goat Cheese; Wild Greens with Grilled Quail; Ragout of Lamb and Fresh Peas; Fava Beans and Salt Cod in Green Garlic Cream; Gratin of Forest Mushrooms; Rosemary-Orange Sorbet; Figs Baked with Honey and Lavender; Green Almond Ice Cream; and Pear Beignets.

Chase, Sarah Leah. *Pedaling Through Burgundy*. **Paperback: 239 pages, 95 recipes. Workman, 1995.**

Chase, coauthor of *The Silver Palate Good Times Cookbook* as well as several others, has also worked over the years as a guide for adult bicycle tours through France. In this colorful and attractive book and its companion volume on Provence, she celebrates two of France's most highly regarded culinary regions. Though bicycling is the thread that runs through the books, these are far more about food than exercise. As guidebooks, they are generous with information general enough not to go out of date very soon. As cookbooks, they are funny and well written and lively enough to become kitchen staples.

CONSIDER: Prosciutto-Wrapped Escargots; Warm Chicken Liver Mousse with Crayfish Cream; Toasted Walnut Bread; French Lentil Salad; Dijon Deviled Chicken; Spiced Pork Loin with Beaujolais-Soused Bing Cherries; Salt-Crusted Beef Tenderloin with Creamy Cognac and Mustard Sauce; Warm Apple Tarts Le Montrachet; Colette's Lemon Tart; and Raspberry and Cassis Bavarian Cream.

Chase, Sarah Leah. *Pedaling Through Provence*. **Paperback: 239 pages, 95 recipes. Workman, 1995.**

This book and its companion volume on Burgundy are perhaps done a bit of a disservice by their titles, which

110

might indicate to certain exercise phobics that they are about bikes, shoes, helmets, and Tour de France–type exertion. Though there is plenty of travel information, loosely slanted toward those abroad on two wheels, these books are really about the food of two of France's finest culinary regions. If you like keen and colorful observation on the fabulous cuisines of beautiful places, don't hesitate to grab one or both works.

CONSIDER: Green Olive, Almond, and Armagnac Tapenade; Poor Man's Bouillabaisse; Quayside Calamari Salad; Provençal Leg of Lamb with Roasted Red Pepper Sauce; Long-Simmered Chicken with Lots and Lots of Garlic; Apricot and Almond Cream Tart; Apple Clafoutis; and Lavender Honey Ice Cream.

Child, Julia, Louisette Bertholle, and Simone Beck. *Mastering the Art of French Cooking,* Volume 1 (revised). Hardcover and paperback: 718 pages, black-and-white illustrations throughout. Alfred A. Knopf, 1983.

Child, Julia, Louisette Bertholle, and Simone Beck. *Mastering the Art of French Cooking,* Volume 2 (revised). Hardcover and paperback: 610 pages, black-and-white illustrations throughout. Alfred A. Knopf, 1983.

We consider these the holy grail of cooking, as these two volumes are probably more responsible for the way we cook and eat in America today than any other single work. Combined with Julia Child's *French Chef* cooking program on public television, an entire generation raised on processed foods and fifties recipes as bland as the decade were transformed by *Mastering the Art*. Retail sources were scarce in those days, and aided by these books, enthusiastic budding gourmets rushed into their kitchens to make their own breads, brown sauces, and boudins. It was a time heady with learning and culinary growth, and we shouldn't forget now how it all began. Some have criticized the length of these recipes. If you can't read or if you have no patience, perhaps these are not the books for you. But following any one dish from beginning to end will teach you more about the art of cooking than any abbreviated recipe. Besides all the invaluable techniques for everything from making an omelet to forming a tart crust, particular favorites of ours in Volume 1 include the entire soup chapter (especially the Cream of Mushroom Soup, Garlic Soup, and Provençal Vegetable Soup with Garlic, Basil, and Herbs); the Roast Squab Chickens with Chicken Liver Canapés and Mushrooms; the excellent Boeuf Bourguignon (a dinner party standard); the somewhat old-fashioned but very good Veau Prince Orloff, leg of veal braised, then re-formed with a filling of creamy onions, minced mushrooms, and rice; and the sumptuous Charlotte Malakoff aux Fraises, almond cream molded with ladyfingers and fresh strawberries.

The second volume contains a new collection of recipes, plus more advanced techniques for working with dough and charcuterie. We've stopped more than one dinner party cold with the incredibly savory Boned, Stuffed Lamb Baked in Pastry—not a project for a beginner—as well as the Gratin d'Aubergines, Provençal— eggplant sliced and baked with Swiss cheese and plum tomatoes.

Ducasse, Alain, with Linda Dannenberg. *Ducasse Flavors of France.* **Hardcover: 288 pages with color photographs, 120 recipes. Artisan, 1998.**

The most honored French chef of the last decade has at last produced a cookbook. Not exactly a household word in America (simultaneously operating an almost unheard-of *two* Michelin three-star restaurants doesn't leave one a lot of time for TV appearances), Ducasse is nevertheless the leading figure in French cooking today. His signatures—combining cooked and raw ingredients, using such by-products as pan drippings, and a quest for the true taste of things—are well represented in a collection of dishes divided between the elegantly simple and the maddeningly complex. One recipe requires the making of a beef stew that simmers for seven and a half hours, the juices of which are then used to sauce fish; the meat and vegetables from the stew are reserved for "another use."

CONSIDER: Grilled Sea Scallops with Black Truffles and Brown Butter; Chicken Fricassee with Morel Mushrooms; Sautéed Pumpkin Slices Crusted with Cracked Szechuan Pepper; and Country-Style Tart of Caramelized and Raw Pears.

Grausman, Richard. *At Home with the French Classics.* **Paperback: 424 pages with black-and-white illustrations, more than 250 recipes. Workman, 1988.**

For years, Grausman toured the country as the official U.S. representative of the Paris-based Le Cordon Bleu, where he trained. In his debonair, low-key, soft-spoken style, he taught legions of American cooks the fine points of classic

French technique. In 1997 he was awarded a Presidential Medal for bringing culinary courses to inner-city schools. His total comprehension of the cuisine gives him the impressive ability to translate French classics for the modern American kitchen. A popular recipe is his easy chocolate mousse that, with minor adjustments, can be transformed into a cake, a chocolate roll, or a soufflé.

CONSIDER: Roast Duck with Peaches; Chicken with Sherry Vinegar; Steak au Poivre; Cold Poached Salmon with Green Mayonnaise; and White Beans with Garlic and Tomatoes.

Loomis, Susan Herrmann. *French Farmhouse Cookbook*. Hardcover and paperback: 541 pages, 250 recipes. Workman, 1996.

This book's foreword by Patricia Wells is a signal of the authenticity to come. Like Wells, Loomis and her family live in France, a process of immersion that translates to the page and makes the reader's experience that much richer. As in previous works, Loomis proves adept at getting to know the people who raise, farm, or forage for the ingredients that make up much of what they cook. The mostly rustic recipes she learns from them are not typical, and most are simpler than the classic French food you may be familiar with.

CONSIDER: Basil Tapenade; Dandelion, Apple, and Bacon Salad; Pumpkin and Chestnut Soup; Chicken Braised in Beer; Simple Roast Duck; Hearty Pork and Vegetable Stew with Buckwheat Dumplings; Swiss Chard and Artichoke Gratin; Hazelnut Pound Cake; Prune Cream Tart;

Lemon Cake with Strawberries; Farmhouse Crème Caramel; and Walnut Butter Cookies.

Manière, Jacques, translated and interpreted by Stephanie Lyness. *The Art of Cooking with Steam.* **Paperback: 318 pages with technical drawings, 180 recipes. William Morrow, 1995.**

Manière, who died in 1991, was one of France's most creative and influential restaurant chefs. Upon publication, his *Le Grand Livre de la Cuisine à la Vapeur* was hailed as an essential work of French cookery. This English-language version, translated and reworked for American kitchens by Stephanie Lyness, a cooking teacher and food editor, makes the heart of Manière's brilliantly innovative cuisine available to the home cook. Steamed food is naturally lighter and more flavorful, requiring no special equipment. Clean, clear, sometimes simple but just as often complex and multilayered, these recipes really illustrate an entirely new way of cooking.

CONSIDER: Warm Asparagus with Soft-Cooked Eggs and Lemon Butter; Gratin of Endive with Ham and Gruyère Cheese; Cod Steaks with Caper-Anchovy Vinaigrette; Chicken with Fresh Ginger and Scallions; Fillet of Veal with Red Pepper and Paprika Cream Sauce; and Apricot Flan with Kirsch.

Marshall, Lydie. *A Passion for Provence: Home Cooking from the South of France.* **Paperback: 320 pages, 140 recipes. HarperCollins, 1995.**

For years Marshall, a native of Paris, taught small groups of students the intricacies of authentic French food at her La Bonne Cocotte cooking school, located in her charming Greeenwich Village townhouse. Now based in Nyon in Provence, she gives week-long programs at her chateau. This volume, titled Chez Nous in its hardcover days, contains recipes that represent home cooking at its best, with a minimum of ingredients raised to maximum levels of flavor. Her reliable recipes are distinctive for their simplicity and elegance. With Marshall, the finished dish is always more than would appear from the sum of its parts. Marshall's earlier cookbooks—*Cooking with Lydie Marshall*, now out of print, and *A Passion for Potatoes*—are well worth seeking out.

CONSIDER: Country Onion Tart; Fish Steaks in Papillote with Mint and Pernod; Chicken Fricassee with Preserved Lemons; Veal Shanks Braised with Pearl Onions and Tarragon; Gratin of Eggplants with Red Peppers and Feta Cheese; Blueberry and Raspberry Summer Pudding; and Pear and Almond Tart.

Olney, Richard. *The French Menu Cookbook*, revised edition. Hardcover: 295 pages, 32 menus, 130 recipes. David R. Godine, 1985.

A complete revision of a classic that was long out of print, this is a book by one of the world's most readable food experts. An American who has lived in France for many years, Olney is a legend among students of fine cuisine, who were delighted at this book's return. Acknowledging that even a menu made up of non-French dishes may nevertheless be French in spirit, Olney attempts to illustrate the "sensuous and aesthetic" concepts that make a French menu French. Divided by season and variously labeled formal, informal, simple, elaborate, or festive, the menus in this book are a fine introduction to Gallic meal-planning. Despite the clarity of the recipes, this is sophisticated food that will challenge all but the most experienced cooks.

CONSIDER: Pike Dumplings Lyonnaise; Veal Cutlets à la Tapenade; Artichoke Puree; and Apple Mousse with Peaches.

Vergé, Roger, with Adeline Brousse. *Roger Vergé's New Entertaining in the French Style*. Hardcover: 159 pages with color photographs, 50 recipes. Stewart, Tabori, and Chang, 1996.

This is a lightened and streamlined version of a book written nearly ten years ago by one of France's greatest chefs. The book begins with a long section titled "Before the Guests Arrive," which deals with selecting wine and cheese, arranging flowers, and other stage-setting matters. All are laid out in the style of the chef's famed Moulin de Mougins restaurant in Provence. The book is lavishly filled with evocative, sun-dappled photographs by Pierre Hussenot. For a summery "Herbs of Provence" menu, Vergé gives us Artichoke and Wild Thyme Soup, Mussels and Fennel in Saffron Cream Sauce, and Lavender Ice Cream with Small Anise Cookies. In "An Autumn Luncheon," he suggests Creamy Morel Quiche, Veal Chops with Anise and Garlic, and Light Reinette Apple Soufflé.

CONSIDER: Warm Rock Lobster Salad with Orange Butter Sauce; Mougins-Style Olive Tart; Roast Rack of Lamb with Thyme Flowers; and Crepes in Honey with Provençal Pine Nuts.

Wells, Patricia. *At Home in Provence with Patricia Wells: Recipes Inspired by Her Farmhouse in France.* Hardcover: 349 pages with color photographs, 175 recipes. Scribner, 1996.

Here is the fantasy of many a cook fulfilled: Find a lovely but run-down farmhouse somewhere in France (Provence, say), then spend leisurely years remodeling it, planting new gardens, making wine from the ancient vineyard, preserving olives from your own trees, baking bread in the outdoor oven, and learning to cook and eat like a native. Lucky Patricia Wells (and husband Walter), for whom this fantasy is reality, and lucky us, for she generously shares Chanteduc and all its rich and fragrant atmosphere in this inspiring book. A friendly cast of French neighbors gifts Wells (and us) with wonderful recipes and an international crowd of famous chefs stop by to help out with dinner, while outside, the seasons of Provence turn, always bringing something new and delicious to the table.

CONSIDER: Smoked Trout Tartare; Roasted Tomato Soup with Fresh Herbs; Spicy Red Pepper Spaghetti; Duck with Lime and Honey; Creamy Olive Oil and Parmesan Potato Puree; Vanilla Bean Ice Cream with Fresh Cherries; and Lemon Lover's Tart.

Wells, Patricia, and Joel Robuchon. *Simply French.* Hardcover and paperback: 368 pages with 100 color photographs, 125 recipes. William Morrow, 1991.

Like many chef's books, this luxurious tome contains a surfeit of dream ingredients—especially black truffles and foie gras. Yet Patricia Wells, food columnist for the *Interna-*

tional Herald Tribune and esteemed cookbook writer, has done a marvelous job of translating the tastes and style of a man who is arguably one of the greatest culinary talents in France into a collection of recipes perfectly suitable to an American kitchen. They say if you get two recipes you love from a cookbook, it's worth the price. There are so many winners in this one, it's hard to choose. Scattered throughout are helpful and often creative cooking tips from both Wells and Robuchon.

CONSIDER: Mussels with Cream, Mushrooms, Leeks and Fennel, Joel Robuchon's version of the traditional French mussel ragout called mouclade (the addition of just a few extra ingredients raises his version to the level of divine); Potato Puree, a.k.a. mashed potatoes, awash in a sea of sweet butter; Salmon on a Bed of Creamy Cabbage; Pork Loin with Sage, Leeks, and Juniper; Beef Tenderloin Roasted in an Herb-Infused Salt Crust; and Bittersweet Chocolate Tart—simple, silky, and sensational.

Wolfert, Paula. *The Cooking of South-West France*. Hardcover: 356 pages, 217 recipes. Dial, 1983.

Wolfert is one of the best food writers we have, and all of her works are veritable classics. Here she casts her passionate and thorough eye over the Gascony region of France, the area known especially for its ducks and geese, foie gras, and truffles. This book is strangely more relevant now than it was when it was first published, mostly because certain ingredients, such as fresh, high-quality ducks and duck parts (that is, the legs and boneless breast) are much more available than ever. Heavily influenced by such French greats as André Daguin, Lucien Vanel, André Guillot, and Alain Dutournier, Wolfert offers a wealth of recipes so rich in taste you'll think you've stumbled onto a gold mine.

CONSIDER: Asparagus with Asparagus Sauce; Fillet of Beef with Roquefort Sauce and Mixed Nuts; Straw Potato Cake Stuffed with Braised Leeks; Ragout of Duck Legs with White Onions and Prunes; Prune and Aramagnac Ice Cream; Fruit Terrine; and Basque Cake with Pastry Cream Filling.

Italian Cooking

Bettoja, Jo, and Anna Maria Cornetto. *Italian Cooking in the Grand Tradition*. Hardcover: 304 pages, over 150 recipes. Dial, 1982.

Many years ago, Georgia beauty Jo Bettoja traveled to Europe as a Ford model. There she fell in love with an Italian hotelier, married, and transformed herself into a highly accomplished Italian cook. From a palaccio around the corner from the fountain of Trevi, she started her cooking school, Lo Scaldaviande, with Anna Maria Cornetto, a native Roman who hails from a long line of fine cooks. Here the two women offer a collection of seasonal menus, many from family heirloom collections, that are unmistakably original—many simple, some more complex, all with a hint of the celebratory about them. One excellent recipe is for a savory liver pâté, lightened with apples and celery, sparked with anchovies, rosemary, and capers. There's even a

Roman version of the Sicilian timbale: "Macaroni with Ragu and Cream Sauce in a Pastry Drum."

CONSIDER: Roast Veal Shank with Sautéed Zucchini and Sweet and Sour Baby Onions; Beef Braised in Coffee (espresso, of course); and Chocolate and Amaretti Pie.

Bianchi, Anne. *From the Tables of Tuscan Women.* Hardcover: 312 pages, 150 recipes. Ecco, 1995.

Located in western Tuscany, away from Florence and Sienna, Lucca is a lesser-known but still rich region of forest, sea, and hill towns, where the people balance an easygoing way of life with a fierce passion for good cooking and eating. In this book Bianchi, an upcoming writer and a highly regarded cooking teacher, profiles nine women of Lucca, giving a personal dimension to this wonderful food. Their distinctive dishes are Frito Misto de Pesce (mixed fried seafood); Cacciucco (fish soup served over toasted bread); and Castagnaccio (sweet chestnut flour cake).

CONSIDER: Crostini with Baby Clams; Focaccia Stuffed with Cheese; Mushroom Stew; Cotechino Sausage with White Beans and Sage; Cold Vegetable Minestrone; A Desperate Woman's Fettuccine; Risotto with Cognac; Pork Roast in Milk; Rabbit in Orange Sauce; Lamb with Olives; Epiphany Cookies; Country-Style Ricotta Cake; Apple Custard Tart; and Aniseed Wafers.

de Blasi, Marlena. *Regional Foods of Northern Italy.* Hardcover: 368 pages, 200 recipes. Prima Publishing, 1997.

In simpler days, we spoke knowledgeably of Northern and Southern Italian food, believing the former featured cream and butter, while the latter relied on tomato sauce and olive oil. Now that the various administrative regions of Italy have separately been plundered for their unique cuisines, and each has been accorded at least one cookbook of its own, the division is seen as approximate at best. For this attractive and well-written work, the bisection is made more for convenience (a volume on Southern Italian cooking is in the works). The author, an American food journalist and culinary historian, is married to a Venetian, and by virtue of extended habitation and travel in her adopted land has come across an array of dishes that seem authentic and yet fresh.

CONSIDER: Gratinéed Mussels with Pancetta and Fennel; Pasta with Olives and Wild Mushrooms; Red Wine Trout; Beef Braised in Barolo; Sausages with Black Grapes; Pears Roasted with Pecorino; and Dried Fruit Tart.

Bugialli, Giuliano. *Giuliano Bugialli's Foods of Tuscany.* Hardcover and paperback: 304 pages with color photographs, 160 recipes. Stewart, Tabori, and Chang, 1992.

Bugialli wrote this book to celebrate the particularly spare and elegant cuisine of his home Italian state. Noted for his scholarly historic research, precise recipes, and disdain for much of Italy's modern cuisine, Bugialli has produced a book of classic food, which despite his natural sense of restraint also manages to be a colorful and passionate tribute to the Tuscan way of life. Years ago Bugialli wanted his first book to include *Tuscany* in the title, but the publisher refused, believing readers wouldn't be interested in so narrow a subject. Times have changed.

CONSIDER: Panzanella (bread salad); Country-Style Minestrone; Pontremoli-Style Pasta and Beans with Pesto; Grilled Whole Chicken with Arugula Sauce; Shrimp and Potatoes Baked with Fennel; Artichokes in Caper Sauce; Orange Almond Cake; Rice Fritters; Cherries Baked in Red Wine; and Marinated Whole Peaches with Mint.

Bugialli, Giuliano. *Foods of Sicily and Sardinia and the Smaller Islands*. Hardcover: 303 pages with color photographs, 180 recipes. Rizzoli, 1996.

Sicily has rated a flurry of cookbooks recently, none more opulent than this, into which Sardinia and "the smaller islands" (Elba and Capri among others) have been incorporated for good measure. Bugialli, one of Italy's finest teachers and food writers, is off his home turf of Tuscany but quite comfortable with food that is mostly simple, occasionally baroque, in the Sicilian way. An expensive oversized, photo-packed coffee table book, this is still a work to take to the kitchen. The text, the many evocative photographs of markets, fishermen, and farms, and the clearly written recipes combine to irresistible effect.

CONSIDER: Zucchini Pancakes; Swordfish Marinated in Aromatic Herbs; Potato Gnocchi with Squab Sauce; Chicken in Sicilian Bread Crumb Sauce; Osso Bucco with Artichoke Sauce; Pistachio Cake; Italian Bread Pudding; Ricotta Fritters with Rose Water; and the potent lemon liqueur called Lemoncello.

Callen, Anna Teresa. *Food and Memories of Abruzzo, Italy's Pastoral Land.* **Hardcover: 448 pages with black-and-white photographs, 200 recipes. Macmillan, 1998.**

Anna Teresa Callen is one of this country's best-loved cooking teachers. When she began her food career nearly forty years ago, though, no one had heard of regional Italian food, nor had they any interest in the remote hill towns of her native Abruzzo. Only after she had written three other cookbooks and attracted legions of loyal followers to her classes was she able to publish the book she always wanted to write celebrating her roots, complete with family photos. It's fun to glimpse the young Callen, who was Miss Abruzzo at the time, in native costume, posing naturally with a jug on her head and a hand on her hip, looking for all the world like the next Sophia Loren. Recipes are both personal ones she has developed over the years and authentic dishes collected from her family, friends, and restaurants all over Italy.

CONSIDER: Maccheroni alla Chitarra ("guitar" macaroni); Shrimp and Bean Antipasto; Mussels with Saffron; Eggplants in Savory Sauce; Fava Bean and Pecorino Cheese Soup; Pasta and Beans with Clams and Mussels; Artichokes in Marsala Wine; Risotto with Lamb and Fennel; Grilled Mackerel; Shrimp with Grappa; Conger Eel on a Spit, an Abruzzo Christmas Eve tradition; Chocolate and Ricotta Pudding; Frangipani Crepes; and Apple Tart with Almond Brittle.

Field, Carol. *In Nonna's Kitchen: Recipes and Traditions from Italy's Grandmothers.* **Hardcover: 451 pages with**

black-and-white photographs of the grandmothers, 200 recipes. HarperCollins, 1997.

For this book, Field, a noted writer on the foods of Italy, goes to the grandmothers—the *nonnas*—for reminiscences and recipes of an older Italy that is almost gone. Ranging from weathered farm wives to Armani-clad urbanites, the grandmothers tell their vivid and sometimes very personal stories to Field in a series of interviews scattered throughout the book. Their lives may have been hard or easy, but through them all runs the thread of good food, much of it simple, direct, and drawn straight from the land and the seasons. As usual with Field, the recipes (aside from a number of glaring typos) are well-tested and fresh; few clichés of modern Italian cookbook writing are found here.

CONSIDER: Crostini with Pureed Fava Beans; Zucchini Soup with Ribbons of Sweet Basil; Pecorino Cheese Bread; Prune- and Fig-Filled Ravioli with Cinnamon-Scented Butter; Beef the Pizza Maker's Way; Bread Pudding with Pear Sauce; and Lemon-Flavored Ricotta Cake.

Field, Carol. *Italy in Small Bites*. Hardcover: 293 pages, 185 recipes. William Morrow, 1993.

This book celebrates *merende*, an entire class of Italian mini-meals that strict American nutritionists would deride as between-meal snacks. For food-loving Italians, particularly those of an earlier era, when work was often physical and calories were not an issue, *merende* provided an energy boost designed to chase the mid-morning and mid-afternoon doldrums. Field, a noted writer on Italian food, has meticulously researched these almost-forgotten snacks, and packed this book with lively, mostly simple, and very tasty things to eat. In our modern lives, she says, these little bites can serve as hors d'oeuvres, or two or three can be combined to provide a lunch or light supper.

CONSIDER: Suppli al Telefono, deep-fried risotto balls with a heart of molten mozzarella; Frico, lacy baked cheese crisps; Frittata of Leftover Pasta and Eggs; Sweet Peppers with Anchovy Sauce; Cornmeal Flatbread with Walnuts; Bread with Cracklings and Black Pepper; Sweet Fig Focaccia; Custardy Rice Pudding Torte; and Ricotta-Filled Chestnut Crepes.

Hazan, Marcella. *Marcella Cucina*. Hardcover: 471 pages with color photographs throughout; 175 recipes. Harper-Collins, 1997.

Wouldn't you love to go grocery shopping in Venice with the godmother of Italian cuisine? Here's your chance. In this her fifth cookbook, she strikes a lovely personal note—cooking for her husband, Victor—that she weaves throughout. Most of the recipes share Hazan's hallmark simplicity and emphasis on pure, fresh flavors; all bear her distinctive stamp of including nothing that is not essential. For example, Roast Boned Leg of Lamb Abruzzi-Style with Potatoes calls for only six ingredients, plus salt and pepper. Because of her savory no-nonsense but loving way with food and exact, clear explanations of different cooking processes (Hazan was trained as a biologist), the book is packed with information.

CONSIDER: Risotto with Red Cabbage and Pancetta; Boiled Fava Beans with Olive Oil and Sage; Turkey Breast

Salad with Pomegranate; Fricasseed Chicken with Garlic, Capers, White Wine, and Jerusalem Artichokes; and Semifreddi with Nuts and Dried Fruits.

Hazan, Marcella. *Essentials of Classic Italian Cooking.* **Hardcover: 688 pages with technical drawings, 500 recipes. Alfred A. Knopf, 1992.**

Marcella Hazan did for Italian cooking what Julia Child did for that of France, setting out its rules, techniques, ingredients, and recipes with such thoroughness and understanding that the fundamentals of a large and varied cuisine were within our grasp. With the publication of this volume, Hazan's first two books (*The Classic Italian Cookbook* and *More Classic Italian Cooking*) were combined, updated, and enlarged into one truly essential work; fifty new recipes have been added, and fat has been reduced wherever possible. Italian food is accessible food, says Hazan, for there is no haute cuisine in Italy, only la cucina di casa—home cooking.

CONSIDER: Cold Trout in Orange Marinade; Crisp-Fried Whole Artichokes; Bean and Red Cabbage Soup; Baked Green Lasagne with Meat Sauce, Bolognese Style; Risotto with Spring Vegetables, Tomato, and Basil; Halibut Steaks Sauced with White Wine and Anchovies; A Farm Wife's Fresh Pear Tart; Polenta Shortcake with Raisins, Dried Figs, and Pine Nuts; and Strawberry Gelato.

Jenkins, Nancy Harmon. *Flavors of Tuscany.* **Hardcover: 282 pages with color and black-and-white photographs, 100 recipes. Broadway Books, 1998.**

Jenkins, who has lived at least part of the year in eastern Tuscany for the last quarter-century, stands out in the pack of Italian food writers. Here she seeks to preserve traditional Tuscan country food as urban, industrial Italy moves away from its past. Readers who find anything other than Italian-American tomato-sauce cookery boring will not be impressed by these simple, subtle, seasonal dishes, but others will cherish them and celebrate their preservation.

CONSIDER: Omelet with Fresh Sage; Rice-Stuffed Tomatoes; Cornmeal, Kale, and Bean Soup; Pasta with a Seaside Sauce; Deep-Fried Artichokes; Oven-Roasted Tuna Steaks with a Sweet Red Pepper Sauce; Peppery Grilled Chicken; Spit-Roasted Pork Loin (prepared with only garlic, rosemary, salt, olive oil, and red wine); Flatbread for the Grape Harvest; Pepper Cake for Christmas; Ricotta Cheese Cake from Mugello; and Biscotti di Prato.

Jenkins, Nancy Harmon. *Flavors of Puglia*. Hardcover: 262 pages with black-and-white photographs, 100 recipes. Broadway Books, 1997.

A harsh land with a cuisine of poverty, Puglia—the "boot heel" of Italy—seems an unlikely place for a culinary investigator such as Jenkins, who lives in and has celebrated far more glamorous Tuscany. Nevertheless, she finds a simple, home-based cuisine, without the influence of chefs or great restaurants, that remains much as it was centuries ago. Surrounded on two sides by the sea, settled by Greeks and later the Spanish, Puglia has the lean, relatively meatless, and very healthful traditional Mediterranean diet about which we have heard so much. Greens, grains, and beans are the stars, and specialties include a puree of fava beans and a dish of flat egg noodles (tagliatelle) tossed with chickpeas and topped with more noodles, crisply fried.

CONSIDER: Marinated Fish with Vinegar and Mint; Soup with Winter Greens and Meatballs; Crisp Oven-Roasted Chicken and Potatoes; Oven-Baked Penne with Eggplant; Double-Crusted Onion Calzone; Sponge Cake with Pear Marmalade; Lemon Tart; and Fried Christmas Pastries.

Kasper, Lynne Rossetto. *The Splendid Table: Recipes from Emilia-Romagna, the Heartland of Northern Italian Food.* Hardcover: 530 pages with color photos and black-and-white illustrations, 200 recipes. William Morrow, 1992.

When territorial Italians talk of great food, says Kasper, they speak of the cuisine of Emilia-Romagna as second only to that from their own home regions. A lush land, blessed with mountains, river valleys, and a seashore, Emilia-Romagna is home to prosciutto, Parmigiano-Reggiano, and balsamic vinegar, an essential trio of ingredients that appears often in the cuisine. The food is rich, says Kasper, meaning deeply layered and flavorful, not caloric, and ranges from elegantly simple dishes to the baroque remnants of the area's Renaissance past. In this evocative book, ten years in the making, sensible modifications of ingredients and techniques produce authentic Italian flavor in the modern American kitchen.

CONSIDER: Chicken and Duck Liver Mousse with White Truffles; Lasagne of Wild and Fresh Mushrooms; Braised Pork

Ribs with Polenta; Sweet Fennel Jewish Style; Home-Style Jam Cake; Caramelized Almond Tart; and Frozen Chocolate Pistachio Cream with Hot Chocolate Marsala Sauce.

Kramer, Matt. *A Passion for Piedmont: Italy's Most Glorious Regional Table*. Hardcover: 336 pages with color photographs, 200 recipes. William Morrow, 1997.

It is debatable that Piedmont enjoys the *best* cuisine in Italy, but Kramer's spirited exploration makes clear that its food certainly ranks near the top. Isolated in the northwestern part of the country, sharing a long—if mountainous—border with France, Piedmont is the most French of the Italian states (mayonnaise and béchamel sauce are staples). Specialties include Gorgonzola, risotti of all kinds, and brilliant antipasti. A Portland-based food and wine writer who has visited often and even lived in Piedmont, Kramer opens up a relatively unexplored region to our unquenchable thirst for great Italian food.

CONSIDER: Fried Zucchini Flowers; Anchovies in Red Sauce; Salad of Chicken Breasts and Prosciutto; Chestnut Soup with Milk and Rice; Risotto with Sausage and Rum; Capon with Honey-Hazelnut Sauce; Calf's Liver with Lemon and Sage; Sweet Cornmeal Cake; Fresh Chestnut Mousse; and Barolo-Flavored Cookies.

Luongo, Pino. *A Tuscan in the Kitchen: Recipes and Tales from My Home*. Hardcover: 240 pages with color and black-and-white photographs, 140 recipes. Clarkson Potter, 1988.

This is an inspiring but aggravating book. Luongo, a noted Italian restaurateur, is such a passionate advocate for the food of his home region, Tuscany, that you want to rush to the kitchen and get cooking. Looking further, however, you find that this exuberant cook does not believe in measured quantities of ingredients, nor, except for pastry-making, does he give precise oven temperatures; timings are also approximate. This is how good cooks cook, he says, and while some confident types will plunge right in, others will be stymied, and no one will be certain that their "Tuscan" food will taste anything like it does in Tuscany. That said, there is a wealth of information found here and every page is an ardent tribute to Tuscany and her simple, elegant cuisine.

CONSIDER: Mixed Wild Mushrooms with Prosciutto; Ribollita (Baked Bread and Vegetable Soup); Spaghetti with Goat Cheese and Pepper; Grilled Tuna with a Marinade of Pesto and Vinaigrette; Baked Peaches Stuffed with Walnuts and Chocolate; Sweet Polenta; and the cookies known as "Ugly But Good."

Plotkin, Fred. *Recipes from Paradise: Life and Food on the Italian Riviera*. Hardcover: 480 pages with black-and-white and color photography, 200 recipes. Little, Brown, 1997.

Food goes in cycles of fashion, and apparently the cuisine of the Riviera has come around to receive its due. This, one of two excellent recent books on the food of that most glamorous and beautiful stretch of the Mediterranean coast, concentrates on the Italian portion, chiefly that in the region of Liguria, with touches of nearby Emilia-Romagna and Tuscany. The pestos, focaccias, fritters and other fried dishes, savory pies, seafood, and simple fruit-based desserts that are the heart of Ligurian cooking are fully and evocatively explored.

CONSIDER: Spinach Toast with Raisins and Pine Nuts; Trenette (flat pasta) with Pesto, Potatoes, and String Beans; Sea Bass Baked in Salt; the towering seafood salad called Capon Magro; Pork Loin with Black Olives; Stuffed Peaches; Candied Chestnuts; Apple Fritters; and Bitter Almond Cookies.

Schwartz, Arthur. *Naples at Table: Cooking in Campania.* Hardcover: 416 pages, more than 200 recipes. HarperCollins, 1998.

Perhaps it's natural that a man who covers restaurants in Brooklyn and Queens would be the one to bring home the idiosyncrasies, passion, and love that go into the cooking from this Southern Italian region, one of the first Italian cuisines to arrive on these shores and perhaps the least understood—until now. Aside from obviously extensive research into the food, history, and customs of this individualistic area that was linked to Sicily and Greece for centuries, Schwartz has a reporterly way of approaching food, asking people interesting questions to dig out information that might otherwise remain buried, providing perfect recipes/answers.

CONSIDER: Marinated Fresh Anchovies; Pizza with Potatoes and Onions; Prosciutto Brioche with Cheese and Tomato Sauce; Bean and Escarole Soup; Spaghetti with

Eggplant and Mozzarella; Fish Fillets with Olives, Capers, and Lemon; Quail of Mondiagone, braised with pancetta and rosemary in white wine with peas; Zuppa Inglese; Baked Stuffed Peaches; and Almond and Orange Sponge Cake.

Scicolone, Michele. *A Fresh Taste of Italy*. Hardcover: 391 pages with color and black-and-white photographs, 250 recipes. Broadway Books, 1997.

Scicolone has been visiting Italy for twenty-five years, and she has written a number of fine books on its cuisine. In this handsome work, she seeks out a combination of authentic but undiscovered dishes and creative new flavors, all designed to be of everyday use to the modern American cook. The book's front matter is particularly helpful, especially the ingredient profiles of the major culinary regions. The book has many sidebars, elegant color photos (but murky black-and-white ones), and good wine recommendations.

CONSIDER: Warm Bean Salad with Grilled Shrimp; Parmesan Custards with Mushrooms; Spinach and Ricotta Gnocchi; Bluefish with Lemon, Garlic, and Mint; Chicken with Fennel-Sausage Stuffing; Roman Artichoke Stew; Parmesan Focaccia; Apples in White Wine with Rum Cream; Figs with Honey and Mascarpone; and Biscotti-Stuffed Baked Pears.

Scicolone, Michele. *The Antipasto Table*. Hardcover: 262 pages, 200 recipes. William Morrow, 1991.

For those who find a restaurant's antipasto table far more enticing than its dessert cart, this book is for you. Organized by main ingredient, these antipasti are mostly light and simple to prepare, although the book progresses to recipes based upon chicken and other meats that might be more suitable as light main courses. Indeed, in the modern, tapas-influenced, "small plates" way of things, the author suggests a number of all-antipasto menus in which a little of this and a little of that add up to a full and very satisfying meal.

CONSIDER: Spinach and Ricotta Tart; Broccoli with Garlic Chips; Eggplant and Pepper Terrine; Roasted Stuffed Artichokes with Pine Nuts and Raisins; Green Bean Salad with Potatoes and Mint; Fig Crostini; Focaccia Stuffed with Tomatoes and Anchovies; Mussels Baked with Prosciutto; and Salt Cod and Olive Salad.

Simeti, Mary Taylor. *Pomp and Sustenance: Twenty-five Centuries of Sicilian Food*. Paperback: 339 pages with black-and-white photos and illustrations, 175 recipes. Henry Holt, 1991.

Italy is a country composed of many smaller political entities, rather roughly forced into union. The unwillingness of these entities to blend seamlessly means that there remain obvious culinary differences among them that persist to this day. This is good news for food writers like Simeti, who married into Sicily and found an unexpectedly rich and interesting region to investigate. It's good news for the reader as well: Given Sicily's long and turbulent history (Greeks, Romans, Arabs, and Normans successively controlled it) and its relative isolation, the cuisine is unique. As a resident cook and a light-handed scholar, Simeti serves up her Sicilian food with pleasant dollops of history and local color, bringing the rugged island to life. Biscuit Books brought out a new hardcover edition of this classic in 1998. Look, too, for Simeti's eloquent narrative of Sicily, *On Persephone's Island*, laced with myths, food, and facts.

CONSIDER: Pasta Con Le Sarde (pasta with fresh sardines, fennel, pine nuts, and currants—the island's most famous dish); Caponata (sweet and sour eggplant); Rianata (pizza with anchovies, tomatoes, cheese, and oregano); Torrone di Mandorle (almond brittle); Granita di Gelsomina (jasmine ice); and Cassata Siciliana (sponge cake filled with fruit and ricotta).

Tihany, Adam D., Francesco Antonucci, and Florence Fabricant. *Venetian Taste.* **Hardcover: 192 pages with color photos, 100 recipes. Abbeville, 1994.**

For centuries a political and trading power on the world scene and a cultural crossroads as well, Venice is one of the few cities whose cuisine deserves a book all its own. Tihany, a restaurant designer, and Antonucci, his partner in and the chef of Remi, a chain of Venetian-influenced restaurants, teamed with food writer Fabricant to create this mouthwatering tribute. Taking much of its inspiration from the sea that surrounds it, and often seasoned by the rich spices whose trade it once controlled, the food of Venice is recognizably Italian, but with a fresh and welcome twist.

CONSIDER: Crunchy deep-freed green olives (great with drinks); Arugula Salad with Parmesan Cheese and Walnut-Olive Dressing; Spaghetti with Oven-Dried Tomatoes; Fennel Soup with Lobster; Tuna Ravioli with Ginger

Marco Polo (the restaurant's signature dish); Rosemary Biscotti; Figs with Zabaglione; and Tirami-Su.

Tornabene, Wanda, and Giovanna Tornabene, with Michele Evans. *La Cucina Siciliana di Gangivecchio.* **Hardcover: 324 pages with color and black-and-white photographs, 280 recipes. Alfred A. Knopf, 1996.**

Located on a remote mountainside in northeastern Sicily, Gangivecchio was once a Roman outpost and then a fourteenth-century Benedictine monastery; it is now a restaurant with a world-class reputation. Operated by the Tornabenes—mother, daughter, and son—the restaurant serves food that is elegant, simple, and overwhelmingly flavorful. With the help of writer Evans (who also took the photos), this work comes as close to cookbook perfection as it is possible to get. Nevertheless, *La Cucina* may not reach the audience it should because of its cumbersome title. Look beyond the multiple syllables, however, and you find a sunny, vivid, and heartwarmingly human book that will have you heading for the kitchen (or perhaps to Sicily) in short order.

CONSIDER: Sun-Dried Tomatoes with Basil, Garlic, and Parmesan Cheese; Spaghetti with Seafood Baked in Foil; Steamed Swordfish with Oregano and Garlic; Sautéed Rabbit with Olives and Capers; Spring Chicken Salad; Wild Berry Tart; Unbaked Chocolate Cake; Ricotta and Lemon Pudding; and quintessential Cannoli.

Wells, Patricia. *Patricia Wells's Trattoria.* **Hardcover: 338 pages with 16 pages of full-color photographs, more than 150 recipes. William Morrow, 1993.**

Although Wells is primarily known for her top-quality French cookbooks, here she turns her attention to neighboring Italy, and its trattoria-style food. She certainly understands the food well enough to translate ideas gleaned from small family restaurants all over Italy into simple ingredients and directions quick enough for the contemporary cook.

While we don't agree with Wells's feeling that risotto should "always be mounded, steaming hot, in the center of warmed individual shallow bowls" and find the metric measures given in parentheses distracting, there's no denying that this book is filled with tantalizing dishes you don't see everywhere else.

CONSIDER: Lemon-and-Oregano-Seasoned Tuna Mousse; Baked Sea Bass with Artichokes; Chicken Cooked Under a Brick; Tagliatelle with Arugula and Garlic Sauce; Chicken Cacciatora; Parma Cotta (almond-vanilla creams); Fragrant Orange and Lemon Cake; and Risotto Gelato.

Jewish Cooking

Friedland, Susan. *The Passover Table*. Paperback: 96 pages with color photographs, 40 recipes. HarperCollins, 1994.

Gorgeous full-color photos—one for each recipe—set this apart from any other Jewish cookbook we've seen. So do the recipes, which while not great in number, are distinctive for their simplicity, variety, and appeal. Friedland, known for the quality books she has produced as executive editor of HarperCollins's cookbooks, writes of Passover food with authority and affection. All holiday basics are here: chopped liver (with real schmaltz), gefilte fish (made from scratch), chrain (get out your grater), and both an all-vegetable and a "full" (complete with meat) Tzimmes. She even includes a lucid description of how to make Rossl, fermented beets, an indispensable but often overlooked ingredient in authentic borscht.

CONSIDER: Carrot and Apple Kugel, flavored with

nutmeg and lemon; Birmelos, fried balls of matzo dough dipped in honey syrup and rolled in a coating of cinnamon, sugar, and ground almonds; Turkish Sweet and Sour Artichokes; even a Moroccan Tagine of Chicken with prunes, lemon, ginger, and toasted almonds.

Goldstein, Joyce. *Cucina Ebraica: Flavors of the Italian Jewish Kitchen*. Hardcover: 206 pages with color photographs, 145 recipes. Chronicle Books, 1998.

There have been Jews in Italy for 2,000 years, says Goldstein. In fact, the oldest Jewish community in the world is in Rome. During this time, a distinctive and delicious Jewish Italian cuisine has developed. Influenced by transplanted Sephardim from Spain and Portugal, who first brought such New World essentials as peppers and tomatoes to Italy, and by Ashkenazim from Central Europe, these foods of the Italian Jews adhere to the Jewish dietary laws yet manage to remain ineffably Italian. Goldstein, a noted cooking teacher and prolific author, first began researching these heritage dishes when offering a Passover menu at Square One, her now-closed San Francisco restaurant. She found great interest among patrons and a wealth of historical information, which led her to this fascinating and mouthwatering book. The recipes here may seem intrinsically Italian (and after 2,000 years, why not?) but, in fact, says Goldstein, certain techniques of preparation and the ways in which they are combined for serving can only be seen as Jewish. As a group, they seem subtle but satisfying, lighter than more familiar Italian dishes, and straightforward to prepare. This is a book that will please all who like well-researched historical writing and who enjoy fine Italian cooking.

CONSIDER: Crostini with Mascarpone, Gorgonzola, and Hazelnuts; Polenta and Anchovy Fritters; Passover Soup with Chicken Dumplings and Eggs; Pasta with Tuna Sauce; Artichokes with Mint and Garlic, Roman Style; Florentine Gratin of Salt Cod and Spinach; Braised Meat with Butternut Squash; Warm Ricotta Soufflé Pudding; and Double-Crusted Carrot and Ginger Tart.

Hofman, Ethel G. *Everyday Cooking for the Jewish Home.* **Hardcover: 393 pages, 350 recipes. HarperCollins, 1997.**

Hofman, a former president of the IACP, grew up Jewish in the Shetland Islands north of Scotland, and learned at an early age the importance of locating kosher ingredients. She has also come to appreciate that given the wanderings of the Jewish people, their cooking now extends to all corners of the globe, with Jewish dietary laws transforming the local dishes wherever Jews have settled. In this book of everyday cookery for busy families, she includes foods from Morocco to Romania. Both great Jewish traditions—the central European Ashkenazic and the Iberian Sephardic—are acknowledged, and the increasingly generous array of kosher convenience products is relied upon whenever possible. The result is a book stuffed with an international lineup of quick and tasty dishes that any busy family might well enjoy.

CONSIDER: Roasted Eggplant and Olive Hummus; Kibbutz Minted Peach Soup; Homestyle Gefilte Fish; Middle Eastern Grilled Trout; Lamb Ragout with Brandied Dried

Fruits; lots of kugels, knishes, latkes, and blintzes; Marbleized Mandelbrot; Hasty Hamantaschen; Sour Cream Coffee Cake; and Cranberry Kissel.

Marks, Copeland. *Sephardic Cooking*. Paperback: 541 pages, 600 recipes. Donald I. Fine Books, 1994.

Anyone interested in the variety of Jewish cooking that blankets half the globe and the migration patterns that led to these cuisines will find this book fascinating. Here Marks, the intrepid adventurer and explorer par excellence of exotic cuisines, returns to his roots. Born into a prominent Jewish family of gourmet food purveyors in Vermont, in his travels he has recorded both the indigenous cuisine of the particular country and that of the Jewish population. This collection takes us from Georgia, Russia, and Uzbekistan down to India, where he identifies three different types of Jewish cooking, across Iran, Iraq, Syria, Lebanon, Turkey, and Israel, down into North Africa to Egypt, Libya, Tunisia, and Morocco, across to Spain and Portugal, and up through France, Italy, and Yugoslavia. In so doing, he records not only the pure Sephardic cooking of the Jews who fled Spain during the Diaspora, but the food of the non-Ashkenazi Jews *before* they migrated to the Iberian Peninsula, when their cultural and religious center was Baghdad. In some cases, such as with the black Jews of Cochin in southern India, a community that is rapidly dying out, Marks believes he has documented their entire cuisine.

CONSIDER: Carrot Conserve, flavored with cardamom, almonds, and pistachio from Persia; Fish in Red Sauce from Tangier, a zesty first course traditionally served on Friday

ETHNIC AND INTERNATIONAL COOKBOOKS

nights, which includes whole garlic cloves and fava beans; and Poultry in Walnut Sauce from Georgia: braised chicken, turkey, or duck served with a spicy walnut and pomegranate sauce loaded with garlic and both fresh and ground coriander.

Marks, Gil. *The World of Jewish Cooking*. Hardcover: 406 pages with black-and-white photographs and archival illustrations, 500 recipes. Simon & Schuster, 1996.

Far more complex than is usually explained, Jewish cooking is one of adaptation. This is food that, as the author says, is eaten "from Alsace to Yemen," not to mention Ethiopia, Italy, and Morocco. As a chef and rabbi, Marks was uniquely qualified to gather this collection of international recipes. Sidebars expand upon Jewish practices, holidays, and history, as well as explaining the larder of ingredients this world-spanning cookbook utilizes.

CONSIDER: Italian Braised Eggplant (Caponata); Ukrainian Pastry Turnovers (Piroshki); Bukharan Lamb; Yemenite Chicken Fricassee with Fruit and Nuts; Jewish-Style Fried Artichokes; Syrian Bulgur and Tamarind Salad; Iraqui Stuffed Dumplings; Ethiopian Pancake Bread (Injera); Babka with Almond Paste Filling; Schnecken; Ashkenazic Honey Cake; and Sephardic Pastry Horns.

Nathan, Joan. *Jewish Cooking in America* (revised). Hardcover: 513 pages with black-and-white archival photographs, 335 recipes. Alfred A. Knopf, 1998.

It is a mistake to reduce Jewish cooking to the set of dietary laws upon which it is based, says Nathan. Beyond

143

those restrictions, the food can be that of one of seventy or more countries, none more significant than the United States, which has the world's largest Jewish population. America had a major impact on the cooking of the Jews who relocated here (as their cooking had an influence on it). The result is a rich, varied, and delicious cuisine that is spelled out in great detail in this award-winning book, revised in time for Nathan's PBS series of the same name. It is chockful of period photographs, anecdotes, and chatty, informative sidebars.

CONSIDER: Bookie's Chopped Chicken Liver; Pickled Herring with Mustard Sauce; Salmon Seviche (Mexican marinated raw fish); Moroccan Bastilla (rich phyllo hors d'oeuvres); Chicken Jambalaya; Wolfgang Puck's Jewish Pizza; and Cincinnati Linzertorte.

Roden, Claudia. *The Book of Jewish Food: An Odyssey from Samarkand to New York.* Hardcover: 668 pages with black-and-white photographs, 800 recipes. Alfred A. Knopf, 1996.

The best and most thorough exploration of Jewish food from around the world is this volume, honored by the James Beard Foundation as Book of the Year. Food always tells a story, says Roden; for Jews, it is one of "uprooted and migrating people and their vanishing worlds." Divided into the two great schools of Jewish cuisine—Ashkenazic (from Central Europe) and Sephardic (more Mediterranean)—this book is a "learned, loving, and delicious" tribute to both. It may be that Egyptian-born Roden feels more empathy with her Sephardic roots, or it may be that such food is inherently more colorful, but the Ashkenazic section of the book seems a little less lively.

CONSIDER: Potato Salad with Herring and Apples; Matzo Brei; Chopped Liver; Chicken Soup with Knaidlach; Hungarian Chicken Paprikash; Spicy Eggplant and Pepper Salad; Calcutta Fish Cakes; Fresh Fig Compote; Coconut Creamed Rice Pudding; and Phyllo Coils with Sweet Pumpkin Filling.

Mediterranean Cooking: Greece, Spain, Portugal, North Africa, Turkey

Algar, Ayla. *Classical Turkish Cooking: Traditional Turkish Food for the American Kitchen*. Paperback: 320 pages, 175 recipes. HarperCollins, 1999.

Turkey stands at the crossroads of Europe and Asia, a location that has indelibly shaped its remarkable cuisine. This enduring work, one of a very few on the subject, begins with a long section on Turkey's political and religious history and culinary customs that goes on for many pages. Too many, perhaps, for the average cook, but for those who demand a rich sense of place along with their exotic food, the wealth of information will be just right. So will much of the cuisine, a heady blend that ranges from China through ancient Persia to dishes from the modern Mediterranean era. It's all thoroughly enticing, and subtle adaptations for the American kitchen make the food very doable.

CONSIDER: Bulgur and Lentil Soup with Red Peppers

and Mint; Filo Cheese Rolls; Sea Bass Grilled on a Bed of Fig Leaves; Morsels of Lamb on a Bed of Smoked Eggplant Cream; Green Olive, Walnut, and Pomegranate Salad; Sweet Saffron Rice with Pistachios and Almonds; Chilled Summer Fruit in a Rose Petal Syrup; and Apricot Ice.

Anderson, Jean. *The Food of Portugal: Recipes from the Most Original and Least-Known Cuisine in Western Europe*. Paperback: 304 pages with color photographs, 130 recipes. Hearst Books, 1994.

For the paperback edition, this prizewinning book has been revised by Anderson, a noted food and travel writer and a longtime champion of the culinary, cultural, and physical attractions of Portugal. Though it shares a larder with neighboring Spain, Portugal looked seaward as it went colonizing and acquired influences from abroad that render its cuisine refreshingly different. Anderson has been visiting Portugal for over thirty years, and this is as much travelogue as cookbook. Photos by the author give a hint of Portuguese color, and glossaries of culinary terms, wines, and cheeses will help prepare the traveler for an experience that, if the recipes are any indication, will be wondrous indeed.

CONSIDER: Fresh Figs with Smoked Cured Ham; Caldo Verde (sausage and collard greens soup, the national dish); Pork with Clams Alentejo-Style; Creamed Salt Cod; Shrimp with Hot Peppers; Broa, a yeast-raised cornbread; Caramelized Flan; Almond Tart Ritz Hotel; and the meringue cookies called Suspiros (sighs).

Andrews, Colman. *Catalan Cuisine*. **Hardcover: 331 pages, 150 recipes. Atheneum, 1988.**

This book's subtitle is "Europe's Last Great Culinary Secret," and it appears, in fact, that Andrews has run across a genuinely different and overlooked cuisine. Currently the editor of *Saveur* magazine, he spent more than two years unlocking the secrets of Catalonia. Loosely located in northeastern Spain, the region remains most influenced by its ancient Roman occupiers. It is food, says Andrews, that is fresh and vital, forthright and vivid, but with a clear—and exciting—connection to the past. Many ingredients, which match those in Spanish cooking, will be familiar to Americans (onions, tomatoes, eggplants, garlic, olive oil, fresh herbs), but the treatments and combinations are unexpected, exotic, and even a bit mysterious.

CONSIDER: Quail in a Pomegranate Sauce; Pork Sausages with White Beans; Scrambled Eggs with Wild Mushrooms, Truffles, and Cheese; Sweet Red Peppers Stuffed with Duck; Mint Sorbet; Cinnamon Ice Cream with Warm Strawberry Coulis; and the crème brûlée-like Catalan "Burnt Cream."

Andrews, Colman. *Flavors of the Riviera: Discovering Real Mediterranean Cooking*. **Hardcover: 313 pages with color photographs, 120 recipes. Bantam, 1996.**

Deeply steeped in the sometimes subtle, sometimes vivid cuisine of what is the glamorous coastal facade of a hard and fairly uncompromising land, this book creates the indelible impression of a completely new—or different—

place. This is Andrews's knack, and here he does for the Riviera what he did in *Catalan Cuisine* for that portion of Spain, which is simple mythmaking. The authenticity is unprovable and probably beside the point; the people, the atmosphere, and the food are what counts. If this volume doesn't make you want to visit the Riviera, it will at least have you off to the kitchen in short order.

CONSIDER: Stuffed Squash Blossoms; San Remo Style Cold Minestrone; "Crazy Little Lasagne" with Mortar-Made Pesto; The Real Salade Niçoise; Rabbit with Anchovies and White Wine; Lamb with Olives and Artichokes; Clams with Broccoli and Potatoes; Monegasque Lemon Tart; Walnut Cake with Honey and Ricotta; and Pandolce—the holiday sweet bread from Genoa.

Barrenechea, Teresa, with Mary Goodbody. *The Basque Table—Passionate Home Cooking from One of Europe's Regional Cuisines*. Hardcover: 232 pages, 130 recipes. Harvard Common Press, 1998.

The northwestern Basque region, along the coast of Biscay Bay, has never quite fit in with the rest of Spain. It speaks a language very different from Castilian, Catalan, or Portuguese, for example, and rebelliously continues to consider separating itself from the mother country entirely. It goes on its own way culinarily, as well, its food similar to, but unlike that of, its Spanish or—just across the Pyrenees— French neighbors. Basaque-born Barrenechea runs a New York City restaurant specializing in her native foods and earns high marks for authenticity. There is a nueva cocina (nouvelle cuisine) in the Basque country, but this book (with jacket blurbs from both Paula Wolfert and Julio Iglesias!) deals with simple, gutsy, and appealing home-style dishes. Fresh seafood (also salt cod) stars here, along with plainly grilled and roasted meats and game, and there are plenty of vegetables, good olive oil, garlic, and the occasional hot chile and splash of sherry or wine. Tapas-like pinchos start every meal with a few savory bites, and desserts are rustic but satisfying. If this sounds like something you want to eat right now, and that might well be good for you if you did, you've gotten the point of this book.

CONSIDER: Eggs Stuffed with Anchovies and Tuna; Salt Cod Croquettes; Foie Gras with Apples; Frog Legs Sizzling in Garlic; Roasted Red and Green Pepper Salad; Lentil-Chorizo Soup; Oxtails Bilbao-Style; Braised Rabbit in Red Rioja Wine Sauce; Chicken Breasts with Garlic and Parsley; Red Snapper Guernica-Style; Almond Tart; Cream-Cheese Ice Cream with Red Berry Sauce; and Christmas Fruit Compote.

Casas, Penelope. *The Foods and Wines of Spain.* Hardcover: 457 pages, 290 recipes. Alfred A. Knopf, 1982.

If you want to know how Spain lives, eats, and drinks its wine, this is still the book to buy. Casas, who studied Spanish growing up and eventually married a Spaniard, was discovered by Craig Claiborne. Invited to sample authentic Spanish cuisine in her New York home, he wrote about her in *The New York Times* and eventually talked her into writing this book. Now that one of Spain's finest products, serrano ham, is again being allowed into the United States, it is perhaps time to return to this well-researched and well-written book and delve more deeply into the food of a fascinating country.

CONSIDER: Clams in Spicy Tomato Sauce; Mushrooms in Garlic Sauce; Mallorcan Chorizo Spread; White Gazpacho with Grapes; Seafood Paella; Spit-Roasted Chicken Brushed with Honey and Cumin; Roast Suckling Pig; Greens with Raisins and Pinenuts; Caramel Flan; Orange Ice Cream Cake; and Strawberry Meringues.

Casas, Penelope. *Tapas*. Paperback: 220 pages with color photographs, over 300 recipes. Alfred A. Knopf, 1985.

It's hard to know which came first: tapas, "The Little Dishes of Spain," as the book is subtitled, or the craze for sampling small dishes of food. The concept of these little bites, enjoyed singly as a snack or in groups to compose a meal of delightful variety, has spawned any number of tapas-style restaurants as well as subsequent cookbooks, many with little or no link to Spanish cooking. Here, from Spanish cooking teacher and scholar Casas, we get the real thing. These recipes can serve anywhere from a snack or appetizer to a grand buffet, depending upon how many tapas you make. If you have any hesitation about how to group these tempting dishes, Casas adds a selection of suggested menus. By and large the recipes are easy, but dishes run the gamut from complex to startlingly simple.

CONSIDER: Sausages with Sweet and Sour Figs; Clams in Sherry Sauce; Cumin-Flavored Mushroom Salad; Grilled Baby Squid; Salmon Baked in Foil; Stuffed Pork Loin, with colorful layers of carrot, pimiento, hard-boiled egg, and chorizo; Shrimp in Garlic Sauce; Spanish Potato Omelet; and Creamed Blue Cheese and Brandy.

Goldstein, Joyce. *The Mediterranean Kitchen*. Paperback: 410 pages, 300 recipes. William Morrow, 1998.

A noted San Francisco cooking teacher who eventually succumbed to the lure of restaurant work, Goldstein cooked for several years at Alice Waters's Chez Panisse Café before opening her own establishment, Square One. Trained as a painter, she felt the same creative challenge in cooking, and when arriving for the first time in Italy, discovered that the sunny, sensual Mediterranean was a place in which, as M. F. K. Fisher has said, she felt more at ease in her skin. The Mediterranean remains her culinary palate and canvas, and this book, with more authentic recipes and fewer flights of fancy than her later works, has the feel of a classic.

CONSIDER: Grilled Tuna Salad with a Moroccan Salsa; Grilled Bread with White Bean Puree and Wilted Greens; Portuguese Pasta with Sausage and Clams; Chicken with Tomato Sauce, Hot Pepper, and Pancetta; Dilled Turkish Meatballs with Eggplant Puree; Steamed Apricot Pudding; Caramel Pot de Crème; Baked Apple in Phyllo Crust; and Lemon-Almond Pie.

Kochilas, Diane. *The Food and Wine of Greece: More than 300 Classic and Modern Dishes from the Mainland and Islands of Greece*. Hardcover: 354 pages, black-and-white illustrations, over 300 recipes. St. Martin's, 1990.

Written by a food authority who lives both in New York and in Greece, this book has an air of authenticity that goes beyond the expected. Here you'll find recipes you don't see everywhere else. Besides the ubiquitous lamb, there are interesting preparations for veal, beef, pork, even goat, sausages, and assorted innards. You'll also find savory preparations for chicken, rabbit, pheasant, and quail. Seafood is simply grilled and complexly stewed. Besides the standard fish and shrimp, Kochilas doesn't shrink from offering delectable preparations for octopus, squid, and snails.

CONSIDER: Stewed Chicken with Feta and Green Olives; Chicken with Red Sauce and Quince; Rabbit Braised with White Wine and Rosemary; Grape Leaves Stuffed with Lentils and Rice; Artichoke Heart and Broad Bean Stew; Clay-Baked Chickpeas; Golden Semolina Pudding; and Rich Walnut Torte.

Marks, Copeland. *The Great Book of Couscous*. Paperback: 333 pages, 350 recipes. Donald I. Fine Books, 1997.
While Marks claims there are at least 300 varieties of couscous throughout North Africa, the title of this very interesting cookbook is misleading, because much more than couscous is revealed here. Through recipes, cultural observations, and travel tips, Marks provides a lively jaunt around North Africa. Beyond finding a dozen and a half varied kinds of couscous—Seven Vegetable Couscous and Fish Couscous among them—the reader is treated to an entire range of recipes from the distinctive cuisines of Morocco, Algeria, and Tunisia. Sweet Lamb for Ramadan contains cinnamon, raisins, sugar, prunes, pears, and orange blossom water, but no salt, Marks points out, which might induce thirst in those fasting during the day. A savory fish

with potatoes in tomato sauce, we are told, comes from the island of Jerba, where Ulysses encountered the lotus eaters. Jewish cooks and food historians will find this book of special note, because separate sections from each country are given over to Jewish recipes of the region, heavily influenced by their Spanish origins. Be aware that the titles don't give enough away; many of the dishes are much more enticing than their English names.

CONSIDER: Savory Couscous Casablanca Style; Lamb and Fresh Quince Ragout; Steamed Fava Bean Salad; Fish in Sweet-and-Sour Raisin Sauce; Chicken with Fresh Fennel; Honey Twists; and Custard with Dates and Nuts.

Morse, Kitty. *Cooking at the Kasbah.* Hardcover: 156 pages with color photographs, 100 recipes. Chronicle Books, 1998.

Recipes from sun- and spice-dazzled Morocco are always welcome, as is the arrival of this rich volume, generously blessed with color photographs. Both scenes of life in Morocco and opulent studio photos of finished dishes contribute to the exotic, even foreign atmosphere. Morse grew up in Casablanca, has written about the vegetarian cooking of Northern Africa (for Chronicle's Vegetarian Table Series), and leads annual culinary tours to what must surely be one of the world's least assimilated places. For the record, kasbahs are walled fortress-villages built by Berbers and Arabs.

CONSIDER: Harissa; Saffron Vegetable Soup; Ratatouille with Dates; Tagine (a kind of stew) of Lamb, Zucchini, Potatoes, and Sun-Dried Tomatoes; Couscous Casablanca Style; the spectacular phyllo-wrapped, sugar-dusted spiced chicken "pie" called B'Stila B'Djej; honey-drenched "gazelle horns" of fruit-filled phyllo; and Sweet Pomegranate Couscous with Buttermilk.

Ozan, Ozcan. *The Sultan's Kitchen.* **Hardcover: 156 pages with color photographs, 130 recipes. Periplus Editions, 1998.**

The author, chef/owner of Boston's most highly regarded Turkish restaurant, rates the cuisines of his native land, France, and China as the three greatest in the world. The omissions from his list may be debatable, but the inclusion of Turkey has merit. Ozan's book stands out among other good Turkish cookbooks by virtue of its profuse and voluptuously rich color photographs, which do more to validate Turkish cooking's exotic appeal than mere words ever could. Regional classics like hummus, baba ghanouj, and stuffed grape leaves appear, but so do more compelling recipes.

CONSIDER: Red Lentil, Bulgur, and Mint Soup; Mussels Stuffed with Rice, Pine Nuts, and Currants; Ground Lamb–Filled Dumplings with Yogurt-Garlic Sauce; Chicken with Creamy Pureed Eggplant; Pistachio Semolina Cake; Baklava; Saffron Pudding; and Feta Cheese Cakes.

Wolfert, Paula. *Mediterranean Grains and Greens.* **Hardcover: 356 pages, 150 recipes. HarperCollins, 1998.**

Passionate and intelligent, with an adventurous soul and an inquisitive palate, Wolfert places taste above all. Her recipes are complex, satisfying, and always interesting. Here she returns to her almost scholarly investigation of the cuisines of the countries that ring the Mediterranean. The focus of her fascination this time is, as the title says, food based upon grains and greens. That's not to say there is no meat or fish in the book—we can't wait to try the Tunisian Fish Couscous with Pumpkin and Leafy Greens and the Black Sea–Style Lamb Smothered with Nettles and Leeks—but the main emphasis is on these basic ingredients. Wolfert's energy and enthusiasm are contagious; this is a must for any serious cook.

CONSIDER: Mustard Greens with Black-Eyed Peas and Rice; Middle Eastern Chard and Lentil Soup; Sautéed Tuscan Kale with Garlicky White Beans; and Purslane and Samphire Salad with Tapenade Toasts.

Mexican and Central and South American Cooking

Bayless, Rick, with Deann Groen Bayless. *Authentic Mexican: Regional Cooking from the Heart of Mexico.* Hardcover: 384 pages with black-and-white illustrations, over 230 recipes. William Morrow, 1987.

How a gringo from Oklahoma traveled with his wife along the highways and byways of our closest Latin neighbor, fell in love with the food, the culture, the people, and their art, and returned to open what is arguably the best Mexican restaurant in the country is a story not to be missed. This volume derives from the notebooks Bayless kept through at least eight years of travel over tens of thousands of miles, "much of it by bus." It offers a loving and tantalizing picture of the kind of food served in Mexican homes, in markets, and in cantinas—both traditional and authentic and, speaking from experience, unbelievably tasty. Bayless has captured the true flavors of each dish,

while paying a little more attention to presentation and re-
ducing fat just enough to suit modern nutritional standards.

CONSIDER: Shredded Beef Salad with Avocado and
Chile Chipotle; Duck in Smooth Pumpkin Seed Sauce;
Charcoal Grilled Baby Onions with Lime; White Rice Pilaf
with Corn; Roasted Chiles and Fresh Cheese; Pecan Pie
with Raw Sugar and Spices; and Fresh Prickly Pear Ice.

**Bayless, Rick, with Deann Groen Bayless and JeanMarie
Brownson. *Rick Bayless's Mexican Kitchen: Capturing
the Vibrant Flavors of a World-Class Cuisine*. Hardcover:
448 pages with color photographs, over 150 recipes.
Scribner, 1996.**

After almost ten more years of travel in Mexico and well-
deserved success, Rick Bayless argues that southwestern—
i.e., Tex-Mex—food, while tasty, is not really Mexican, and
he pleads with us to try the real thing. Yet again he offers a
knockout collection of authentic-tasting recipes, tailored
to the American kitchen. Inspired by the cooking at his
award-winning Chicago restaurants—Frontera Grill and
Topolobampo—he has held on to all the authentic flavors
while further refining the food. Ingredients and techniques
are explained in depth. Having won James Beard's Best Regional Restaurant, Best Chef, and most recently Humani-
tarian of the Year awards, he is a cook you can trust.

CONSIDER: Tomatillo-Braised Pork Country Ribs
with Mexican Greens; Smoky Shredded Chicken with
Potatoes and Roasted Tomatoes; Spicy Mushroom Tamales; Yucatecan Grilled Fish Tacos; Smoky Peanut
Mole with Grilled Quail; Tropical Trifle of Mango and

Almonds; and Modern Mexican Chocolate Flan with Kahlua.

Idone, Christopher. *Brazil: A Cook's Tour*. Hardcover: 216 pages with color photographs, 100 recipes. Clarkson Potter, 1995.

Brazil is a huge and dazzlingly complex country, one that finally gets its culinary due in this vivid and attractive book—part travel guide, part culinary investigation. With wonderfully evocative photographs by Idone (a founder of the Manhattan catering company Glorious Foods and a noted author), this is about as close to the Brazilian experience as it's possible to get without boarding a plane for Rio. Taking into account the various cultural influences (native Indian, Portuguese, Dutch, and African, among others), Idone wanders marketplaces, restaurants, and home kitchens from São Paulo to the jungles of the Amazon. Travelers can use the book to plan a trip, while stay-at-homes will want to get busy in the kitchen.

CONSIDER: Potent Caipirinha Cocktails; hot sauce–splashed fried Codfish Balls; Heart of Palm Soup; Grilled Shrimp on Sugarcane Spears; Sweet Corn Puree Steamed in the Husks; the rib-sticking national meats-and-beans dish called Feijoada; Star Fruit Sorbet; Passion Fruit Mousse; and Brazil Nuts Dipped in Chocolate.

Kennedy, Diana. *My Mexico*. Hardcover: 550 pages with color photographs, 300 recipes. Clarkson Potter, 1998.

When a writer produces books of the size, substance, and single-mindedness that Kennedy does, there is a temptation, with each new arrival, to claim it as her masterpiece. This book, oversized and generously filled though it is, is by the author's own admission personal and eccentric, and perhaps best considered a brilliant addition to a brilliant career, rather than a capstone. (We are already looking forward to the next one.) It is "her" Mexico that British-born Kennedy shares with us here, one she hardly expected to know when she moved there over four decades ago. The planned stay of a year or two turned into a lifetime—and a lifetime's work for Kennedy, who has written four other books in English and two in Spanish, championing the varied cuisines of Mexico. She writes in a different climate than she first did in the early seventies and finds a welcome increase in this country in the availability of authentic ingredients. Her own efforts and those of others have also elevated the general knowledge of how wondrous and rich Mexican food can be. This is a regionally organized book (there is also a chapter on cooking wild mushrooms), recalling her many trips around what is a very big country, and the writing is as interesting as the recipes are enticing.

CONSIDER: Black Bean and Masa Snacks; Pork in a Pumpkin Seed Sauce; Shrimp Pozole; Red Enchiladas from Aguascalientes; Chicken for a Wedding; Mushrooms Cooked with Mint; Rice Fritters in Pasilla Chile Sauce; Candied Peanuts; Chocolate-Flavored Tamales; and Dona Rosa's Bread Pudding.

Kennedy, Diana. *The Art of Mexican Cooking.* Hardcover: 526 pages with color and black-and-white photographs, 200 recipes. Bantam, 1989.

At the time she assembled this masterful collection, Kennedy had lived in Mexico for over thirty years, a fact that has always given her work the kind of depth and authenticity lacking in many other books on the subject. Here she continues to celebrate the traditional and popular fare of a very large and complex country, taking into account the increasing availability of necessary ingredients on this side of the border. She argues that techniques are not difficult (tricky steps have photos by way of illustration) but different, and as always we gringos have a lot to learn about the real food of Mexico.

CONSIDER: Squash Flower Soup; Casserole of Chicken Tacos and Green Sauce; Fish Tamales from Tamaulipas; Ancho Chiles with Chorizo and Potato Filling; Pit-Barbecued Chicken; Pork in a Simple Red Mole; Oaxacan Beef Stew; Hot as a Dog's Nose Salsa; Coffee Caramel Custard (Flan); Pineapple Rice Torte; and Poached Guavas in Syrup.

Martinez, Zarela. *The Food and Life of Oaxaca: Traditional Recipes from Mexico's Heart*. Hardcover: 342 pages with black-and-white photographs, 200 recipes. Macmillan, 1997.

Among the states that make up Mexico, none casts a stronger spell than Oaxaca. Located south of Mexico City, Oaxaca is a rugged and mountainous land that also boasts a Pacific coastline. Originally home of the ancient Zapotec Indians, Oaxaca today remains among the most unspoiled of regions, and Oaxaca City is one of the most beautiful, serene, and pleasant places on earth. Martinez, a noted

New York City restaurateur, while not from Oaxaca, has made it her particular field of study, and this book is a wonderful window into the daily life and cuisine of this very special place. The rich and celebratory cooking is centered around the famed seven moles (chile-based sauces) of Oaxaca.

CONSIDER: Tiny Omelette Soufflés with Dried Shrimp; Roast Corn and Pork Soup; Turkey Tamales with Mole Negro; Pumpkin Seed Sauce with Chicken; Ixtepec-Style Stewed Beef with Fruit; Crabs in Chipotle Chile Sauce; Layered Cake with Almond Filling; Coconut-Filled Meringue Cookies; and Avocado Ice.

Martinez, Zarela. *Food from My Heart: Cuisines of Mexico Remembered and Reimagined.* Hardcover and paperback: 354 pages, 175 recipes. Macmillan, 1992.

With illustrations by Milton Glaser, a foreword by Budd Schulberg, and a blurb on the dust jacket from Gael Greene, this book clearly shows Martinez's New York City star power. Born on a ranch in Sonora, Mexico, and trained as a social worker, this former El Paso caterer has clearly come a long way. In this book, she tells the story of her childhood and later years in Mexico, illustrating the moving and well-written chapters of her life with recipes that reinforce the experiences. Fate eventually led to her being tapped by Paul Prudhomme to help cook for a culinary event in New York City, media attention followed, and soon Zarela the restaurant and Zarela the culinary star were born. Long sections of this colorful book on authentic ingredients, Mexico's culture, and her regional cuisines are invaluable.

CONSIDER: Cold Avocado Soup; Chicken Wings with Chipotle Sauce; Crab Enchiladas; Braised Chicken in Spicy Fruit Sauce; Meatballs Like Mama Makes; Jalisco-Style Hot Roast Pork Sandwiches; Clams Mexicana; Red Snapper Hash; Beans Cowboy Style; Sweet Tamales; Walnut Christmas Cookies; Mango Mousse; and Oaxacan Sweet Fritters.

Novas, Himilce, and Rosemary Silva. *Latin American Cooking Across the U.S.A.* **Hardcover: 331 pages with black-and-white photographs, 200 recipes. Alfred A. Knopf, 1997.**

Part of the landmark Knopf Cooks American Series (and edited by the veteran Judith Jones), this book celebrates the rich diversity of Latins cooking their native cuisines in this country. Sometimes *nuevo*, sometimes old-fashioned, these recipes present a fine survey of the possibilities and will only be of increasing interest as the number of Latin Americans and the accessibility of authentic ingredients grow. (The book is also available from Knopf in Spanish, under the title *La Buena Mesa*.) Long headnotes introduce us to various cooks from various Latin countries, while sidebars discuss ingredients and other practicalities.

CONSIDER: Peach-Habanero Salsa; Crabmeat and Avocado Salad with Lime Mayonnaise; Puerto Rican Chicken in Almond Sauce; Pork Enchiladas with Poblano Chile Cream Sauce; Jerk Lamb Shish Kebabs; Three-Milks Cake; Coconut Bread Pudding; and Bananas Stuffed with Rum Butter Cream.

Ortiz, Yvonne. A *Taste of Puerto Rico*. Hardcover: 273 pages, 200 recipes. Dutton, 1994.

Like many of the island cuisines of the Caribbean, Puerto Rican food is simpler and less exotic than one would expect from a tropical "paradise." Though various cultures from the Spanish to the Chinese have had influence, the relative isolation of island life has meant, until recent years, reliance mostly upon what can be grown locally. For expatriate Puerto Ricans this is soul food, and gives crucial lessons for younger generations born elsewhere. Zesty seasoning mixtures enliven traditional dishes, and revisionist chefs, like the author, have begun to create Nuevo Puerto Rican recipes that are lighter and livelier. The book is a useful blend of old and new and a nice addition to the Caribbean bookshelf.

CONSIDER: Puerto Rican White Cheese and Tomato Salad; Salt Codfish Fritters; Cold Mango and Rum Soup; Puerto Rican Tamales; Coconut Shrimp; Roasted Chicken with Honey-Rum Glaze; Pork and Eggplant Stew; Stovetop Coffee Flan; Passion Fruit Bread Pudding; and Piña Colada Cake.

Quintana, Patricia. *The Taste of Mexico*. Hardcover and paperback: 303 pages with color photographs, 225 recipes. Stewart, Tabori, and Chang, 1986.

While it is a culinary given these days to say that much of what we know about Mexican cooking lacks depth, a handful of writers have managed to begin spreading enlightenment. Some slight advantage may go to Quintana, if only for the rich color photographs with which this book is packed. One full-page picture, of a basket of varied and beautiful fresh wild mushrooms, might well have been taken in France. Organized by region, and with dishes ranging from pre-Hispanic Mayan fare to modern, upscale restaurant creations, this book presents a richly diverse, fascinating, and aching-to-be-discovered culinary treasure trove.

CONSIDER: Mango Daiquiris; Spit-Grilled Baby Goat; Red Chiles Stuffed with White Cheese; Mazatlan Smoked Swordfish Salad; Crepes Filled with Mushrooms and Cilantro; Fish Tamales; Pork in Green Pumpkin Seed Sauce; Hibiscus-Blossom Sherbet; Buñuelos (fritters in spiced sweet syrup); and Chestnut Flan.

Quintana, Patricia, with Jack Bishop. *Cuisine of the Water Gods.* **Hardcover: 322 pages, 200 recipes. Simon & Schuster, 1994.**

Flanked by the sea on two sides, Mexico has a long coastline and a rich history of seafood cookery. It is said that Montezuma, the great Aztec chief, established a relay of runners to carry fresh fish from the sea inland to Teotihuacán, outside of what is now Mexico City, in less than a day. Quintana, known for works packed with photos, goes the literary route here, writing extensively on the subject. Each chapter is based upon the distinctive dishes of one of the numerous coastal Mexican states, and each is introduced by a short monologue in the voice of an imagined fisherman, explorer, cook, or other sea-influenced person of that region. This chorus adds a mythic quality to the book, which is already impressive for its insights and unfamiliar but delicious-sounding recipes.

CONSIDER: Pickled Oysters Guaymas Style; Tuna Taquitos with Guacamole; Crab Soup with Ginger; Plantain Tamales Stuffed with Seafood; Rice with Clams; Pan-Fried Fish with Ancho Chiles and Lemon Mayonnaise; Eggnog Mousse; Fruits of the Guerrero Coast with Coconut Ice Cream; and Banana Nut Cake.

Rojas-Lombardi, Felipe. *The Art of South American Cooking*. Hardcover: 504 pages, 250 recipes. Harper-Collins, 1991.

The late Rojas-Lombardi, a Manhattan chef, was born in Peru. Growing up in a food-intensive household influenced by Incan, Spanish, German, and black African cooks, he was uniquely equipped to undertake this sweeping work, the most complete and accessible treatment of South American cooking to date. From the Spanish-influenced seafood cuisine of coastal Chile to the Portuguese dishes of Brazil, and from the beef-herding grassland cooking of Argentina to the rich agricultural heritage of his mountainous native country, Rojas-Lombardi brings the food of an entire continent together in a collection of recipes that are lively, unusual, and intriguing.

CONSIDER: Tuna Ceviche; Duck Empanadas; Roast Beef in a Black Pepper Crust; Feijoada, the national dish of Brazil; Seafood Tamales; and Quinoa Pudding.

Schlesinger, Chris, and John Willoughby. *Big Flavors of the Hot Sun: Hot Recipes and Cool Tips from the Spice Zone*. Hardcover: 487 pages with color photographs and technical drawings, 240 recipes. William Morrow, 1994.

"The food I like best—casual, a little rough around the edges, and filled with big, bold tastes—is found in places where the weather is hot." So says Schlesinger, a noted chef and the coauthor of a number of lively cookbooks. The focus of his interest here is the Spice Zone, that belt of tropical weather on either side of the equator where the food is often as hot as the climate. Sometimes authentic, sometimes strictly a figment of his fevered imagination, these recipes will appeal to anyone who likes their meals big-flavored and bold. Though written in the spirit of an ongoing beach party (one chapter is entitled "Let's Get Stewed in a Strange and Exotic Way"), this book is founded on serious culinary fundamentals.

CONSIDER: Smoked Eggplant and Tomato Soup with Rosemary-Garlic Butter; Grilled Lamb Chops with Sweet Mint-Chile Glaze; Grilled Shrimp BLTs with Smashed Avocados; North African Roast Chicken Thighs with Raisins, Almonds, and Apricots; Banana-Papaya Fool; and Peach Shortcake.

Tausend, Marilyn, with Miguel Ravago. *Cocina de la Familia*. Hardcover: 413 pages, 200 recipes. Simon & Schuster, 1997.

This award-winning book of compelling recipes and colorfully moving stories comes from Mexican families now living in the United States. These transplanted cooks maintain contact with their homeland by making the dishes their grandmothers taught them. As gathered by Tausend, coauthor of *Mexico the Beautiful*, each recipe is identified by its Mexican place of origin as well as by the

American city in which it was collected. Most remain authentic, while a few have undergone minor sea changes. Besides good ingredient and technique information, there are fine headnotes and essays on such essentially Hispanic American places as New Mexico, California, and Texas.

CONSIDER: Caesar Salad with Chipotle Chile; Green Chile and Corn Soup; Tacos of Charcoal-Grilled Beef; Tequila Shrimp and Pasta; Green Mole with Pork and Vegetables; Lentils and Chorizo; Wild Greens with Pinto Beans; Pumpkin and Pine Nut Yeast Rolls; Chocolate Rice Pudding; Eggnog and Raisin Ice Cream; and Ancho Chile Flan.

von Bremzen, Anya. *Fiesta!* Hardcover: 388 pages with color and black-and-white photographs, 200 recipes. Doubleday, 1997.

A Moscow-born food and travel writer, von Bremzen won a James Beard Award for her book on Russian cooking, *Please to the Table.* Now living in the largest and most diverse Hispanic community in New York (Jackson Heights in Queens), she celebrates the world of Latin hospitality and festive culinary style in this lively and colorful work, also a Beard Award winner. Though it includes dishes from Spain and Portugal, the book concentrates primarily on Central and South America, plus the Caribbean, with the occasional nod to Mexico. Sidebars provide plenty of ingredient and cultural information, while snapshot-quality photos provide authentic, nonglitzy Latin color.

CONSIDER: Bahian Coconut-Peanut Dip; the addictive corn cake-and-cheese snacks called Arepas; Galician

White Bean Soup with Greens; Skirt Steak, Cuban Style; Pork Loin with Picadillo Stuffing; Yellow Rice with Carrots and Orange Zest; Passion Fruit Mousse Cake; Peruvian Pumpkin Doughnuts; and Mango Flan.

Zaslavsky, Nancy. *A Cook's Tour of Mexico: Authentic Recipes from the Country's Best Open-Air Markets, City Fondas, and Home Kitchens.* **Hardcover: 366 pages with drawings and photographs (both color and black and white), over 150 recipes. St. Martin's, 1995.**

You can use this entrancing book two ways: Buy a ticket to Mexico and travel state by state, following Zaslavsky's suggestions for "Places to Go and Things to Eat." She offers names and addresses of gift and craft shops, markets, bazaars and restaurants. Or go to your local market or Latin grocery, recipe in hand, and return home to simulate the trip in your kitchen. Either way, you'll have a ball. Though the author is a professional photographer and designer, and by her own description a passionate though amateur cook, the recipes have been collected from experts all over Mexico.

CONSIDER: Chile-Marinated and Grilled Chicken with Herbs and Vinegar from Jalisco; the traditional Ceviche; Shrimp in Garlic; Creamy Pumpkin Seed Salsa; Scrambled Eggs with Tomato Sauce and Fried Tortilla Chips; Vinegared Chicken with Flavors of the Yucatan; Beef Filet with Onion, Potato, and Serrano Chile.

Vegetable and Vegetarian Cooking

Bishop, Jack. *Pasta e Verdura: 140 Vegetable Sauces for Spaghetti, Fusilli, Rigatoni, and All Other Noodles.* **Hardcover: 326 pages, 140 recipes. HarperCollins, 1996.**

This collection of vegetable-based sauces for pasta is a natural extension of the recent crowd of books dealing with the Italian way of cooking vegetables. A bright, fresh, and attractive book, it is organized by main ingredient from A (artichokes) to Z (zucchini). An editor of *Cook's Illustrated* magazine, Bishop is not content to merely serve up delicious recipes. Each section opens with how to buy, store, and prepare the vegetable in question as well, making this useful book even more valuable. Also nice is information on cooking, saucing, and serving pasta; pairing a sauce with its ideal pasta shape; stocking a pasta pantry; and getting at least some of the fat out of pasta sauces.

CONSIDER: Arugula Puree with Walnuts and Goat Cheese; Broccoli in "Hot" Pink Tomato Sauce with Basil;

Sautéed Cauliflower with Garlic, Raisins, and Pine Nuts; Caramelized Vidalia Onions with Black Olives and Rosemary; Marinated Black and Green Olives with Fresh Herbs; and Grilled Peppers with Red Wine Vinegar and Tarragon.

Brown, Edward Espe. *Tassajara Cooking*. Paperback: 255 pages with technical drawings, 200 recipes. Shambala, 1973.

This classic vegetarian work is one of a handful of cookbooks still in print a quarter of a century after being published. In today's welter of vegetarian books (are all of them really necessary?), a modest paperback like this can get overlooked, which would be a shame. Tassajara is the location of Zen Mountain Center, a Zen Buddhist practice center in Marin County, California. Imbued with the Buddhist philosophy, this work is lively, readable, and spiritual, with tasty food that does include eggs and dairy products. Brown, who coauthored *The Greens Cook Book*, is both ethereal ("The way to be a cook is to cook") and pragmatic. One caveat: measurements and cooking times are not given.

CONSIDER: Guacamole; Sauced Sweet and Sour Carrots; Yams on the Half Shell; Spinach Goes Bananas with Sesame; Cucumber and Cantaloupe Salad; Chili Beans; Baked Eggplant Moussaka; Tahini Shortbread; Peanut Butter Balls; and Prune-Apple Special.

Emmons, Didi. *Vegetarian Planet*. Hardcover and paperback: 576 pages, 350 recipes. Harvard Common Press, 1997.

Emmons, chef at Boston's Delux Cafe, had an advantage over some of her predecessors when setting out to write this award-winning vegetarian work—namely fifteen to twenty years more general culinary sophistication. Where early vegetarian writers labored to make wondrous fare out of little more than brown rice, cheese, and broccoli, Emmons has sun-dried tomatoes, kaffir lime leaves, roasted garlic, chipotle chiles, and mangoes in her repertoire and a foundation of increasingly well-traveled food writing to build upon. The result is as mouthwatering and thorough a vegetarian work as you are likely to find. Big, too, since it's a big world out there, and packed not only with recipes (some of which use dairy products and eggs) but chatty sidebars on all sorts of related subjects.

CONSIDER: Korean Vegetable Pancakes; Green Grape and Tomatillo Gazpacho; Sweet Potato Vichyssoise; Shocking Beet Vinaigrette; Ratatouille with Soft Basil Dumplings; Tofu and Pumpkin-Seed Burgers; Smoky Mexican Lasagna; Lavender Rice Pudding with Raspberries; Pomegranate Ice with Mascarpone Cream; and Lemongrass-Ginger Cheesecake.

Fletcher, Janet. *Fresh from the Farmer's Market*. Paperback: 207 pages with color photographs, 75 recipes. Chronicle Books, 1997.

This is a pretty book, based upon the seasons at the farmer's market. Some may think them boutique produce shops for the rich, but according to Fletcher, they support independent farmers, preserve and distribute heirloom varieties that might otherwise vanish, and promote community ties. Within seasonal chapters, the produce and fruits are listed alphabetically, which means springtime apricot desserts begin the book. The effect is not chaotic, but rather one of random abundance, just like a good farmer's market. For some reason there are no chiles, which will puzzle those who have visited Santa Fe's excellent farmer's market, but much of the rest of what you will want to cook is here, along with selection and storage information.

CONSIDER: Artichokes Roman Style with Garlic and Mustard; Roasted Corn Soup; Fingerling Potato Salad with Fennel; Pizza with Mozzarella and Arugula; Pappardelle with Asparagus and Fava Beans; Risotto with Savoy Cabbage, Lemon, and Parsley; Pomegranate Apple Jelly; Chunky Peach Preserves; Fresh Fig Galette; Tapioca Pudding with Strawberry Rhubarb Sauce; and Blackberry Macaroon Torte.

Goldstein, Darra. *The Vegetarian Hearth: Recipes and Reflections for the Cold Season*. Hardcover: 316 pages, 120 recipes. HarperCollins, 1996.

Anyone, writes Barbara Kafka on this book's dust jacket, can be a vegetarian in summer. When cold weather comes, however, and sturdy food is wanted, going meatless can be tough. Until now, that is. For Goldstein, winter's limited larder and icy weather are challenges to the cook's creativity and the diner's inner resolve. Here are thoughtful essays on everything from the English celebration of Shrove Tuesday to buckwheat to Tolstoy (Goldstein's book on the food of the former Soviet state of Georgia was an IACP book of the year). The mostly simple, hearty recipes are international in scope, though wintry places like Russia and Northern Europe naturally get the lion's share of the attention.

CONSIDER: Mushroom and Barley Soup; Stilton Bread Pudding; Sweet Buckwheat Crepes; White Bean and Potato Pie; Garlicky Winter Greens; Savory Sauerkraut; Cinnamon Walnut Wreath; Sour Rye Bread; Baked Apples with Cider; Gingerbread with Hot Orange Sauce; and Snow Ice Cream.

Greene, Bert. *Greene on Greens*. Paperback: 432 pages, 450 recipes. Workman, 1994.

This popular and durable book by one of the country's best-loved food writers is about far more than mere "greens" (although there is a substantial chapter dealing with that entire leafy family). Instead, a whole garden's worth of vegetables—from artichokes to zucchini—are here presented in Greene's uniquely chatty style. Personal anecdotes are followed by solid consumer information, which then gives way to exuberant but balanced recipes designed to show off the vegetable in question. There is lots of good sidebar material, too. The vegetables may be the stars, but the cook will also harvest plenty of glory.

CONSIDER: Artichoke Risotto; Curried Chicken with Avocado; Amish Carrot Dumplings; Clam and Corn Chowder; Dandelion Greens with Prosciutto; Squash and Sausage Ratatouille; Tomato Devil's Food Cake with Tomato Buttercream Frosting; Carrot-Vanilla Tart; Yam Ice Cream; and The Ultimate Pumpkin Pie.

Hesser, Amanda. *The Cook and the Gardener—A Year of Recipes and Notes from the French Countryside.* Hardcover: 608 pages, 240 recipes. W.W. Norton, 1999.

Hesser, who graduated with a Grande Diplome from La Varenne cooking school and is a *New York Times* "Dining Out" reporter, once worked as private chef for La Varenne's founder, Anne Willan, and her family. Living and cooking at Chateau de Fey, in Burgundy, Hesser found her job and her life inextricably entangled with the seasons of the French countryside and with the crotchety chateau gardener M. Milbert. Locked in the age-old relationship between the gardener who grows the produce and the cook who transforms it, the old Frenchman and the young American woman developed a grudging friendship. After all, together they completed a cycle, one that, in this book at least, leads to a rich, detailed, and moving account of life at the Chateau as the garden wakes from its Burgundian winter and warms into summer abundance.

Hesser's recipes are French, or at least French-inspired, and simple, full of le *gout de terroir*—the flavor of the earth. Hungers change with the seasons, too, and anticipation for the arrival of the first asparagus or for the cherry trees to ripen provides inspiration and appetite. The personal essays that accompany the recipes are wonderfully written and the food is enticing.

CONSIDER: Cold Asparagus Soup with Mint; Creamy Leeks and Tarragon on Toast; Cool Pea-and-Potato Salad; Skewered Beef with Tomatoes and Marjoram; Pork Tenderloin with Peaches; Pheasant with Sorrel; Red Snapper with

Fennel Seed, Tomatoes, and Vermouth; Slow-Roasted Zucchini with Balsamic Vinegar; Rhubarb-Ginger Preserves;
Green Tomato Chutney; Flatbread with Vine Grapes and
Rosemary; Pear and Almond Tart; Raspberry Ice Cream
with Herb Syrup; and Lavender Sorbet.

**Jaffrey, Madhur. *Madhur Jaffrey's World of the East Vege-
tarian Cooking*. Paperback: 460 pages with line drawings,
more than 400 recipes. Alfred A. Knopf, 1981.**

Any cookbook still in print seventeen years after publication has to have a lot going for it. This title was clearly
way ahead of its time, so it's not surprising that it seems so
contemporary today. Jaffrey, an Indian actress turned food
writer and cooking teacher, was prescient to see the importance of vegetarian cuisine when she did, and she has a fine
palate with which to express it. There are no compromises
on ingredients; authenticity comes first here, which means
this book is packed with delicious diversity. To collect the
recipes, Jaffrey, originally from Delhi, traveled extensively
throughout India, Asia, the Eastern Mediterranean, and the
Middle East. Her Lebanese recipe for Tabbouleh is the best
we've seen, yielding a lemony parsley salad flecked with
tomato and cracked wheat. While there is a chapter on eggs
and another on milk products, the majority of the recipes
feature vegetables and grains.

CONSIDER: Usha's Hot and Spicy Hyderabadi Tomato
Chutney (India); Miso Soup with Carrots and Mushrooms
(Japan); Cold Noodles with Sesame Sauce (Japan); Yogurt
with Fresh Mint, Raisins, and Walnuts (Iran); Thai Fried Rice.

Katzen, Mollie. *Mollie Katzen's Vegetable Heaven*. Hardcover: 224 pages, 200 recipes. Hyperion, 1997.

This new work by one of the leading writers on vegetarian cooking (and the companion volume to a PBS cooking series) features food that is "lighter, simpler, and tastier" than might previously have been the case. Like a lot of food writers, not just vegetarians, Katzen is trying to shorten the time we spend in the kitchen and yet still turn out a home-cooked meal. To that end the book is strong on soups and on medium-sized dishes that can be combined in various ways as the cook desires. Not as adventurous as some current meatless cookbooks, this one seems designed to mainstream vegetarian cooking for a television audience.

CONSIDER: Persian Eggplant Dip; Kung Pao Lettuce Cups; Tunisian Tomato Soup with Chickpeas and Lentils; Green and White Beans Under Garlic Mashed Potatoes; Rice Noodles with Cashew-Coconut Sauce; Blackberry Buckle with Warm Vanilla-Lemon Sauce; Cherry Upside-Down Gingerbread; Miniature Chocolate Soufflé Cakes; and Homemade Butterscotch Pudding.

Katzen, Mollie. *The Enchanted Broccoli Forest* (revised). Paperback: 303 pages, 220 recipes. Ten Speed Press, 1995.

This is a revised edition of the classic vegetarian cookbook published in 1982. Given its odd title, wobbly illustrations, and hand-lettered recipes, it would be easy to dismiss the book as quaint—if it weren't for its enduring popularity. It resembles a scrapbook of treasured family recipes and reads like advice from a hip, friendly grandmother, qualities no less welcome nearly twenty years later. The revision has lightened the fat and calories of many of the dishes, bringing old-fashioned cheese-and-nuts vegetarian food into the modern era. That title, since you asked, comes from a recipe in which broccoli stalks are served standing upright in a dish of brown rice pilaf.

CONSIDER: Curried Peanut Soup; Deviled Egg Pie; Enchiladas Filled with Cheese and Surprises; Apple and Cheddar Soufflé; Tofu, Spinach, and Walnut Loaf; Cottage Cheese–Dill Bread; Cherry-Berry Pie; Oatmeal-Yogurt Cake; and Fresh Strawberry Mousse.

La Place, Viana. _Verdura_. Paperback: 388 pages, 290 recipes. William Morrow, 1991.

The particularly creative Italian way with vegetables has been celebrated in a number of cookbooks, few better and none more attractive or more interesting than this one. La Place's roots are in California, but her restaurant training and her heart are both intensely Italian—conditions that made her well-suited to produce this earthy, inspired collection of (almost) meatless fare. Her philosophy is that we have grown out of touch with the earth and its seasons, and that one of the best ways to recapture that mysterious force is to eat fresh vegetables at their respective peaks of perfection. Less familiar vegetables such as cardoons, chayote, and brocciflower appear alongside Italian stalwarts like artichokes, radicchio, and eggplant. A brief concluding chapter of fresh fruit desserts is a pleasant surprise.

CONSIDER: Tomato and Peach Salad; Grilled Bread with Sautéed Mushrooms and Herbs; Summer White Bean

Soup with Tomato Salad Topping; and Baked Red Pepper Frittata.

Lee, Karen, with Diane Porter. *The Occasional Vegetarian.* **Hardcover: 272 pages, over 200 recipes. Warner, 1995.**

Karen Lee keeps a fairly low profile, but she's been one of New York's top caterers and Chinese cooking teachers for years. Lee is not Chinese; she developed her early food sensibilities in a three-month sojourn in France and has returned there often. This explains why she was such an early and deft practitioner of blending East and West flavors. Here she brings her prodigious talents to vegetarian recipes designed to appeal, as she professes, not only to hard-core vegetarians, whoever they may be, but to the legions of people like her (and us), who are naturally lightening their diet by eating meatless meals several times a week. Lee's appetizing offerings come in a wide range of styles and tastes, with strong emphasis on both Mediterranean and Asian—all doable and delicious.

CONSIDER: Penne with Roasted Tomato and Leek Sauce; Roasted Vegetable Cassoulet; Vegetable Lo Mein; Grilled Shiitake Mushrooms on Arugula; Chinese Charred Vegetable Pasta; Barefoot Contessa's Low-Fat Ginger Cake; Bananas Baked with Buttered Rum; Peach and Cherry Cobbler; and Drop-Dead Chocolate Cake.

Madison, Deborah. *The Savory Way.* **Paperback: 444 pages, 200 recipes. Broadway Books, 1998.**

This award-winning cookbook went out of print and immediately achieved cult status. Now available again as a paperback, it is no less attractive a work, and while it is meatless, any cook interested in good, fresh food will welcome its return. Madison has a way with vegetarian fare, celebrating seasonal vegetables, fresh herbs, pastas, beans, grains, and fruits with an appealing and personal style. Sometimes light, sometimes rich, occasionally labor-intensive but mostly not, this food is always deeply flavorful—savory, in fact, and while at times elegant, at its heart, as the author says, it's simple home cooking.

CONSIDER: Moroccan-style bread, stuffed with pistachio-and-jalapeño butter; Potato Salad with Tomatillo Sauce; Winter Vegetable Stew Baked in a Clay Pot; Cold Noodles with Peanut Sauce; Popped Millet Griddle Cakes; Smoked Chile Salsa; Wild Blackberry Sherbet; Apricot Upside-Down Cake; and Chocolate Chestnut Log.

Madison, Deborah. *Vegetarian Cooking for Everyone*. Hardcover: 742 pages with color photographs, 1,400 recipes. Broadway Books, 1997.

These days, many cookbooks claim to be bibles. Madison's tantalizing tome is, indeed, the Five Books of Moses of vegetarian cooking and the 1998 winner of the IACP Cookbook of the Year Award. Maybe it's because Madison herself is not a total vegetarian that she brings such a comfortable, extra-flavorful touch to meatless cooking. The recipes here are designed so that many can serve as the main event for a committed vegetarian or as a side dish along with meat, fish, or poultry for people who want to incorporate more vegetables and grains into their ordinary diet.

The immensely appealing dishes are original and call for a modicum of ingredients, which are used in intriguing ways.

CONSIDER: Rajas (Mexican-style roasted pepper strips and onions); Potato Soup with Mustard Greens; Butternut Squash Ravioli with Sage; White Bean and Vegetable Stew; Basic Buttermilk Biscuits; Ginger Cream Scones; Pear-Almond Upside-Down Cake; and Barley Sesame Flatbread.

Madison, Deborah, with Edward Espe Brown. *The Greens Cookbook: Extraordinary Vegetarian Cuisine from the Celebrated Restaurant.* **Hardcover: 396 pages, 260 recipes. Bantam Books, 1987.**

This is vegetarian food (eggs and dairy products are used) of the highest order—fresh, colorful, and satisfying in every way. Taking their inspiration from various world cuisines, particularly the Mediterranean, the authors (she was the San Francisco restaurant's founding chef, while he worked there in many capacities and authored, among other works, *The Tassajara Bread Book*) serve up a distinctive meatless cuisine that could probably have evolved only in California. Using many of the same fine sources for rare just-picked produce as Alice Waters's Chez Panisse, Greens' food is often simple, always extraordinary.

CONSIDER: Romaine Hearts with Buttered Croutons and Roquefort Vinaigrette; Roasted Eggplant Soup with Saffron Mayonnaise; Creole Egg Salad Sandwich; Spring Pasta with Artichokes, Mushrooms, and Peas; Black Bean Enchiladas; Buckwheat Crepes with Mushrooms; Rhubarb-Apple Betty; Meyer Lemon Mousse; and Blackberries with Rose Geranium Leaves.

The Moosewood Collective. *New Recipes from Moose-wood Restaurant.* **Hardcover: 302 pages with hand-tinted photographs, 200 recipes. Ten Speed Press, 1987.**

This was the first cookbook by the seventeen-member collective that operates Moosewood Restaurant following the departure of Mollie Katzen, whose original *Moosewood Cookbook* brought the Ithaca, New York, eatery to national attention. Since this later work is a group effort, there is necessarily less individual personality on the page, but there is no shortage of fine, mostly meatless cookery, much of it internationally inspired. Dairy products and eggs are used, as is seafood, which gives the food a lot of breadth. In the ten years that passed between the publication of Katzen's work and this one, vegetarian cooking grew up, resulting in much more sophisticated food, with considerably less fat. Also gone are the hand-lettered recipes, which will be seen as an improvement by many.

CONSIDER: Asian Asparagus Salad; Mexican Vegetables on Cornbread; West African Ground Nut Stew; Creole Beans and Rice; Baked Pasta with Cauliflower and Cheese; Flounder Florentine; Apple and Cheddar Cheese Pie; Pots de Crème au Chocolat; and Spice Cake with Prunes and Pecans.

Peterson, James. *Vegetables.* **Hardcover: 429 pages with color and black-and-white photographs, 300 recipes. William Morrow, 1998.**

On the dust jacket of this large and thorough book is a promotional quote from Madeleine Kamman that seems almost blasé: "Another excellent book by James Peterson."

One might almost yawn, were the scope and quality of Peterson's books not always so impressive. Vegetables being a friskier topic than sauces and seafood, Peterson's previous subjects, this book is lighter and perhaps better suited for the home cook. It begins with a list of vegetables from A to Z, giving buying and storing information and recommended cooking methods for each, followed by "The Dishes," in which vegetables are variously prepared, including occasionally with meat.

CONSIDER: Roasted Asparagus; Creamed Corn; Green Celeriac Rémoulade; Baked Squash with Butter and Maple Syrup; Endive and Bacon Gratin; Grilled Porcini; Truffle Risotto; Choucroute Garnie; Creamed Spinach Puree; Broccoli Rabe with Olives, Garlic, and Anchovies; Pork and Beans; and Glazed Turnips with Foie Gras.

Robertson, Laurel, Carol Flinders, and Brian Ruppenthal. *The New Laurel's Kitchen*. Paperback: 511 pages with illustrations and many charts, 500 recipes. Ten Speed Press, 1986.

The now not-so-new *The New Laurel's Kitchen* is a thorough updating of an even earlier work, a classic vegetarian cookbook. This version lightens dishes that have survived the test of time. Certainly there is a spiritual aspect to the book, with its emphasis on values that sustain the earth and its philosophy of no junk food, no junk lives. More than a mere recipe collection, it includes thorough sections on nutrition in pregnancy, weight control, and diets against disease. The emphasis is on home cooking, says Laurel, in contrast to the welter of "gourmet" meatless cookbooks on the market. Home is where friends and family are, and good food and good health are the greatest gifts.

CONSIDER: Fresh Corn and Tomato Soup; Green Bean Stroganoff; Lasagne al Forno; Spinach Crepes; Chard Pizza; Helen's Polenta with Eggplant; Many Bean Stew; Appley Bread Pudding; Oatmeal School Cookies; Fruit Tzimmes; and Yogurt Cheese Pie.

Ross, Rosa Lo San. *Beyond Bok Choy: A Cook's Guide to Asian Vegetables*. Hardcover: 191 pages with color photographs, 70 recipes. Artisan, 1996.

This book leaves few mysteries of a shopping trip to Chinatown's wondrous produce stores unsolved, and for the dedicated Asian cook with access to big-city markets, this is an indispensable (though not meatless) work. Each vegetable includes a description and photograph of it, information on buying and storing it, and tips for its cultivation, for those whose green thumbs (or small-town markets) lead them to grow their own bok choy. Each vegetable also comes with a recipe—some authentically Asian, some of Ross's creation (she teaches and caters in Manhattan)—designed to show off its best qualities. The shape and size of the book make it handy to take shopping, but it's a little hard to cook from.

CONSIDER: Meatballs Braised in Chinese Cabbage; Authentic Beef with Chinese Broccoli; Spicy Amaranth; Green Papaya Pancakes; Stem Ginger with Shredded Duck; Kohlrabi Tossed in Butter; and Garlic Chive Dumplings.

Sahni, Julie. *Classic Indian Vegetarian and Grain Cooking.* Hardcover: 511 pages with technical drawings, 230 recipes. William Morrow, 1985.

A follow-up to Sahni's masterwork on classic Indian cooking, this book is equally comprehensive, informative, and mouthwatering. With an ancient tradition of meatless cooking and a dazzling variety of seasonings, ingredients, and culinary customs considerably different from those of the West, India would seem to be a logical resource of fresh vegetarian ideas. And indeed, those who are vegetarian due to either spiritual belief or health concerns will find a wealth of information and good eating here. Those who merely want to broaden their knowledge of Indian cooking in general will also be well served. Lengthy sections on essential equipment, ingredients, and techniques are followed by a wide range of meatless recipes.

CONSIDER: Steamed Sourdough Split Pea Cakes with Sesame and Coriander; Cold Malabar Avocado Coconut Soup; Hearty Blue Mountain Cabbage and Tomato Stew; Spicy Eggplant in Ginger-Tamarind Sauce; Beets Smothered with Beet Greens; Sweet Potato Puffed Bread; Mustard-Flecked Hot Tomato Chutney; Nirvana Rice Pudding; Indian Mango Ice Cream; Coconut Dumplings; and Watermelon Sherbet.

Sass, Lorna. *Lorna Sass's Complete Vegetarian Kitchen.* Paperback: 492 pages, 250 recipes. William Morrow, 1992.

Among the reasons given for choosing a vegetarian diet, the ecological one is the most interesting, perhaps because it gets invoked less often than the others. Meat production wastes resources, says Sass, and does massive environmental harm. Eating a meat-centered diet, which she believes leads to many diseases, is also wasteful in terms of both life lost and dollars spent on health care. This is a strong stance, and the book (titled *The Ecological Kitchen* in its hardcover version), though a warm, friendly, and interesting read, is unsparing in its avoidance of animal foods; no dairy products or eggs are used. Sass also relies heavily on pressure cooking, steaming, and stir-frying—methods that use less energy. Organic ingredients are emphasized. For those wishing to adopt this kind of diet, the book will be useful indeed.

CONSIDER: Multibean Minestrone; Quinoa and Potatoes with Caraway; Pasta with Stir-Fried Greens and White Beans; Hot Thai-Style Broccoli; Tempeh Chili; Savory Blue Corn Muffins; Lemon Poppyseed Cake; and Down-Home Bread Pudding.

Sass, Lorna. *Lorna Sass's Short-Cut Vegetarian*. Paperback: 162 pages, 100 recipes. Quill, 1997.

Confessing to a longtime philosophy of "everything from scratch" (she pioneered the modern pressure-cooker revolution), Sass finally admits to finding an acceptable brand of canned beans and marks it as the moment this book's concept came to her: There are tricks and shortcuts out there that can help get vegetarian meals on the table faster than ever, without sacrificing quality or flavor. Sass's advice on choosing necessary equipment and setting up the shortcut pantry will help prepare the kitchen for getting down to work. There are recipes for pressure-cooker beans, just in case you still don't like canned, but most of these vegan recipes will help you produce healthful, completely meatless, lower-fat recipes in less time than you ever thought possible.

CONSIDER: Pinto Salsa Dip; Greek Leek and Potato Soup; Grain Salad with Lemon-Tahini Sauce; Asian Slaw; Smoky Black Bean Chili; Thai-Inspired Red Bean and Sweet Potato Stew; Fettuccine with Spinach Pesto; and Banana French Toast with Mango Sauce.

Shaw, Diana. *The Essential Vegetarian Cookbook*. Paperback: 611 pages, 600 recipes. Clarkson Potter, 1997.

This recent entry in the rather overwhelming vegetarian cookbook market is large and thorough. It begins with good advice on starting a vegetarian lifestyle, including general nutritional concerns, especially during pregnancy. The book then offers a number of well-balanced sample meatless menus for each of the reasons one goes vegetarian: to lose weight, to control diabetes, etc. Sidebars in the question-and-answer format reveal a lot of culinary information; all recipes include not only nutritional counts (the majority of the food is low in fat) but estimates of prep and cooking times as well. Stylistically the food is fresh and modern, and while many recipes are vegan, much use is also made of eggs.

CONSIDER: Chilled Cream of Carrot Soup with Ginger and Lime; Pierogi; Orange-Sesame Tempeh Soba; Lemon-Spiked Lentil Salad; Baked Eggs on Polenta with Spinach; Moo-Shu Mushrooms; Chunky Bean Burritos with Spicy

Tomato Sauce; Spinach Strudel; Grilled Tofu in Mideast Marinade; Pumpkin Bran Muffins; Chocolate-Cherry Sorbet; and Lemon-Berry Pudding.

Sommerville, Annie. *Fields of Greens: New Vegetarian Recipes from the Celebrated Greens Restaurant.* **Hardcover: 437 pages, 289 recipes. Bantam Books, 1993.**

When it comes to the food of Greens, the vegetarian restaurant at the San Francisco Zen Center, more, apparently, is more, as this volume testifies. Sommerville, who trained under Deborah Madison (author of the original *Greens Cookbook*) and succeeded her as Greens' chef, has a style so seamlessly similar to her mentor's that the two books are effectively a single work. The food is as fresh, lively, and meatless as ever (eggs and dairy products are used), although there is a new emphasis on gardening, following the Zen Center's establishment of its own organic truck farm.

CONSIDER: Grilled Potato Salad with Chipotle Vinaigrette; Curried Spinach Soup with Toasted Coconut; Chinese Noodle Salad with Citrus and Spicy Peanuts; Nectarine-Almond Streusel Coffee Cake; Steamed Chocolate Cake; Lemon Pots de Crème; and Rhubarb-Strawberry Cobbler.

Thomas, Anna. *The New Vegetarian Epicure.* **Hardcover and paperback: 449 pages, 325 recipes. Alfred A. Knopf, 1996.**

Thomas's first two "epicure" books were published in the 1970s and helped pioneer the meatless movement. Now

Thomas, along with so many of her fellows, is working in a lighter, more sophisticated, and better traveled vein. The resulting food is infinitely more attractive and more healthful. (Thomas, it must be noted, a more imaginative writer than many, had a head start on this process.) This handsome work is a menu book, which implies sharing with others, and so there is a spiritual message as well: "Food is not a chore; it's a gift."

CONSIDER: Roasted Eggplant Dip; Fresh Corn Tamales; Black Bean Chili; Artichoke Frittata; Polenta with Leeks and Gorgonzola; Couscous with Moroccan Spices; Charred Tomatoes with Garlic and Olives; Roasted Yams and Green Tomatoes; Wild Mushroom Cobbler; Fresh Peach Ice Cream; Coffee Flan; Orange Slices in Grand Marnier and Cognac; Chocolate Caramel Nut Tart; and Pear Sorbet.

Waters, Alice. *Chez Panisse Vegetables*. Hardcover: 344 pages with color botanical illustrations, 250 recipes. HarperCollins, 1996.

For twenty-five years Chez Panisse, the landmark Berkeley, California, restaurant, has been in the forefront of American cuisine. Based in the European tradition, the restaurant and Waters, its founder and chef, have pioneered a style of cooking that has become synonymous with California. Much of the emphasis at Chez Panisse is on vegetables, and small specialty growers of tasty but lesser-known varieties supply the kitchen with a wealth of fresh and unusual fare. At last Waters and Chez Panisse's many chefs have put their considerable knowledge of growing, handling, and cooking fine vegetables into a book. Beautifully illustrated by Waters's longtime collaborator, Patricia Curtan, the book is handsomely designed and packed with usually simple, always delicious, vegetable (not vegetarian) recipes. Running from A (Amaranth Greens) to Z (Zucchini), the food is incredibly enticing.

CONSIDER: Grilled Asparagus with Blood Oranges and Tapenade Toast; Carrot and Cilantro Soup; Fresh Black-Eyed Peas with Pancetta and Caramelized Onions; Hearts of Escarole with Apples and Roquefort; Fennel-Infused Broth with Halibut; Wild Mushroom and Greens Ravioli; and Winter Squash Pizza.

Willinger, Faith. *Red, White, and Greens: The Italian Way with Vegetables*. Paperback: 352 pages, 150 recipes. HarperCollins, 1999.

Though not the first—and probably not the last—book dealing with Italian vegetable cookery, this is surely the most thoroughly researched and engagingly written. In the by-now-established way of things, it deals with its vegetables from A to Z. Note that this is a book *about* vegetables, not a vegetarian work; meat, seafood, and dairy products occasionally appear. Willinger, who lives in Florence and writes about eating all around Italy, knows her onions, not to mention her cardoons. The Italian knack, it seems, lies in doing something simple that transforms a familiar vegetable into an extraordinary one. Many of the recipes have been shared with the author by native cooks, a sure way to compile a welcome array of nontrendy dishes. Discussions of varieties are useful (even the Italians now get out-of-season Mexican asparagus, just as we do), and the historical and cultural ramifications are explored.

CONSIDER: Giuliano's Garlicky Artichoke Spaghetti; The Mother of All Bean Recipes; Torquato's Cauliflower and Sausage; Staff Lunch Lentil and Rice Soup; New-Wave Eggplant Parmigiana; Fabio's Walnut, Pecorino, and Garlic Salad; Cesare's Fish Baked on Potatoes; Squash Risotto; and Francesca's Zucchini Carpaccio.

Low-Calorie, Reduced-Fat, and Spa Cooking

Bernard, Melanie, and Brooke Dojny with Mindy Hermann, R.D., and C. Wayne Callaway, M.D. *American Medical Association Family Health Cookbook.* **Hardcover: 135 pages, over 350 recipes. Pocket Books, 1997.**

This may be the book that actually inspires you to start eating well—not occasionally, in binges, but consistently, all the time. Close to fifty pages of really helpful information about diet, weight, optimal nutrition at different ages, and specific health problems provide a motivational read that's full of hard facts simply explained. The recipes are based upon the food pyramid. Reduced in fat and using meat in small portions for flavor and nutrition, they are both nutritionally sound and incredibly appealing. Steakhouse Salad, a toss of lean beef with artichokes, potatoes, Portobello mushrooms, arugula, radicchio, Italian bread, and mustardy balsamic vinaigrette, would be welcome on any table.

CONSIDER: Sweet Corn and Shrimp Salad; Almond Meringues with Purple Plum Compotes; Thai Grilled Chicken and Broccoli on Napa Cabbage; New Mexican White Clam Pizza; and Double Chocolate Brownies.

Brody, Jane. *Jane Brody's Good Food Book: Living the High-Carbohydrate Way*. Paperback: 732 pages, 350 recipes. Bantam Doubleday Dell, 1987.

Fad diets come and go and come again, but sound general advice on healthful eating remains pretty much constant: Eat less fat and animal protein, eat more complex carbohydrates, watch salt and sugar intake, and exercise moderately but regularly. This is the premise of Brody's massive book, which has had much to do with transforming our attitudes toward grains, beans, pasta, and potatoes. Fruits, nuts, sprouts, and vegetables are also celebrated. She lays out a general plan for eating more healthfully with the same firm, friendly, and practical voice that has characterized her writing for *The New York Times* for years. This is not a vegetarian book, and it is not a weight-loss plan as such, though weight will be lost if all the precepts are observed.

CONSIDER: Cocktail Knishes; Hot and Sour Chinese Soup; Turkey Tetrazzini; Buckwheat Noodle Stir-Fry; Brown Rice Curry with Vegetables and Shrimp; Deep-Dish Spinach Pizza; Carrot Cake; Spicy Poached Pears; Pumpkin Cookies; Apple-Ricotta Pie; and Pineapple Sherbet.

Jacobi, Dana. *Soy!* Paperback: 244 pages, 75 recipes. Prima Publishing, 1996.

So convincing are the arguments for working soybeans

and soy-derived products into our diets that books on the subject abound. One of the earliest and best is this simple paperback. The author touches on the health claims only briefly (chiefly her own nearly symptom-free passage through menopause) before getting into the nuts and bolts of handling soy foods and incorporating them into your diet. Vegan vegetarians already know much about tofu, miso, tempeh, soy milk, textured vegetable protein, and so on, but the rest of us have much to learn; this pragmatic and knowledgeable book is a good place to begin.

CONSIDER: Corn and Smoked Tofu Chowder; Sun-Dried Tomato Dip; Sweet and Sour Tofu Stir-Fry; Mushroom Chili; Macaroni and Cheese au Gratin; Eggless Egg Salad; Nutty Mushroom Tofu Burgers; Incendiary Thai Kebabs; Zucchini Muffins; Chocolate Silk Pie; Banana Coconut Bread Pudding; Apple Cranberry Crumble; and Gingerbread.

Jones, Jeanne. *Canyon Ranch Cooking: Bringing the Spa Home.* **Hardcover: 438 pages with color photographs, 280 recipes. HarperCollins, 1998.**

For Mel and Enid Zuckerman, the owners of the famed Canyon Ranch Spas (in Tucson and the Berkshire Mountains), "wellness is not a destination, it's a journey." This heavy, handsome book, with photos by Tom Eckerle, is written by Jones, their longtime menu consultant. Known for getting the fat out of favorite foods, Jones has worked out a balanced dietary approach, heavy on the carbohydrates, but also including protein, fiber, a bit of fat, and a pinch of salt. Lots of water, this book, and the fantasy of being coddled while being briskly exercised are then all it takes to bring the spa home (the book concludes with just such a plan for a weekend of health and fitness). Thirty-four Canyon Ranch fat-trimming tips and techniques can also be applied to your favorite home recipes.

CONSIDER: Canyon Ranch Guacamole (made with pureed asparagus, not avocado); Zucchini Bisque; Salad Niçoise with Grilled Tuna; Szechuan Chicken; Corn and Quinoa Casserole with Roasted Vegetables; and Pumpkin Crème Brûlée (140 calories and 2 grams of fat).

Mattson, Robin. *Soap Opera Café: The Skinny on Food from a Daytime Star*. Hardcover: 292 pages with black-and-white photographs throughout, over 150 recipes. Warner, 1997.

Why would a couple of top chefs like Emeril Lagasse and Daniel Boulud endorse a collection of reduced-fat recipes by a leading soap opera diva? Because they are that good. Unlike some celebrity cooks, Mattson has solid credentials: She graduated from the Los Angeles International Culinary Academy and hosted her own TV food program. And who is better equipped to fight fat than an actress who faces the camera every day? Mattson has her own distinctive light style, which features contemporary ingredients and an accent on flavor with striking visual presentation. Her own recipes, along with a sampling from fellow actors and star chefs, are interspersed with charming, surprisingly humorous anecdotes. Each recipe is followed by a nutritional analysis that includes calories, fat, and cholesterol per serving.

CONSIDER: Light and Lemony Tabbouleh; Mango Tango Soup; Cajun Roast Turkey Breast with Bourbon Gravy; Maple-Marinated Shrimp Kebabs; and Low-Fat Chocolate Soufflé.

Pepin, Jacques. *Simple and Healthy Cooking*. Hardcover: 354 pages with color photographs, illustrations by the author, 200 recipes. Rodale Press, 1994.

Pepin may have retained much of his French accent, but his cooking has moved forward with the American times, as this low-fat foray illustrates. Here the master chef brings his talent to creating food that is relatively simple to prepare and low in fat, but delicious. Pepin's success comes not in eliminating *anything*, as he puts it (butter and other high-fat ingredients do appear), but in using moderation and diversity. He also understands that the recommended levels of fat in the diet are meant to be achieved over the long haul; an occasional dish may exceed the limits without ruining the overall plan. To emphasize this point, the book begins with forty low-fat menus, helping to chart a fat-reducing course.

CONSIDER: Hot Thai Soup with Noodles; Ratatouille Dip with Endive; Salmon Sausage with Chipotle Sauce; Turkey Cassoulet; Angel Cake with Chocolate Sauce; and Crepes with Caramelized Apples and Pecans.

Raichlen, Steven. *Steven Raichlen's Healthy Latin Cooking*. Hardcover: 410 pages with color photographs, 200 recipes. Rodale Press, 1998.

The Latin American diet is not intrinsically unhealthful,

points out Raichlen, but with prosperity and the American emphasis on large amounts of meat at most meals, it has become that way. "Return to your roots" is at least part of the message of this book, which will be welcomed by Latins (a Spanish-language version is available) as well as by anyone who enjoys the foods of Mexico, Brazil, Cuba, and beyond. Plant foods are the most significant segment of the revised food pyramid for Latins. These include not only vegetables, beans, and fruits but nuts, an important source of unsaturated fats that are key in the traditional Latin diet. Known for his success at cutting the fat while keeping the flavor, Raichlen here gives side-by-side nutritional analyses for standard as well as his revised versions of many classic Latin dishes.

CONSIDER: Pork Empanadas; Gazpacho; Salt Cod Fritters; Nicaraguan Tamales; Beef Fajitas; Argentinean Mixed Grill; Pork in Oaxacan Mole; Guava Cheesecake; Flan; and Arroz con Leche (Rum-Raisin Pudding).

Rodgers, Rick. *Mr. Pasta's Healthy Pasta Cookbook.* Paperback: 260 pages, 150 recipes. Hearst Books, 1994.

Known for imaginative recipe development, lively writing, and professional thoroughness, Rodgers brings to what could be just one more book in the skinny and/or pasta categories a real vision of just how tasty reduced-fat and -calorie pasta can be. Assuming healthful pasta as a part of a sensible, non-crash-diet eating plan, Rodgers discusses nutrition, then gets on with solid culinary information. Twenty-five recipes for flavored fresh pastas are given (along with brief evaluations of leading pasta machines on the market), though most recipes call for purchased fresh or dried pasta varieties. As with the best of lower-fat cookery, family and guests won't even notice how good these recipes are for them.

CONSIDER: Faux Fettuccine Alfredo (7 fat grams versus 48 in the traditional recipe!); Grilled Tuna with Pesto Pasta Salad; Broccoli Rabe and Sausage with Ziti; Updated Chili Mac; Shellfish and Mushroom Lasagne; Clams in Tequila-Spiked Tomato Sauce on Vermicelli; Stir-Fried Thai Noodles with Shrimp and Tofu; Fish and Pasta Soup Niçoise; and Apricot-Raisin Kugel.

Sass, Lorna. *The New Soy Cookbook*. Paperback: 120 pages with color photographs, 40 recipes. Chronicle Books, 1998.

If soy-derived foods are indeed as miraculous as they are touted as being, there will surely be a need for more than one book explaining the best ways of buying, storing, and cooking such mysteries as tofu and tempeh. This recent addition to the soy-help lineup features the work of one of our best vegetarian writers complete with color photographs, a touch that may serve to convert doubters who assume all soy foods are putty gray. Sass's soy information is sound and practical, and her recipes—mostly vegetarian, a few containing seafood—are vividly flavored and easy to prepare.

CONSIDER: Thai-Inspired Shrimp and Tofu Cocktail; Red Lentil Soup with Indian Spices; Tempeh with Quick Homemade Tomato Sauce and Olives; Down-Home "Barbecued" Tofu; Cauliflower Slaw with Creamy Dill Dressing;

Pumpkin Tart with Pecan Crust; and Chocolate–Grand Marnier Sauce.

Sax, Richard, and Marie Simmons. *Lighter Quicker Better*. Hardcover: 416 pages, 200 recipes. William Morrow, 1995.

These talented food writers here apply their culinary skills to the goals of lowering calories and fat while producing satisfying results. Coauthors for a number of years of a lighter-cooking column for *Bon Appétit* (Simmons now continues solo after Sax's untimely death), they do not include nutritional counts for each recipe, but through sidebars and headnotes explain how they have slightly modified dishes to greatly reduce fat and calorie counts. The food, especially in the meatless main dish and dessert chapters, is so good you'll hardly know it's good for you.

CONSIDER: Smoked Salmon Mousse; Curried Cream of Carrot Soup; Southwestern Style Meat Loaf; Spaghetti and Little Herbed Meatballs; New Vegetable Paella; Sweet Potato Biscuits; Broiled Caramelized Pears with Toasted Almonds; Spicy Gingerbread with Warm Cider-Lemon Sauce; and Deep, Dark Devil's Food Cake.

Schneider, Sally. *The Art of Low-Calorie Cooking*. Paperback: 256 pages with color photographs, 125 recipes. Stewart, Tabori, and Chang, 1993.

The hardcover version of this attractive work was published in 1990 and created quite a sensation. Among a crowd of rather utilitarian low-calorie cookbooks, its oversized format and luminous photographs (by Maria Robledo, who did much to define the look of *Martha Stewart Living Magazine*) caused it to stand out. Schneider's goal was to develop dishes so delicious, no one could tell they are low-calorie, and she certainly achieves it here. Working with excellent ingredients, which intrinsically pack big flavors, and designing dishes where just a touch of something rich makes an impact, Schneider brought a creative, fine-dining sensibility to the low-fat cooking game.

CONSIDER: Artichoke Bottoms and Chicory with Warm Walnut Dressing; Yellow Pepper and White Bean Soup with Sage; Pasta with Swiss Chard, Cognac, and Cream; Cajun Meat Loaf; Divine Inspiration Pan-Smoked Salmon; Cassoulet; Pot-Roasted Beef with Ancho Chiles and Sweet Spices; Warm Cherries with Zabaglione; Phyllo Pear Tart with Fried Raspberries; Pineapple Upside-Down Cake; and Chocolate Chestnut Truffles.

Shulman, Martha. *Entertaining Light: Healthy Company Meals with Great Style*. Hardcover: 465 pages, 300 recipes. Bantam Books, 1991.

There are rigorous nutritional goals in this attractive, recipe-packed book: no more than 30 percent of calories from fat in any menu; no menu over 1,000 calories. Those statistics are of less importance, however, than Shulman's sense of culinary style, which is impeccable. A caterer and food writer who has over the years hosted what she calls a Supper Club in her home for up to thirty paying guests, Shulman loves to cook and entertain, and she doesn't see why extreme fat and calories *or* extreme deprivation should be a part of the process. Raised in Texas but living in Paris, she brings a worldly sense of design to the creation of a party. Some chapters are in the form of menus, which are supported by preparation timetables; others cover such useful turf as "Hors d'Oeuvres You Can Eat with One Hand"; "Come Over, I'll Make a Salad"; and "Choosing Wines."

CONSIDER: New Potatoes Filled with Corn and Sage Salad; Dried Porcini Soup with Tarragon Bruschette; Asparagus and Herb Lasagna; Black Bean Chili; Roast Turkey with Wild Rice and Chestnut Stuffing; Baked Apples with Whiskey and Honey; Prune Ice Cream; Orange Biscotti; and Maple Pecan Pie.

Stroot, Michel. *The Golden Door Cookbook*. Hardcover: 302 pages with color and black-and-white photographs, 200 recipes. Broadway Books, 1997.

Known as "the world's most luxurious spa," The Golden Door, in Escondido, California, has been pampering and slenderizing ladies (and some gents) for decades. Now Stroot, the executive chef, with the help of cookbook veteran Mary Goodbody, has collected some of the spa's notoriously tasty dishes into a cookbook. At home you must necessarily supply your own serenity, and the exercise may be optional, but the food, which for many is the most memorable part of a Golden Door stay, will be all yours. Each recipe has full nutritional information, and each is designed to derive less than 20 percent of its calories from fat.

CONSIDER: Potato Skins with Ricotta Sun-Dried Tomato Dip; Tortilla Bites with Spa Guacamole and Turkey; Hot and Sour Shrimp Soup; Lobster-Filled Papaya; Curried Ratatouille with Tofu and Quinoa; Roasted Mahimahi with Tomatillo Salsa; Stir-Fried Tamarind Chicken with Shiitake Mushrooms; Apricot Cobbler with Berries; Exotic Fruit Salad with Mint and Gingersnap Crumbles; and Apple Pizza.

Single-Subject
Cookbooks

Pasta and Asian Noodles

Bugialli, Giuliano. *Bugialli on Pasta.* Hardcover: 363 pages with color photographs and technical drawings, 200 recipes. Simon & Schuster, 1988.

Thanks to pasta's popularity, there is too much undirected "creativity," says Bugialli. As an advocate for, and a master of, traditional Italian cooking, he has written this book—among the handful of pasta cookbooks worth owning—to set the record straight. The result is a passionate, mouthwatering treatise on pasta Italian style. Bugialli can be dogmatic, but always within the context of the proper Italian way. Early chapters are organized around the other main ingredient—pasta and beans, pasta and vegetables, pasta with fish; later chapters cover flavored pastas, fresh regional pastas (a standout), and even dessert pastas. The recipes are so enticing, no one will feel shortchanged, in either the pasta or the creativity department.

CONSIDER: Spaghetti with Black Truffles; Naked Ravioli with Gorgonzola; Lasagne with Shrimp and Mussels; Pasta with Duck, Parma Style; Red Pasta with Onion-Flavored Pesto; and honey-drizzled Chocolate Pasta Dessert "Nests."

della Croce, Julia. *Pasta Classica*. Hardcover and paperback: 160 pages with color and black-and-white archival illustrations, 125 recipes. Chronicle Books, 1987.

We love pasta, but enthusiasm alone is not enough, and many modern American notions about pasta cause Italians to shudder. Acquiring a sense of history, classic proportions, and time-tested combinations is the surest way of coming up with something good to eat. It's also absolutely necessary before setting out to "invent" some new pasta dish (assuming, after educating ourselves about the genuine article, invention retains any appeal). To acquire that sound pasta education, turn to this handsomely designed work, one of only a handful of pasta books worth owning and cooking from. More than a third of this profusely illustrated volume is given over to a much-needed discussion of pasta history and basics, but don't assume it is a work of dry scholarship.

CONSIDER: Pasta and Bean Soup; Sweet Potato Gnocchi with Almond Sauce; Tagliarini with Fish and Lemon Sauce; Spinach Lasagne Bolognese; Corn Pasta with Zucchini and Red Peppers; and Wide Chocolate Noodles with Veal Sauce.

De'Medici, Lorenza. *Lorenza's Pasta*. Hardcover: 192 pages with color photographs and archival illustrations, 200 recipes. Clarkson Potter, 1996.

This is a big and lavishly produced book, perhaps too much so, since the deliberately scratched and damaged, fresco-like color photographs, no doubt intended to add rustic authenticity to the project, tend to detract from the sound simplicity of the recipes. De'Medici, once the editor of Italian *Vogue*, is a stylish grandmother and PBS food program host who operates a cooking school on the grounds of the family's wine and olive oil estate, Badia a Coltibuono, in Tuscany. Tuscan food is among Italy's most restrained, and in the extensive how-to section that opens the book, De'Medici campaigns, as do all Italian teachers, against the American pasta excesses of too much sauce, too much cheese, and too much creativity. She is a masterful pasta maker: We once saw her, dressed all in Armani, whip up a batch by hand—and she didn't get a speck of flour on her beautiful clothes.

CONSIDER: Angel Hair and Asparagus Soup; Shells with Broccoli and Saffron; Trenette with Radicchio and Goat's Cheese; Fettuccine with Caviar and Ricotta; Linguine with Pork and Eggplant; Tortelloni with Swordfish and Olives; and Green Lasagna with Lamb and Sweet Bell Peppers.

Hazan, Giuliano. *The Classic Pasta Cookbook*. Hardcover: 160 pages with color photographs, 100 recipes. Dorling Kindersley, 1993.

In the way of other books from this publisher, there is color photography on virtually every page of this mouthwatering tribute to pasta. Hazan, son of Italian food writer Marcella, lives and works in the United States but has inherited his love of pasta as well as his mastery of classic Italian cooking from his mother. The result is a pasta book that is boldly modern in appearance, but traditional in approach—as an educational tool, it's hard to imagine a better pasta book. Hazan begins with a catalog of pasta shapes, always working to pair a sauce with its ideal pasta matchup, resulting in taste and texture perfection. General advice on making and serving pasta is followed by eleven classic sauces; then traditional and modern recipes complete this imaginative work.

CONSIDER: Spaghettini with Shrimp, Tomatoes, and Capers; Fettuccine with Zucchini and Saffron Cream; Buckwheat Noodles with Fontina and Swiss Chard; Rigatoni with Lamb Ragu; Bow Tie Pasta with Smoked Salmon and Roasted Bell Peppers; and Artichoke Tortelloni with Pink Tomato Sauce.

Passmore, Jackie. *The Noodle Shop Cookbook*. Hardcover: 246 pages, 170 recipes. Macmillan, 1994.

This book was clearly ahead of the current passion for noodles, Far Eastern style. Passmore has an extensive culinary experience throughout the region, and she delves deeply into the noodles of seven separate cuisines. Though the book lacks the sexy magic of color photographs, the in-depth discussion of noodles and other essential ingredients more than compensates. The book has vividly contrasting recipes from China, Singapore, Malaysia, Indonesia, Thailand, Vietnam, and Japan, so it's unlikely that the reader will feel any sense of limitation—only hunger pangs. There is a chapter of vegetarian recipes, as well as one of Passmore's own improvisations on the noodle theme.

CONSIDER: Shrimp Noodle Soup with Chinese Greens; Sichuan Fireball Dumplings; Chicken in a Creamy Crabmeat Sauce over Egg Noodles; Dan Dan Spicy Peddler's Noodles; Seafood Coconut Curry Soup; Pork and Long Beans on Soft Fried Egg Noodles; Hot Thai Noodles; Curried Noodles for the New Year; Shrimp Ball and Roast Pork Soup Noodles; and Classic Cold Soba (buckwheat noodles).

Simonds, Nina. *Asian Noodles: Deliciously Simple Dishes to Twirl, Slurp, and Savor.* Hardcover: 131 pages with color photographs, 75 recipes. William Morrow, 1997.

Love noodles and crave Asian food? If so, this book is for you. Slim, but packed with mouthwatering "pasta" recipes (and delectable photographs by Christopher Hersheimer), it is an indispensable addition to the good cook's international bookshelf. Noted as a teacher of Chinese cooking, Simonds has cast her well-trained eye for noodle-based comfort food all over the Asian arena. The result is a work with solid buying and cooking information and a group of recipes that will have you reaching for the ginger and the pasta pot in short order. The recipes are diverse in taste and texture, quick to prepare, healthful, often economical, and always satisfying.

CONSIDER: Noodle-stuffed Vietnamese Spring Rolls; Ginger Scallops with Thin Noodles; Spicy Korean Beef Noodles served in lettuce-leaf packets; Cinnamon Beef

Noodles; Red-Hot Sichuan Noodles; Thai Pork with Slippery Noodles and Pineapple; and Hot-and-Sour Shrimp Lo Mein.

Teubner, Christian, Silvio Rizzi, and Tan Lee Leng. *The Pasta Bible*. Hardcover: 240 pages with color photographs and archival illustrations, 150 recipes. Penguin Studio, 1996.

Teubner, the photographer/chef who headed the teams responsible for *The Chocolate Bible* and *The Chicken and Poultry Bible*, now brings his opulent visual style to the world of pasta. Pasta has a long history, a large set of fundamental technique requirements, rich visual possibilities, and an almost primal attraction. After a discussion of which grains are employed in making pasta and of how pastas are made, there are pages and pages of illustrations of pasta shapes—both fresh and dried; there is also sensible advice on how to cook pasta. The recipes range far and wide, including, it must be noted with satisfaction, plenty from noodle-rich Asia. While there are simple little recipes, there are also quite a few more fantastic ones.

CONSIDER: Greek Tomato Soup with Orzo; Crispy Wonton Soup; Bucatini Served in a Block of Parmesan; Basil-Flavored Noodles with Salami Sauce; Penne with Tomatoes and Eggplant; Ravioli Stuffed with Lamb; Rice Noodles with Pork and Tofu; Cannelloni with Seafood Stuffing; Spaetzle; and sweet Noodle Pudding with Chestnuts and Cherry Compote.

Rice

Alford, Jeffrey, and Naomi Duguid. *Seductions of Rice.* Hardcover: 480 pages with color photographs, 200 recipes. Artisan, 1998.

Americans are finally beginning to get the idea that there's more to rice than raisin-studded diner pudding and Uncle Ben's. We now appreciate the remarkable variety and importance of rice in diets around the globe and understand the difference a diet with a generous amount of complex carbohydrates can make to our health. Most rice-eating cultures are familiar only with their own indigenous rice(s), so this book travels to all points in order to create a kind of anthropology of rice. The authors, international food photographers, cover the world, differentiating a multitude of rice types, giving the best ways of cooking them, and pairing them with dishes from Thailand to Oaxaca. Cooking tips and ideas for recipes often come from the cooks on the street, while lots of photos reinforce the local color.

CONSIDER: Beef and Lettuce Congee; Sweet Rice and Pork Dumplings; Smoky Red Pepper Chicken; Winter Stir-Fry with Root Vegetables; Risotto with Salami and Red Beans; Senegalese Festive Rice and Fish; Classic Low-Country Pulao with Chicken and Bacon; Jamaican Rice and Peas; and Oaxacan Rice Pudding.

Owen, Sri. *The Rice Book: The Definitive Book on Rice, with Hundreds of Exotic Recipes from Around the World.* Paperback: 402 pages, 200 recipes. Griffin, 1993.

America eats less rice than almost any other country, although an increasing interest in the goodness of grains in general is changing this. For Owen, who is a native of Indonesia, rice is a fundamental of life and cooking, and this prizewinning book is her effort to share that importance with those for whom rice is not quite yet as significant. There are, as the subtitle promises, many exotic recipes, but there is also a long introductory section on the types of rice, their cultivation and harvesting, nutritional strengths, cooking methods, and even the religious significance of the grain in some parts of the world.

CONSIDER: Puerto Rican Rice and Peas; Wild Rice Croquettes with Ham; Thai Chicken and Galingale Soup with Rice Vermicelli; Jambalaya with Chicken; Rice and Rhubarb Porridge; and Black Rice Sorbet.

Rodgers, Rick. *On Rice: 60 Fast and Easy Toppings That Make the Meal.* **Paperback: 144 pages with color photographs, 60 recipes. Chronicle Books, 1997.**

Rice, one trend-spotting magazine has claimed, is the new pasta. We're not sure about that, but Rodgers wisely thinks that rice is worth celebrating for its own sake. The world's rices (also other toppable grains) are discussed, and then Rodgers, known for his deft recipe development, gets right into the heart of the matter. In such chapters as "From the Sea," "From the Farm," and "From the Ranch," he rings all the possible international changes he can on the book's theme. No long-simmered, mingled-rice dishes like pilaf, jambalaya, or paella are found here. Instead, in the manner of Asian stir-fries, quick imaginative saucy sautés are cooked up in about the same time as the pot of rice over which they are served.

CONSIDER: Portuguese Clams with Linguica Sausage; Brazilian Fish Stew; Chicken and Asparagus with Mustard-Tarragon Sauce; Sirloin and Black Bean Chili; Smoked Pork Chops with Beer-Braised Cabbage; and Erna's Make-in-Your-Sleep Raspberry Rice Pudding.

Simmons, Marie. *Rice, the Amazing Grain: Great Rice Dishes for Every Day.* **Hardcover: 288 pages, 160 recipes. Henry Holt, 1991.**

This is a practical rice book, written for the contemporary American cook. Simmons, a monthly columnist for *Bon Appétit*, sets her respect for rice in the context of recipes that are light, fresh, and uncomplicated. Over half the world's population eats rice as their main starch, says Simmons, and for them it is an affordable, nutritious, low-fat staple that is wondrously versatile. The story of rice cultivation is told, rice varieties are differentiated, and cooking methods are explained, but it is the recipes that really matter, and there are plenty of these, all attractive sounding and approachable.

CONSIDER: Corn and Rice Chowder with Smoked Prawns; Brown Rice, Lentil, and Sausage Salad with Roasted Red Peppers; Josephine's Rice and Beans, Puerto Rican Style; One "Mean" Jambalaya; Orange and Currant Pilaf; Creamy Rice Pudding with Mangoes and Pistachios; Pecan Carrot Cake (made with brown rice); and Orange and Rice Crème Caramel.

Meat and Chicken

Aidells, Bruce, and Denis Kelly. *The Complete Meat Cookbook.* **Hardcover: 604 pages with color photographs and black-and-white technical illustrations, over 230 recipes. Houghton Mifflin, 1998**

The renewed interest in meat—as a special treat to be enjoyed perhaps less often but with full gusto—has left some cooks with an information gap. Many tasty joints, such as lamb shanks, beef short ribs, and fresh ham, are unfamiliar to contemporary cooks more accustomed to boneless cuts. As Aidells and Kelly, both former chefs and coauthors of *Real Beer and Good Eats* and *Hot Links and Country Flavors*, argue as well, modern meat is raised to be leaner, which means less fat to add flavor and tenderize the large muscles. Consequently cooking techniques must be adjusted to add moisture and taste and to help you achieve some of those old-fashioned results Mom used to serve up without a thought.

This book is appealing, complete, and approachable. Clear illustrations and text show what the different cuts of beef, pork, lamb, and veal look like and where they come from on the animal. Text explains nomenclature and how to buy the best. Want to know just what a hanger steak is and how to get one? This is the place to look. Besides plenty of marvelous recipes that use the different cuts, included also are all kinds of ways to enhance flavor— marinades, brines, and rubs—as well as assorted side dishes, sauces, and condiments. Dishes range from Sautéed Filet Mignon with Artichoke and Mushroom Ragù that are "Fit for Company" to assorted ribs, meat loaves, and burgers, which accommodate "Cooking on a Budget" and conjure up memories of meals from the past. A number of quick meat recipes are included, as well as some that are relatively low in fat. There is a small section on sausage making; Aidells is nationally known for the commercial gourmet sausage company that bears his name.

CONSIDER: Braised Lamb Shanks with Fennel and Small White Beans; Thai-Style Barbecued Baby Back Ribs; Braised Pork Butt (shoulder) with Port and Prunes; Roasted Pork Tenderloin with Dried Cranberries and Apples; Philly Cheese Steaks; California Beef Stew with Zinfandel and Roasted Winter Vegetables; Oven-Braised Veal with Portobello Mushrooms.

Barnard, Melanie. *Everybody Loves Meatloaf.* Hardcover: 166 pages, over 100 recipes. HarperPerennial, 1997.

It's true, everybody does love meatloaf. Only sometimes they forget. Here's the perfect little book to remind you of just how good, versatile, and economical all kinds of loaves can be. Because beyond the usual beef, pork, sausage, and mixed meat loaves, Barnard explores plenty of turkey, chicken, seafood, and vegetarian alternatives. Barnard, who has her own cooking program on CNBC every other Friday, is a prolific and dependable author with lots of good ideas. While she explains just what makes a great meatloaf, this is not brain surgery, and the delight of the book is in the variety of its recipes. Beyond the expected, she's taken flavor combinations from popular classics and transformed them into loaf form.

CONSIDER: Bacon and Double Cheeseburger Loaf; Osso Buco Loaf with Gremolata Tomato Gravy; Reuben Loaf; and Sweet and Sour Pork Loaf.

Ellis, Merle. *The Great American Meat Book*. Hardcover: 338 pages with technical drawings and archival illustrations, 300 recipes. Alfred A. Knopf, 1996.

Meat is back—good news for Merle "The Butcher" Ellis and his many fans, none of whom ever really believed it had gone away. As the number of vegetarian cookbooks published each year rises in seemingly exponential fashion, so too does the hunger for steaks, chops, and roasts of every succulent sort. More philosophical types can gnaw over that puzzle, while the rest of us, led by the ever-knowledgeable Ellis, will set about getting dinner on the table. Organized by the various meats in question (beef, lamb, pork, veal, plus "odds 'n' ends" and sausages; there is no poultry), this book discusses the best ways of cooking the fundamental cuts, then gives good, nearly always easy, recipes showing them off at their best.

CONSIDER: Second-Best Chili; Sauerbraten and Potato Pancakes; Basic Smothered Steak with Onions; Fajitas; The Best Burger; Maytag Blue-Stuffed Iowa Pork Chops; Country Ham and Potato Casserole; Curried Lamb Shanks in Wine; Kidneys in Sherry Mustard Sauce; and Moroccan Lamb Sausage (Merguez).

Hibler, Janie. *Wild About Game.* **Hardcover: 311 pages with color photographs and archival illustrations, 150 recipes. Broadway Books, 1998.**

Game is a trend on restaurant menus, says this book's publisher, and soon more of us will want to be cooking it at home. While there will always be variables in preparing something from the wild, this book's scope is broad enough, and Hibler's game-cooking experience deep enough, that much of the guesswork has been eliminated. Married to a hunter, Hibler—an author and cooking teacher—has been cooking game for over thirty years, and as a resident of the Pacific Northwest, eating it for longer than that. Her expertise, along with the growing availability of more predictable farm-raised game animals, means the average home cook can experience the joys of cooking and eating game without the drawbacks of strong flavors, tough meat, or stray buckshot—not to mention actually having to go hunting. The internationally influenced recipes here run the gamut from homey and simple to restaurant-complex, and they deal with everything from alligator and antelope to venison and wild turkey—as well as kangaroo, rattlesnake, and possum. Sidebars reprint some very readable quotes on game cookery in American history, and the recipes, necessarily developed to showcase the big flavors inherent in most game, are robust and intriguing.

CONSIDER: Slow-Roasted Duckling with Red Currant Sauce; Pheasant with Chanterelles and Herb Dumplings; Grilled Squab with Gorgonzola and Orecchiette; Cider-Basted Wild Turkey; Buffalo and Beer Pot Roast; Thai Green Curry Turtle Soup; Game Terrine with Roasted Shallot Mustard Sauce; Vietnamese Smoked Pheasant Soup; and Venison Jerky.

Longbotham, Lori. *Summer/Winter Chicken*. Paperback: 111 pages with color photographs, 70 recipes. William Morrow, 1997.

This clever flip book (with the two seasons reversed from each other) is an attractive package (the excellent photos are by Melanie Acevedo), full of savory ideas. Given the vast number of chicken recipes in the world, it makes sense to retreat to a manageably modest work that fills your basic chicken needs. Longbotham, a former editor at *Gourmet*, spices up her work with an international array of flavors, and earns special kudos for keeping the use of boneless chicken breasts to a minimum, knowing, apparently, that chicken cooked on the bone is more flavorful.

CONSIDER: (Summer) Spicy Fried Chicken Salad; Cold Sesame Noodles with Chicken; Chicken Sauté with Peaches and Basil; and All-American Barbecued Chicken; (Winter) Old-Fashioned Chicken Noodle Soup; Chicken with Bacon and Goat Cheese; Chicken and Sausage Gumbo; and Beverly Hills Chicken Pot Pie.

Rice, Bill. *Steaklover's Cookbook.* **Hardcover: 246 pages, 140 recipes. Workman, 1997.**

Steak is hot, steak is in, steak is what we want to eat, and while all sensible folks are watching their diets, steak as a treat is being celebrated as never before. Given the increasing rarity of its appearance on our tables, knowing the best way to buy, store, cook, and serve steak now becomes essential, and so, to that end, Bill Rice has written *the* book on the subject. Following sound advice on finding the steak and getting it home, Rice, the food and wine columnist of the *Chicago Tribune*, serves up recipes for pricey uptown cuts like tenderloin and porterhouse, while not ignoring cheaper "downtown" cuts like chuck and flank. He also gives terrific recipes for dishes that go great with steak.

CONSIDER: The True Steak au Poivre; Surf and Turf Asian Style; Grilled Sirloin with Greek Olive Butter; Lush Chicken Liver Pâté; Herbed Potato Hash; Outrageous Onion Rings; and Rich Raisin Bread Pudding with Bourbon Caramel Sauce.

Teubner, Christian, Sybil Grafin Schonfeldt, and Siegfried Scholtyssek. *The Chicken and Poultry Bible.* **Hardcover: 192 pages with color photographs and archival illustrations, 100 recipes. Penguin Studio, 1997.**

Styled "The Definitive Sourcebook," this bible, unlike Teubner's works on chocolate and pasta, has a less focused subject and so is a less intense culinary experience. Also, while we are fully prepared to be seduced by a plate of pasta or a chocolate dessert, we mostly turn to poultry out of some form of necessity, giving this particular book a more dutiful air than its companion volumes. Which is not to say paging through it won't make you hungry. Historical notes and lots of sound basic information on how the various types of poultry are bred, stored, boned, trussed, stuffed, and so on are impeccably done, while the chapters, mostly organized by cooking technique, are packed with appealing (some quite challenging) recipes.

CONSIDER: Consommé of Guinea Fowl and Tomatoes; French Cream of Chicken Soup; Squab Steamed in Beet Leaves; Champagne Chicken with Lobster; Barbecued Marinated Chicken; Turkey Breast Cordon Bleu; Duck in Cherry Sauce; The Classic Roast Goose; Smoked Chicken Pizza; and Szechuan Chicken.

Sandwiches

Cotler, Amy. *Wrap It Up.* **Paperback: 208 pages, 100 recipes. Three Rivers Press, 1998.**

As the subtitle explains, this delightful little book is filled with "100 fresh, bold, and bright sandwiches with a twist." The twist is that instead of being sandwiched between slices of bread, the fillings here are wrapped up, usually in flour tortillas and other flatbreads, occasionally in lettuce leaves. Since in most cases, the filling is completely enclosed, wraps tend to keep better than ordinary sandwiches and, cut in half on the diagonal, are both attractive and easy to eat. Cotler, who teaches at Peter Kump's New York Cooking School and at New York University, specializes in vegetarian food, and the two chapters on vegetables and beans and legumes are particularly creative.

CONSIDER: Corny Avocado Taco; Antipasto Wrap;

Smoky Eggplant Gyro; Wrap-tatouille; Thyme-Roasted
Vegetables with Chèvre; Crispy Twice-Baked Bean and
Cheese Wrap; Who-Needs-Meat Fajitas with Ancho
Chili Sauce; Chicken Wrap with Sun-Dried Tomatoes;
Deer Isle Lobster Roll; Wasabi-Steamed Salmon and
Cabbage Bundles; and a Carnegie Deli Wrap.

McLaughlin, Michael. *The Little Book of Big Sand-*
wiches. **Hardcover: 95 pages with two-color illustra-**
tions, more than 85 recipes. Chronicle Books, 1996.

It's not often that a great sandwich book comes along,
but this is one you don't want to miss. Who needs a collection of recipes to make sandwiches? Anyone who has
ever eaten one too many tuna fish, egg salad, or ham and
cheese sandwiches. The *big* in the title refers not so much
to the physical size of the preparation as to its bold flavor
and position in the meal. No little teatime nibbles here.
Many of these are knife-and-fork sandwiches. A bonus
to go with the recipes is McLaughlin's colorful, witty
writing, in which he shares many a memory of hand-
held food.

CONSIDER: Focaccia Sandwiches with Mushrooms
(sautéed Portobello caps), Garlicky Greens, and Goat
Cheese; Cobb Sandwiches; Roast Pork and Apple Sand-
wiches with Horseradish Mayonnaise—along with a
Madeira Roast Loin of Pork to begin with; Shrimp on a
Shingle; Griddled Tomato, Pesto, and Three-Cheese Sand-
wiches; and Soft-Shell Crab Sandwiches with Tabasco
Toasted-Pecan Mayonnaise.

Seafood

Brown, Edward, and Arthur Boehm. *The Modern Seafood Cook*. Hardcover: 339 pages, over 250 recipes. Clarkson Potter, 1995.

Ed Brown's first job, at seventeen, was unloading fishing boats that docked near his home on the New Jersey coast. The ocean catch smelled "sweet and salty and green, like a windy day on the shore." At the restaurant for which the bounty was intended, the pearly fresh seafood was "mouthwatering raw and astonishing to eat when prepared." Now, after years of seasoning in restaurant kitchens here and abroad, he is chef of Rockefeller Center's Sea Grill. There, his twin approaches of gentle cooking and subtle embellishment have earned his seafood cookery fine reviews, and have led to the publication of this book, intended to demystify fish cookery for the newcomer as well as to teach old kitchen salts some new tricks. The how-to-shop and how-to-handle sections that are essential to any seafood cookbook are impeccably written here; anyone with access to seafood anywhere near fresh will learn the best ways of selecting, storing, and prepping it. Organized mainly by cooking technique, the recipes have contemporary restaurant flair but are easy enough for the home cook, and though Brown recommends a specific fish variety for each, substitutes are suggested. Particularly interesting chapters include those on Cooking in Wrappers; Dumplings, Fish Cakes, and Croquettes; Po' Boys and Snapper Sandwiches; and an excellent one on preparing sushi and sashimi at home.

CONSIDER: Fishermen's Chowder; Moroccan Lobster Salad; Crab and Avocado Roll; Roasted Whole Grouper with Garlic, Potatoes, and Bacon; Barbecued Shrimp on Sugarcane Skewers with Ginger-Lime Sauce; Big Danny's Thai Fish Cakes; Fat Tuesday Catfish with Dirty Rice; and Soft-Shell Crab Club Sandwiches.

King, Shirley. *Fish: The Basics*. Paperback: 333 pages with technical drawings, 100 recipes. Chapters Publishing, 1996.

This simple, thoughtful, encouraging book that covers the bases while providing easy recipes that can be prepared today, with today's catch, is a find. A reprint of an earlier hardcover, this no-nonsense work spells out the differences between round and flat fish, describes the major varieties of fish and shellfish, and gives good buying and storage information. Its strength, however, is in the recipes. There are not a lot and they are basic indeed, designed for the most part to cook a type and cut of fish rather than a specific variety (though the best varieties are suggested)—sensible, given that the freshness of the fish found at market is far more important than tracking down the main ingredient for a too-specific recipe. The book is a beginner's treasure, though the generic recipe titles only hint at the potential good eating.

CONSIDER: Bake-Poached Fish Fillets; Roast Whole Fish; Deep-Fried Seafood with Seasoned Flour; Steamed Lobster; Seviche; and Seafood Stew.

Le Coze, Maguy, and Eric Ripert. *Le Bernardin Cookbook—Four-Star Simplicity*. Hardcover: 372 pages with color photographs, 110 recipes. Doubleday, 1998.

Le Bernardin is the only four-star seafood restaurant in New York. Founded by French-born Gilbert Le Coze and his sister, Maguy, it set a standard for subtle luxe and pristine seafood presented with what can only be called opulent restraint. Following Gilbert's untimely death several years ago, many wondered if Le Bernardin would decline. So like-minded were the two siblings, however, that Maguy—more than ably aided by her brother's second-in-command, Eric Ripert—has fiercely preserved the restaurant's standing. Now a book celebrating that excellence has been published. It is handsomely designed, silvery and blue like the bounty of the sea, and while the impression must always remain that when it comes to seafood of the Le Bernardin level, access to the finest raw materials is more than half the battle, these recipes will help serious home cooks duplicate much of the restaurant's cuisine at home.

The dishes are a mix of the old and the new (Ripert's style is more Mediterranean and complex than was Gilbert's), and except for a beef salad and a chapter of elegant desserts, it's all seafood.

CONSIDER: Slivered Black Bass with Basil and Coriander; Spiced Tuna Salad with Curry-Peanut Dressing; Gazpacho with Shrimp and Croutons; Pan-Roasted Salmon with Red Wine-Lentil Sauce; Whole Turbot Baked with Lemon, Fennel, and Tomato; Bitter Chocolate Soufflé Cake; Earl Grey Tea and Mint Soup with Assorted Fruit; and Rice Pudding with Dried Lemon, Orange, and Apple-Guanabana Sorbet.

Loomis, Susan Herrmann. *The Great American Seafood Cookbook*. Paperback: 320 pages with black-and-white photographs and technical drawings, 250 recipes. Workman, 1988.

This remains one of the best and most thorough of seafood cookbooks despite its many years in print. Some information may have become dated, but the author's passion for the freshest possible seafood and her inventive recipes are timeless. Not one to sit at her desk imagining the sea, Loomis headed out on trawlers, oyster boats, shrimpers, and skiffs, watching the catch pulled from the ocean and following it back to market and then home. The technical information and drawings are very good, with major and some minor fresh and saltwater seafood varieties covered. The recipes were selected, says the author, to maintain some connection to the people she met in the fishing industry.

CONSIDER: Smoked Sturgeon with Salmon Pâté and

Roe; Crabmeat and Cheese Gratin; Mussels in Balsamic Vinaigrette; Spiced Lamb Patties and Oysters; Maine Lobster Stew; Greek-Style Rosemary-Grilled Swordfish Kebabs; Macadamia Mahimahi in Coconut Milk; Trout with Hazelnuts and Butter; and Steamed Salmon with Corn, Bacon, and Cream.

Peterson, James. *Fish and Shellfish: The Cook's Indispensable Companion*. Hardcover: 413 pages with color photographs and charts, 240 recipes. William Morrow, 1996.

Seafood intimidates many cooks, and even the imposing size of this virtual tome of seafood recipes and information may also be a little scary, but hang in there: Peterson's friendly, reassuring voice and encyclopedic knowledge of seafood cookery have the power to open up a whole new culinary world. A former chef and a professional cooking instructor, Peterson leaves few seafood questions unanswered. The author divides the book into finfish recipes, further divided by technique, and shellfish recipes, the latter dealt with by variety. There is sound buying and storing information, plus good technique photos and less good finished-dish pictures by the author.

CONSIDER: Braised Striped Bass Fillets in Green Curry; Grill-Smoked Trout; Sautéed Tuna Teriyaki; Sushi Hand Rolls; Microwave Seafood Stew; Steamed Mussels with White Wine and Parsley; New England Clam Chowder; and Bay Scallops with Spinach and Saffron Cream.

Revsin, Leslie. *Great Fish, Quick*. Hardcover: 308 pages with color photographs, 100 recipes. Doubleday, 1998.

Revsin, chef at a number of noted Manhattan restaurants over the years, has stuck close to home for this work. Dedicated to the proposition that fish fillets, fish steaks, and shellfish are just as fast, equally healthful, but far more versatile than the ubiquitous boneless chicken breast, this is a book to use daily. Revsin's goal was to peer into the "fishy soul" of the various varieties and prepare each to bring out its best. A wide array of commercially available seafood is described, and sound buying, storing, and substitution information is given. The recipes are brief, easy, and long on flavor, while the writing is lively and mostly very readable, except where it verges on the breathless: The word "veggies" appears far too often. Recipes are grouped by the type of seafood used: mild white fillets, stronger fillets, "sea animals with armor," and recipes combining sea animals.

CONSIDER: Halibut Fillets with Roasted Tomato Vinaigrette; Pan-Fried Perch with Celery Salt, Thyme, and Tartar Sauce; Grilled Red Snapper with Tomatillo Salsa; Broiled Tuna with Caesar Vinaigrette; Crabmeat Hash with Corn and Cheddar Cheese; and Classic Oyster Stew.

Rodgers, Rick. *Simply Shrimp*. Paperback: 168 pages with color photographs, 101 recipes. Chronicle Books, 1998.

Shrimp is America's most popular seafood, according to the author; also the most reliably fresh from coast to coast, he might have added, providing it has been properly handled after defrosting. Good advice on buying, storing, and handling the crustaceans precedes chapters on shrimp appetizers, shrimp in the pot, on the grill, in the salad bowl, from the oven, out of the skillet, and served over pasta and rice. Rodgers does his usual fine job of making the expected changes with the maximum of creativity.

CONSIDER: Salsa Shrimp Cocktail with Tortilla Crisps; Popcorn Shrimp with Shocking Pink Sauce; Grilled Shrimp Caesar Salad; Curried Shrimp and Apple Salad in Pita Bread; Chinese Creamy Corn Soup with Shrimp; Low Country Shrimp, Sausage, and Corn Boil; Fettuccine with Shrimp, Asparagus, and Mint; and Moroccan-Spiced Shrimp on Fruited Couscous.

Soups and Stews

Dragonwagon, Crescent. *Dairy Hollow House Soup and Bread Cookbook.* **Paperback: 406 pages, 200 recipes. Workman, 1992.**

Dairy Hollow House is a renowned country inn in Eureka Springs, Arkansas. Among the specialties of the house, soup and bread count high, leading to this whimsical but knowledgeable and idea-packed volume. A nice section of salad recipes is a bonus surprise. There is more than a little of the flower child in the author (also a writer of children's books), which explains the whimsy as well as her expertise with soups and breads. Good stock recipes, lots of fillips or little soup touches, and even "The Soup"—an add-a-little-of-this-or-that low-fat recipe that makes a fine centerpiece for a weight-loss plan.

CONSIDER: Chicken and Corn Soup with Late Summer Vegetables; Duck Soup with Sweet Potatoes; Fishyssoise; Chilled Avocado Soup Mexique Bay; Old South

Peanut Soup; Rose and Apple Velvet Soup; Bean and Barley Soup Bourguignon; Tomato Soup with Cognac and Orange; Oatmeal Molasses Bread; and Patchwork Slaw.

Famularo, Joe. *Italian Soup Cookbook*. Hardcover and paperback: 288 pages, 150 recipes. Workman, 1998.

The plethora of recent books on Italian soup-making illustrates both the continued popularity of Italian food and the persistent trend toward more casual cooking and eating. Soups (particularly Italian ones) are also apt to be less fat- and calorie-packed than more solid foods, a plus on the health side. Famularo has traveled Italy from one end to the other searching out savory and soul-affirming soups, and his publisher has attractively packaged the collection. A concluding chapter on soup "enhancers" like Grilled Garlic Bread and Sun-Dried Tomato Butter is a nice touch.

CONSIDER: Lentil Soup with Duck; Puree of Escarole with Thyme and Sour Cream; Velvety Fish Soup with Golden Croutons; and Papa Joe's Spicy Savoy Cabbage and Spareribs Soup.

Kafka, Barbara. *Soup: A Way of Life*. Hardcover: 556 pages with color photographs, 300 recipes. Artisan, 1998.

Common among cookbook editors in these competitive days is the desire to publish works so thorough that there will be no need for another on the subject for years to come. While the flow of soup books will surely continue uninterrupted, their authors may be laboring in vain. Kafka has, in her usual way, seized a subject and made it uniquely her own. Handsomely produced (with luscious photos by Gentl and Hyers), filled with soups light or hearty, simple or complex, uncooked or long-simmered, vegetarian or afloat with various meats, poultry, and fish, soups familiar or freshly new, this book comes startlingly close to being the last word on a very large and universal subject. Reading it, you will learn a lot about soup and more than a little about Kafka herself, who lectures in a rather literary and schoolmarmish tone, à la Miss Jean Brodie—no-nonsense, tetchy, and eloquent at once.

CONSIDER: Cabbage and Goose Confit Soup; Green Gazpacho with Citrus and Yellow Squash; Sour Cherry Soup; Miso Soup with Daikon and Spinach; Garlic Soup with Poached Eggs; Chicken in the Pot with Chinese Flavors; Shrimp and Pork Wontons; Cornmeal Dumplings; Aioli; and Horseradish Sauce.

Peterson, James. *Splendid Soups: Recipes and Master Techniques for Making the World's Best Soups.* Hardcover: 524 pages, 300 recipes. Bantam Books, 1993.

Written by a former restaurateur who now teaches cooking, this award winner is impeccably researched and intelligently written and leaves few soups unstirred. No soup book can be said to be complete, but from limpid, low-fat broths to rib-sticking gumbos, all the soups you really want to eat can be found here. Peterson believes in shopping the market, being creative, and improvising when so moved; though the recipes are complete and detailed, there is plenty of general advice, plus charts of soup "patterns" that will encourage the cook to strike out on his own.

CONSIDER: Chinese Corn and Shrimp Soup; Spicy

Cold Cucumber Soup with Yogurt; Medieval Pea Soup with Ginger, Saffron, and Almonds; Grilled Vegetable Soup; Vietnamese-Style Hot and Sour Fish Soup; Shrimp Bisque; Moroccan-Style Lamb Soup with Dried Apricots; Hot Peach Soup with Crème Fraîche; and Berry Broth.

Schwartz, Arthur. *Soup Suppers*. Paperback: 215 pages, 140 recipes. HarperCollins, 1994.

This international collection of 100 main-dish soups and forty soup-friendly accompaniments is one of the best and most useful books on the subject ever written. Schwartz, a popular Manhattan radio host, has exactly the right informative, casual, and no-nonsense voice soup-making requires. The soups are grouped mostly by main ingredient: vegetable, bean and grain, meat, chicken, fish and shellfish. Menu-planning advice, tips on advance preparation, and chapters on breads, salads and appetizers, and desserts round out the book—and the meal. Techniques are simple, directions clear, and flavors bold, while the chatty headnotes are never less than a joy.

CONSIDER: Roumanian Eggplant Salad; Russian Sweet and Sour Cabbage Soup; bulgur-based Three-Bean Vegetable Chili; Sausage, Mushroom and Chick-Pea Pasta Fazool; Thai Chicken and Coconut Soup; Shrimp Gumbo; Creamy Borscht; and Blueberry Apple Crumble.

Villas, James. *Stews, Bogs, and Burgoos: Recipes from the Great American Stewpot*. Hardcover: 306 pages, 150 recipes. William Morrow, 1997.

Few writers know more about regional American fare

than Villas, for the past twenty-five years the food editor of *Town and Country* magazine. His book is packed with coast-to-coast ideas that are firmly based in the American tradition while simultaneously managing to sound fresh and new. Stews should be easy and fairly economical, says Villas, and in these times of more casual entertaining, they make fine company fare. Since you can be fairly certain your guests didn't have stew for lunch, you can also count on their being impressed that you went to what some folks (not the author) consider "trouble" on their account. The final chapter gives thirteen biscuit recipes, since, says Villas, biscuits are the perfect accompaniment to a well-made stew.

  CONSIDER: Prairie Oxtail Ragout; Chasen's Famous Chili; Sheboygan Cider Pork and Apple Stew; Cajun Ham, Sausage, and Shrimp Jambalaya; Ranch Ham Hocks with Sauerkraut; Maui Papaya Chicken Stew; and Bucks County Stewed Spiced Pears.

Wyler, Susan. *Simply Stews: More Than 100 Savory One-Pot Meals.* Paperback: 242 pages, 110 recipes. HarperPerennial, 1995.

Though *essentially* about stews, there is nothing *simple* about this friendly, useful book, simply packed with stews, chilies, ragouts, and curries. Wyler, a former food editor of *Food & Wine*, has a special love of one-dish meals which shows in the imaginative, carefully crafted recipes. Single-dish comfort and slow-simmered convenience are the prime attractions of stews, she says, although more than a few of these dishes are remarkably speedy. "Comfort" can sometimes mean high in fat, but here, modest amounts of fat (which let the cook accomplish the browning necessary for depth of flavor) and rigorous skimming lead to relatively restrained calorie loads for all but the most indulgent of stews. Headnotes come with creative serving suggestions, and many recipes include a crust, topping, side dish, or garnish that further elevates the cuisine.

CONSIDER: Cider-Stewed Chicken with Fall Vegetables; Barbecued Beef Stew with Cheddared Corn Pudding; Lobster Stewed in Whiskey Cream with Grilled Portobello Mushrooms and Asparagus; Tangy Cabernet Beef with Bacon and Onions; Lamb Stew au Ratatouille; Salmon Corn Chowder; and Smoky Vegetable Chili with Pinto Beans.

Various

Aaron, Chester. *The Great Garlic Book*. Paperback: 146 pages with color photographs, 40 recipes. Ten Speed Press, 1997.

Aaron is a specialty garlic farmer, practicing his craft in Northern California's wine country and selling the results to such restaurants as Chez Panisse and the Zuni Café, as well as to private garlic aficionados. He is also a gentleman of some thought and has put together a slim but attractive volume that sings garlic's praises as a garden crop, a food, and a powerhouse of health and well-being. Aaron covers garlic's place in history ("Six Millennium of Allium"), describes the pluses and minuses of many different varieties, and concludes with a section of very appealing recipes collected from restaurants known to celebrate garlic.

CONSIDER: Crabmeat Monaco; Linguine with Garlic and Sage; Forty-Clove Garlic Chicken with Cabernet

Sauce; Wild Mushroom-Roast Garlic Bread Pudding; and
Delmonico Baked Creole Eggplant.

**Barber, Mary Corpening, Sara Corpening, and Lori Lyn
Narlock.** *Smoothies.* **Paperback: 108 pages with color
photographs, 50 recipes. Chronicle Books, 1997.**

While a decent smoothie may be improvised from a
little fruit, juice, and yogurt, true blender beverage artistry
apparently requires the input of three authors to achieve.
Indeed, this book takes its popular subject just about as far
as it's possible to go. There is information on fruit, equipment, ingredients, and techniques, followed by wholesome
smoothies, dairy-free smoothies, decadent smoothies, and
smoothies incorporating alcohol. Nutritional information
for each recipe is given separately at the back of the book.
Happily, not all are lean or low-cal. The importance given
to such a light topic would seem fairly silly were it not for
the ravishing, *Martha Stewart Living*–style photos (by Amy
Neusinger) and the creative recipes.

CONSIDER: Guava Gulp; Peachy Keen; Mango Mad-
ness; Just Dew It!; Tea-licious; Polynesian Power Punch;
Cool Hand Lime; and tequila-spiked Sunset Sipper.

Benning, Lee Edwards. *Oh, Fudge! A Celebration of
America's Favorite Candy.* **Paperback: 303 pages, 290
recipes. Henry Holt, 1990.**

Any cook who has ever had a batch of fudge fail, as well
as anyone with a serious passion for chocolate, will treasure
this book. Benning, a home economist, historical novelist,
and the author of another single-minded cookbook, *Better*

with Buttermilk, set out to answer a simple question: "Why does fudge have to cook for forty-five minutes?" She ended up with what Maida Heatter has called "a Ph.D. in fudge-making." There is a very readable history and lore of fudge followed by "Ten Easy Steps to Making No-Fail Fudge at Home," intermixed with various "Myths of Fudge-Making" endorsed or debunked.

CONSIDER: Plain Vanilla Sugar and Cream Fudge; Gingerbread Brown Sugar Fudge; Chocolate Cashew Ultimate Fudge; Lazy Cook's Chocolate Brownie Fudge; Double-Chip Microwave Fudge; Classic Twice-Cooked Caramel; and even marshmallows from scratch.

Binns, Brigit Legere. *Polenta.* Paperback: 120 pages with color photographs, 40 recipes. Chronicle Books, 1997.

Combine the tender appeal of mashed potatoes, the deep-seated American love of corn, and the undeniable comfort of Italian cooking, and you have polenta. The current and continuing craze for this simple peasant food is thoroughly celebrated in this colorful book. The recipes are, says the author, for "all occasions" and run the gamut from breakfast to appetizers and from main courses to dessert. Polenta in history, polenta choices at the market, and polenta techniques in the kitchen get briefly but thoroughly discussed (lump prevention is covered) before the recipes begin.

CONSIDER: Polenta with Poached Eggs, Smoked Salmon, and Chives; Baked Polenta with Eggplant, Sun-Dried Tomatoes, and Basil Sauce; Soft Polenta with White Truffles and Crème Fraîche; Skewered Chicken Livers, Bacon, and Mushrooms Over Polenta Squares; Polenta Pound Cake with Warm Summer Fruits; and the rich, warm, and comforting Polenta Dolce with Dried Dates and Ricotta.

The Complete Garlic Lovers' Cookbook. Hardcover: 349 pages, 400 recipes. Celestial Arts, 1987.

This authorless compendium, collected from the chefs, home cooks, and cook-off winners associated with the legendary Gilroy Garlic Festival, remains a single-minded and fully dedicated tribute to the "Stinking Rose" and will surely provide garlic lovers with many hours of fragrant cooking and dining pleasure. Gilroy, south of San Jose, is the self-declared garlic capital of the world, and indeed, most of the country's supply is grown in the area. Short sections on garlic buying, storing, and growing conclude the book, but it is the vast number of savory recipes that make this a find. Yes, there are desserts, including chocolate-dipped garlic gloves, Garlic Chip Cookies, and a pudding using two *heads* of garlic that is described as "light and flavorful."

CONSIDER: Baked Stuffed Garlic Clams; Garlic Goddess Cheese Pie; Green Ravioli with Garlic Filling; Garlic Beef Enchiladas; Garlic Chicken with Artichokes and Mushrooms; and Krusty Garlic Kuchen.

Cunningham, Marion. *The Breakfast Book*. Hardcover: 320 pages, 280 recipes. Alfred A. Knopf, 1987.

Like supper, about which Cunningham has also written, breakfast is a cozy, family-oriented meal that is often scheduled out of existence in these busy times. For Cunningham, who supervised the recent revision of *The Fannie Farmer Cookbook*, breakfast is a meal of honest simplicity, a repast that deserves revival. To recapture that mellow morning feeling (whether alone or in the company of loved ones), turn to this quiet, sane, and calming volume. These easy, satisfying, but by no means clichéd recipes will ease you into an otherwise hectic day with a touch of grace, most especially Cunningham's signature silver-dollar-sized sour cream pancakes ("Heavenly Hots"). Rhubarb Ginger Jam is one of a number of quick or no-cook fruit preserves that will add sweet style to your breakfast table.

CONSIDER: Granola Breakfast Bread; Mexican Breakfast Sandwiches; Bacon Scrapple; Cornmeal Buttermilk Pudding; Trout Fried with Oatmeal; Potato Apple Fry; Chipped Ham with Dried Apricots; Fluffy Caramel Coffeecake; and Glazed Cinnamon Rolls.

Cunningham, Marion. *The Supper Book*. Hardcover: 253 pages, 180 recipes. Alfred A. Knopf, 1992.

Supper packs such a nostalgic punch these days because what was once one of the coziest of family meals remains only a memory in many households. To re-create that homey, end-of-the-day experience, open this lively book at almost any page and cook on. Cunningham, the grandmotherly reviser of *The Fannie Farmer Cookbook* and a disciple of James Beard, has really written two books, one simple and familiar, the other more creative but still comforting. All are supper-easy and supper-quick, but not all are to be found in Mom's well-used recipe file. A particularly interesting chapter called "Fringe Dishes" includes everything from Tartar Sauce and Apple Butter to Beet Marmalade and Jasmine Rice.

CONSIDER: Baltimore Crab Cakes; Tomato Rarebit; Posole Salad Soup; Holey Moley Tamale Pie; Minced Chicken in Lettuce Leaves; a lively Grapefruit, Black Olive, and Mint Salad; and Beginner's Coconut Pie.

Czarnecki, Jack. *A Cook's Book of Mushrooms*. Hardcover: 208 pages with color photographs, 100 recipes. Artisan, 1995.

This book is an interesting hybrid, combining technical mushroom forager's information with a sophisticated chef's food sensibility; the typical mushroom hunting guide has rather more utilitarian recipes. Owner of Joe's Restaurant, a Pennsylvania eatery famed for its mushroom cookery, Czarnecki writes passionately about common and uncommon culinary mushrooms. Though cultivated varieties are sometimes used, wild types are favored. Those who do not or cannot collect (or purchase) their own wild produce can still cook from this book, however, since supermarket substitutions are usually suggested. The author's evocative and often funny essays on the joys and mysteries of mushroom hunting will also more than make up for the lack of an actual field trip. Look past the uninspired photographs to find richly savory possibilities.

CONSIDER: Pennsylvania Pasta with Cremini; Breakfast Portobellos with Shiitake; Soft-Shell Crabs with Chanterelles; Crêpe Risotto; Lobster Lasagna with Chèvre and Morels; and Curried Mushroom Soup.

Desaulniers, Marcel. *Salad Days*. Hardcover: 236 pages with color photographs, 80 recipes. Simon & Schuster, 1998.

At the opposite end of the culinary spectrum from his usual subject matter (decadent desserts), Desaulniers here celebrates salads, specifically main course salads that make a "first-class meal." It's important to keep that concept in mind, for most of the salads run to several pages and more than a few sub-recipes. The results are not fridge-cleaning toss-togethers, but salads that celebrate varying temperatures, colors, flavors, textures, and tangy complexity. Most of these are meatless, but are followed by variation recipes that transform them into substantial main courses for carnivores.

CONSIDER: Sliced Beets with Curly Endive, Red Bliss Potato Salad, Honey Mustard Roasted Walnuts, and Meaux Mustard Vinaigrette; and Baby Salad Greens and Sliced Tomatoes with Asiago Cheese, Toasted Pine Nuts, Herbed Olive Flat Bread, Honey-Charred Duck Breast, and Basil Vinaigrette.

Detrick, Mia. *Sushi*. Paperback: 93 pages with color photographs. Chronicle Books, 1981.

Though sushi and sashimi can be replicated by following the descriptions given in this thorough little handbook, it is more of an appreciation and a guide to the dining-out sushi experience than it is a household how-to. To define sushi as the author does: "The most perfect fish and shellfish are served uncooked in gemlike portions with a delicately seasoned rice." Missing at home (not to mention with sushi purchased from a supermarket refrigerator case) is the essential interactive performance of sitting at the sushi bar and letting the master chef entice you with one swiftly assembled treat after another. How to order, what to drink, and the all-important "what is it?" questions are all answered; general sushi etiquette is explained; and ingredients and equipment are discussed for those who can't resist making their own.

DeWitt, Dave, and Nancy Gerlach. *The Whole Chile Pepper Book.* **Paperback: 373 pages with color and black-and-white photographs, 180 recipes. Little, Brown, 1990.**

For all but the most dedicated of chile heads (you know who you are), this book will be all the chile information required. From tracing the first ancient wild ancestor of today's cultivated chiles to identifying chiles in the field to growing chiles in the home garden, this generous book covers it all. Lots of recipes, too, grouped by such chile-loving world regions as the American Southwest, Africa, and India; introductions to these chapters discuss in detail the chile practices of each area. The authors were founders of *The Chile Pepper Magazine* and follow that publication's quirky practice of listing chiles first in the ingredient list, even if they do not come first while preparing the dish.

CONSIDER: Sun-Cured Pickled Jalapeños; Pumpkin Blossom Quesadillas; Fiery Seafood Gumbo; Chicken Paprikás; Burmese Spiced Duck; Curried Lentil Stew; Thai Green Mango and Pork Platter; and Singapore Chile Crab.

Duffy, Gillian. *Hors d'Oeuvres*. Hardcover: 144 pages with color photographs, 80 recipes. William Morrow, 1998.

Duffy, the food editor of *New York* magazine, has assembled a compact and attractive volume of cutting-edge hors d'oeuvres, some of her own devising, others contributed by some of Manhattan's best chefs and caterers: Matthew Kenney, Bobby Flay, and David Waltuck, to name three. While most of the recipes are not complicated, they are all very stylish and tasty, getting a lot of their sizzle from unusual ingredients and eye-catching presentation. Advice on stocking the pantry and on designing hors d'oeuvres, plus suggested party menus and a section of cocktail formulas round out the book, though it is the recipes that are, quite properly, the stars.

CONSIDER: Smoked Chicken and Jalapeño Jack Quesadillas with Chipotle Sauce; Prunes and Smoked Mozzarella Wrapped with Prosciutto; Curried Mussels with Sweet Red Pepper; Terrine of Caviar and Smoked Salmon; Spicy Asian Chicken Wings; and Smoked Trout-Stuffed Eggs.

Fussell, Betty. *Crazy for Corn*. Paperback: 238 pages, over 170 recipes. HarperPerennial, 1995.

In this follow-up to her award-winning *Story of Corn*, Fussell again eloquently sings the praises of the all-American grain we love to eat so many ways. Besides everything you wanted to know about the types of corn and cornmeal available, Fussell offers a distinctive collection of corn recipes. While the use of hard-to-find ingredients is long—a complaint or a compliment, depending upon where you live—Fussell displays a virtuosity in culinary scholarship and a creativity that is dazzling. She whirls about pairing corn in its many guises with elements from all over the world.

CONSIDER: Ecuadorian Corn and Pineapple Salad; Mexican Corn Mushroom in Chève Sauce; Indonesian Corn-Shrimp Fritters; Peruvian Purple Corn Desert; Moldavian Feta Cheese Corn Bread; French Savory Corn Crepes; Puerto Rican Coconut Tamales; Sweet Corn Clam Cakes; and Cherry Cornmeal Biscotti.

Greene, Bert. *The Grains Cookbook*. Hardcover and paperback: 403 pages, 400 recipes. Workman, 1988.

This book, Greene's last, begins with a tribute to the beloved writer. With a big heart, a big appetite, and endless curiosity (not to mention the storyteller's gift), he manages to make plain old good-for-you grains into something downright adventurous. At least fourteen grains are represented in this overstuffed work; buying, storing, and cooking information, plus an anecdotal analysis of each one's place in the larger food scheme of things, is given, followed by recipes that show each off to perfection. Because there is no course of the meal into which Greene doesn't fit grains, this is a far-ranging book.

CONSIDER: Jim-Dandy Jambalaya; Wild Mushroom and Barley Risotto; Chilly, Minty, Tomatoey Bisque with Amaranth; Alsatian Pork with Buckwheat Dumplings; Texas Tabbouli; Opelousas' Paella; Shocking Pink Wild Rice; Gingered Pumpkin Pie (in Gilded Cornmeal Crust);

Apricot Millet Soufflé; Hazelnut and Rice Macaroons; and buckwheat-based Fractured Fudge Cake.

Greenspan, Dorie. *Pancakes from Morning to Midnight*. Paperback: 147 pages with black-and-white photographs, 80 recipes. William Morrow, 1997.

A follow-up volume to Greenspan's book on waffles, this book takes a similar position that there's no time of day when a pancake isn't welcome. Sweet or savory, the recipes are imaginative and inspiring, about equally balanced between homey comforts and startling flights of fancy that, gotten used to, sound delicious. Briefly but thoroughly, pancake history, ingredients, techniques, and equipment are discussed, while do-ahead advice may encourage busy folks to abandon their Bisquick. Where once she "waffled," now she "flips"; so will you.

CONSIDER: Bacon-Cornmeal Softies; Oatmeal Raisin Pancakes with Cinnamon Sour Cream; Fresh Peach Pancakes with Quick Strawberry-Peach Sauce; Potato Pancakes with Applesauce Like Grandma Made; Spicy Buttermilk Crab Cakes Topped with Tomato-Crab Salad; Golden Oniony Ricotta Crepes Topped with Tomato Sauce; Blini; Peanut Butter–Chocolate Chip Pancakes with Cinnamon Ice Cream; Cranberry Blintzes; Rum-Flavored Almond Cream Crepes; and Puffed Pear Pancake.

Greenspan, Dorie. *Waffles from Morning to Midnight*. Paperback: 201 pages with nostalgic black-and-white photos, 100 recipes. William Morrow, 1997.

For those retro types who remember waffles from a

waffle iron rather than popped from a toaster, not to mention those who remember waffles topped with something other than maple syrup (creamed chicken, for example), this book is for you. To Greenspan, "waffling" is a fine art, not a character flaw, and in the recipes for morning-to-midnight waffles and toppings, both sweet and savory, that make up this attractive book, she practices that art with creative panache.

CONSIDER: Crispy Cornmeal Waffles with a fresh orange topping; bacon-studded Hickory and Maple Waffles; Curried Waffle Club Sandwiches with Chutney Mayonnaise; Butterscotch Babies lusciously—and instantly—topped with melted ice cream "sauce"; Creamed Spinach and Rice Waffles with Sautéed Scallops; and Tiramisù Waffles, flavored with cinnamon, rum, and chocolate and topped with an espresso custard sauce.

Griffith, Linda, and Fred Griffith. *Onions, Onions, Onions: Delicious Recipes for the World's Favorite Secret Ingredient.* **Paperback: 384 pages with technique illustrations, 200 recipes. Chapters Publishing, 1994.**

Onions may be the supporting players in dishes cooked all around the world, but for the Griffiths, onions—and the other members of the allium clan—are the stars of the show. Originally intrigued by the growing number of so-called specialty sweet onions (Vidalia, Walla-Walla, etc.) on the market, this husband-and-wife cookbook team found themselves equally drawn to leeks, scallions, garlic, chives, shallots, ramps, and more, all of them essential in developing rich deep flavors in the most savory of dishes. Along with shopping, storing, and cooking information, simple technique drawings, mail-order and gardening sources, wine suggestions, and tips from kitchen professionals for avoiding the teary eyes that go with onion cookery, the Griffiths serve up a batch of recipes so onion packed, you just know they're going to taste great.

CONSIDER: Fresh Oysters with Chive and Corn Vinaigrette; Confit of Red Onions and Cherries; Cream of Onions Soup with Stilton; Roasted Alaska Salmon with Roasted Leek Sauce; and Onion and Apple-Smothered Pork Chops.

Hutson, Lucinda. *¡Tequila! Cooking with the Spirit of Mexico.* Paperback: 158 pages with color folk art illustrations, 150 recipes. Ten Speed Press, 1995.

Tequila: The word evokes dual exclamation points, at least for Texas-born Hutson, who writes with passion and wit in this attractively produced tribute to Mexico's fiery spirit. Despite its growing popularity, tequila is badly misunderstood, she says, and vows in this friendly and profusely illustrated work to set the record straight. From the origins of tequila in Jalisco to the premier brands to the salt-and-lime ritual to stocking the home cantina and much more, this book is the best and liveliest of several recent ones on the subject. Not merely a cocktail book (though there are plenty of these), it also has recipes for dishes that include tequila as an indispensable ingredient, and even a handy, tequila-free one for Menudo, the tripe and hominy soup/stew that is said to be the best cure for a tequila hangover.

CONSIDER: Melted Cheese Flambéed in Tequila; Garden Green Cilantro Salsa with Tequila; Golden Gazpacho Spiked with Tequila; Black Beans and Corn in Peppered Tequila Marinade; Thai/Tex Tequila Coleslaw; Fish Margarita-Style; Grapefruit Tequila Chiffon Pie; Spanish Almond Cake Laced with Tequila Anejo; and Jalapeño Carrot Cake with Tequila/Lime Cream Cheese Frosting.

Lalli, Carole. *Stuffings*. Hardcover: 87 pages with color photographs, 45 recipes. HarperCollins, 1997.

To get any possible confusion out of the way, this book is in no way limited to what you can pack inside the Thanksgiving turkey. It's about stuffed things of all sorts, from seafood to meat, to vegetables, fruits, and, yes, turkey. Some things just beg to be stuffed, says Lalli, a noted book and magazine editor. There's an element of show business in going the extra step or two it takes to stuff a food that would in any case be tasty on its own, and there's more than a little childish sense of delight at cutting into something and finding the delicious surprise inside. No ground will be broken by this modest and attractive work, but much good eating can be had.

CONSIDER: Southwest Stuffed Red Snapper; Stuffed Crab Cakes; Roast Chicken with Polenta Stuffing; Turkey Breast with Rich Chestnut Stuffing; Susan's Mother's Stuffed Cabbage; Leg of Lamb Stuffed with Dried Fruits and Bulgur Wheat; Stuffed Portobello Mushroom Caps; Gingery Baked Apples; and Corn Crepes with Apple and Walnut Stuffing.

Lesem, Jeanne. *Preserving in Today's Kitchen*. Paperback: 264 pages, 168 recipes. Henry Holt, 1992.

About a third of the recipes in this useful book originally appeared in Lesem's *The Pleasures of Preserving and Pickling*, published in 1975. Times change, and so have Lesem and canning in general. This revised and reworked book takes several nice turns, putting Granny-style home-canned goodies within the reach of busy modern cooks. Small batches are emphasized, the blender and food processor are relied upon, and much use is made of the microwave oven. Exotic new arrivals at the fruit stand (pummelo, mango, kiwi) appear and dried fruits and fruit juice concentrates let the canner cut back on sugar. Historical notes, quotes, and kitchen tips appear in multiple—and entertaining—sidebars. A few recipes that use the preserves appear, including Key Lime Marmalade Sherbet and Upside-Down Cake with apple ginger preserve replacing the pineapple.

CONSIDER: Lemon Rosemary Jelly; Peach Melba Jam; Blood Orange Marmalade; Strawberry Preserves; Peppery Pear Relish; Mango Chutney; and Sweet-and-Sour Duck Sauce.

Miller, Mark, with Mark Kiffin and John Harrisson. *The Great Salsa Book*. Paperback: 148 pages with color photographs, 100 recipes. Ten Speed Press, 1994.

There are many salsa books around, but if your budget or the length of your cookbook shelf limits you to only one, make it this small but thorough and imaginative work from one of the Southwest's most noted chefs. Divided into such far-ranging categories as Tropical Salsas, Fruit Salsas, Corn Salsas, and Ocean Salsas, this book rings every possible change on its spicy subject. Besides the traditional medium into which to dip corn chips, Miller's salsas act as sauces, garnishes, and explosive flavor boosters for all sorts of foods, particularly those from the grill. The photos are vivid, technique and ingredient information is thorough, and each salsa comes with a "heat" scale and serving suggestions.

CONSIDER: Golden Tomato, Ginger, and Chipotle Salsa; Wild Mushroom and Sun-Dried Tomato Salsa; Pear and Black Olive Salsa; Corn and Jerky Salsa; Barbados Black Bean Salsa; Thai Peanut Salsa; and Smoked Shrimp Salsa.

Miller, Mark, Stephan Pyles, and John Sedlar. *Tamales*. Hardcover: 178 pages with color photographs, 110 recipes. Macmillan, 1997.

Three of the Southwest's sharpest chefs have joined forces to produce a book celebrating one of the New World's oldest foods. Dumpling-like, masa-based tamales, typically wrapped in one kind of leaf or another and steamed, have been prepared in Latin America for centuries. They are "treasures," say the authors, who clearly relish working within the limited theme-and-variation format this book requires. Although all three chefs have extensive experience traveling and eating in the "tamale zone," this is far more about their creativity at home than it is about authentic recipes, which entire chapters of other works on Latin cuisine can handily supply.

CONSIDER: Smashed Potato Tamales with Carrot-Ginger Broth; Red Snapper Tamales with Red Curry Masa; Barbecued Brisket Tamales with Jicama Slaw; Duck Tamales with Pineapple and Chipotle; and Bittersweet Chocolate Tamales with Anchos, Prunes, and Raisins.

Peterson, James. *Sauces: Classical and Contemporary Sauce-Making,* second edition. Hardcover: 598 pages with color photographs, 500 recipes. Van Nostrand Reinhold, 1998.

The first edition of this substantial work won the James Beard Foundation's Cookbook of the Year Award, and this edition has been updated to cover Asian and Italian sauces, both slighted in the original. Comprehensive enough for the professional chef, thanks to Peterson's friendly, nononsense voice, this book will be of use to the serious home cook as well. Divided into chapters covering a range from salad sauces, vinaigrettes, salsas, and relishes to the classics of haute cuisine, the book includes all major sauces, variations upon them, alternate methods, tips, and the occasional recipe using the sauce in question.

CONSIDER: Brown Chicken Stock; Glace de Viande (Meat Glaze); Miso Sauce; Green Tomato Chutney; Red-Wine Beef Stew; Steamed Bass Fillets with Yogurt Curry Sauce; Spaghetti Alla Puttanesca; Teriyaki-Glazed Steak; and Crème Anglaise.

Rodgers, Rick. *Thanksgiving 101.* Paperback: 192 pages, 100 recipes. Broadway Books, 1998.

Whether you've been celebrating Thanksgiving in your

home for years or this is your very first turkey, this fine little volume is a must. Dedicated to easing and embellishing the preparations for America's number-one food holiday, it's a gem. No one is better qualified than Rick Rodgers, prolific author (among whose previous books are *50 Best Stuffings and Dressings* and *The Turkey Cookbook*) and for years spokesperson for Perdue poultry. Rodgers has roasted more turkeys than any of us have seen in our lifetimes; his information is flawless. "The happiest Thanksgiving cook is also the most organized," suggests Rodgers, who recommends lists, helps with menu planning, marks do-ahead possibilities, and provides helpful timetables wherever possible.

CONSIDER: Cranberry-Ginger Tart with Chocolate Drizzle; Potato Tortilla with Smoked Salmon; Sweet Potato and Peanut Soup; Sausage Gumbo Dressing; and Rosemary and Cracked Peppercorn Sticks.

Routhier, Nicole. *Nicole Routhier's Fruit Book.* Paperback: 482 pages, 400 recipes. Workman, 1996.

Even those who don't think fruit belongs in the main course will find plenty to like in this glorious, seductive volume. Less familiar fruits get a descriptive write-up, while sidebars cover kitchen tips and tidbits. There are menus, too, but since all the dishes come from the book, even fruit lovers may find these meals excessive. The recipes are clear, interesting, and well balanced; only occasionally (as in Strawberry Salsa) does the concept seem forced. There are also substantial chapters on canning, breakfast, beverages, and bread-making, and lots of desserts.

CONSIDER: Apple Coconut Chowder; Minty-Fruity Tabbouleh; Broiled Bluefish with Orange Sauce; Thai Red Chicken Curry with Pineapple; Moroccan Lamb Tagine; Venison Chili with Papaya; Three-Fruit Haroseth; Mashed Potatoes with Roasted Pears; Tangerine Sorbet; Cosmic Chocolate Cake; Chilled Cherimoya Custard; and Lemon-Strawberry Squares.

Routhier, Nicole. *Cooking Under Wraps: The Art of Wrapping Hors d'Oeuvres, Main Courses, and Desserts.* **Hardcover and paperback: 382 pages with color photos and technical drawings, 200 recipes. William Morrow, 1993.**

Routhier knows what the advertising agencies of various fast-food restaurants seem not to, namely that food wrapped up is not a new and trendy marketing concept, but one of the world's oldest and most widespread cooking techniques. This intriguing work circles the globe and finds, in addition to such obvious choices as pita bread and tortillas, wrappers ranging from seaweed, corn husks, and strudel dough to thin-sliced potatoes, crepes, and parchment paper. Those familiar with Routhier's award-winning book on Vietnamese cooking will be pleasantly surprised to find her stretching her international muscles here.

CONSIDER: Potato-Wrapped Pork Chops in Mustard Cream Sauce; sugar-dusted Moroccan Chicken Pie; Chimichangas with Pork and Black Bean Chili; Sausage in Saffron Brioche; Pistachio Baklava; ravioli-like Ukrainian Cherry Vareniki with Whipped Sour Cream; and High-Rise Peach Pie.

Sahni, Julie. *Savoring Spices and Herbs.* **Hardcover: 301 pages with color photographs, 190 recipes. William Morrow, 1996.**

Sahni, a noted teacher of and writer on Indian cuisine, has naturally become somewhat of a spice and herb specialist. Here she celebrates a number of familiar and not-so-familiar spices and herbs in relatively simple, contemporary, and internationally flavored recipes. For readers who have a vague feeling that they aren't getting full use out of their spice cabinets and for those who like big, explosive flavors, this book will be a delight. Concise background information on the herbs and spices being used is followed by a large repertoire of herb and spice blends, which then turn up in an array of mouthwatering recipes.

CONSIDER: Curry-Grilled Scallops; Arroz con Pollo; Marinated Mozzarella with Thyme; Fried Clams with Barbecue Spices; Ginger Ragout of Lamb; Green Beans with Sichuan Peppercorns; Anise-Pistachio Crepes; Dried Fruit Compote with Allspice; Blueberry Tart with Saffron Cream; and Basil-Pineapple Ice.

Sloman, Evelyne. *The Pizza Book: Everything There Is to Know About the World's Greatest Pie.* **Hardcover: 276 pages with illustrations by the author, 200 recipes. Times Books, 1984.**

Sloman, raised on fine cuisine, was transformed into a confirmed pizza-lover after sampling the fabulous pies at Santarpio's in Boston. Despite her career as a French cooking teacher, she continued her quest for the best in pizza, eventually developing a pizza workshop cooking class and then writing this book. Fifteen years after it was published, this book is still in print, and remains the best book on the subject. Combining her passionate love for pizza with a methodical mind, Sloman delves deeply into pizza history, spells out regional differences, and discusses the basic ingredients and essential techniques for making great pizza at home. Follow her amazing thirty-minute pizza recipe, and you can have a hot, from-scratch pie in less time than it takes the deliveryman. Bake her ultimate New York–style pizza and you'll have a pie every bit as good as those from the legendary John's, on Bleecker Street.

CONSIDER: Classic Neapolitan Pizza; Deep-Dish Eggplant-Sausage Pizza; Ratatouille Pizza; Shrimp and Pesto Calzone; Pepe's White Clam Pie; and Pizza à la Spago.

Weir, Joanne. *You Say Tomato*. Paperback: 276 pages, 250 recipes. Broadway Books, 1998.

"More than any other fruit or vegetable, the tomato changed the face of modern cuisine," says Weir, as if the sight and taste of a luscious, vine-ripened beauty wasn't justification enough for an entire book on the subject. A midsized paperback, this is nevertheless jam-packed with recipes, quotes, tips, techniques, tomato legend, history, lore, and more. Weir, a noted cooking teacher who has written on Mediterranean cooking and on summertime cuisine, clearly relishes her topic. Anyone who doubts the importance of the tomato in world cuisine has only to open this book and marvel at the diversity of its excellent recipes.

CONSIDER: Smoky Yellow Tomato Sauce; Roasted

Tomatillo Avocado Salsa; Creamy Tomato Bisque; Pizza with Tomato, Fontina, and Gorgonzola; Spicy Thai Noodles with Pork and Tomato Curry; Spoonbread with Corn and Green Tomatoes; Veal Shanks with Tomatoes, Orange, and Garlic; Tomato Sorbet; Love Apple Chocolate Cake; and Italian Green Tomato Tart.

Weir, Joanne. *From Tapas to Meze.* **Hardcover: 287 pages, 220 recipes. Crown, 1994.**

First courses are frequently the most interesting part of the meal, and nowhere are these morsels more colorfully conceived and vividly flavored than in the Mediterranean region. From tapas, the little snacks of Spain, to meze, the varied hors d'oeuvres of the Middle East, and including as well France, Italy, Greece, Turkey, and North Africa, Weir's book celebrates first courses as few others have. A noted cooking teacher who has worked at Chez Panisse and trained under Alice Waters, Weir sets out the best of these zesty nibbles and talks intelligently about techniques, ingredients, and the inevitable similarities (and differences) between one country's snack and the next.

CONSIDER: Wild Mushroom and Roasted Garlic Flan; Spanish Omelet, Gypsy Style; Tiny Spiced Meatballs with Tomatoes; Provençal Roasted Summer Vegetable Ragout; Shellfish Fritters with Spicy Hot Garlic Mayonnaise; Garlic Flat Bread with Smoked Mozzarella and Tomato Vinaigrette; Grape Leaves Stuffed with Rice, Currants, and Herbs; and Moroccan Carrot, Radish, and Orange Salad.

Wood, Rebecca. *The Splendid Grain.* Hardcover: 394 pages with color photographs and charts, 260 recipes. William Morrow, 1998.

Accorded the production values usually reserved for works on high-ticket ingredients or written by award-winning chefs, this ode to all the splendid grains announces loud and clear that carbohydrates and fiber are every bit as pleasurable on the plate as butterfat and cholesterol. The book won both an IACP/Child and a Beard Foundation award. Wood, a consultant to the natural foods industry and a Colorado-based cooking teacher, takes the larger nutritional aspect of grains very seriously, but recipe inventiveness and eating pleasure are as important to her as where the grains were grown. Cooking and handling information and other sidebar materials are very strong, as is the advice on the best methods for cooking grains, from barley and wild rice to spelt, amaranth, and tef.

CONSIDER: Creole Corn Oysters; Salmon, Wild Rice, and Huckleberry Pot Pie Topped with Biscuits; Quinoa Soup, Saigon-Style; Rye Bread Stuffing with Apples and Sauerkraut; Buckwheat Waffles with Peach Butter; and Couscous Marmalade Torte.

Cookbooks from Chefs, Restaurants, and TV Personalities

Arnold, Sam. *The Fort Cookbook.* **Hardcover: 310 pages with black-and-white photographs and archival illustrations, 190 recipes. HarperCollins, 1997.**

The Fort is a renowned Denver restaurant that for nearly forty years has served up Old West–style vittles to legions of adoring fans. Built of adobe bricks and modeled on the historic Colorado fur-trading outpost known as Bent's Fort, the restaurant is helmed by the legendary Sam Arnold. Gourmand, historian, media personality, and teller of tales, tall and otherwise, Sam, like his restaurant, is larger than life. Though much of the cuisine of this colorful establishment is modeled on authentic period recipes—game and variety meats are particularly celebrated—there are also contemporary and foreign touches that appear just because Sam thinks they taste good.

CONSIDER: Finger Fajitas of Buffalo; Rocky Mountain Oysters in Beer Batter; Old-Fashioned Texas Barbecued Steak; Elk Medallions in Cranberry Cream Sauce; Turkey with Piñon Stuffing; Lakota Indian Fry Bread; Cider-Cooked Trapper's Fruit; Bee-nanas (bananas injected with honey and grilled in their peels); and President Andrew Jackson's Trifle.

Bastianich, Lidia Matticchio. *Lidia's Italian Table*. Hardcover: 320 pages with color photographs, 200 recipes. William Morrow, 1998.

This book is based upon Bastianich's public television series of the same name. A noted restaurateur (of the several she owns, Felidia is the best-known), she may or may not be the "First Lady of Italian Cooking," as the book's jacket so confidently states, but she has been a major force in transforming America's ideas of what Italian food really is. Her childhood in rural Istria, in northeastern Italy, informs her cooking with Yugoslavian and other Central European touches that set her apart. The memoir portions of the book are variously amusing, moving, and entertaining, and the recipes, polished with the assistance of chef and author Christopher Styler, are impeccably written.

CONSIDER: Frico (Cheese Crisps) with Potato-Crab Filling; Prosciutto and Fig Bruschetta; Sauerkraut and Bean Soup; Squash-Filled Ravioli with Marjoram Sauce; Risotto with Squab; Griddle-Crisped Spring Chicken; Roasted Loin of Pork Stuffed with Prunes; Blueberry-Apricot Frangipane Tart; and Sweet Crepes with Chocolate-Walnut Filling.

Bastianich, Lidia, and Jay Jacobs. *La Cucina Di Lidia*. Hardcover: 286 pages with color and black-and-white photographs, 120 recipes. Doubleday, 1990.

Recent fans of Bastianich, who now has a public television cooking series and whose New York restaurant domain has expanded to Kansas City, will want to read this earlier work. Written with the impeccable word artist Jay Jacobs, it's a more personal book than the one based upon her series, and includes some extraordinary dishes from her Italian childhood as well as the specialties of her first Manhattan restaurant, Felidia (owned and operated with her husband, Felice). The authors work to set this remarkable food in a context (not just "add this, stir that"), in this case Lidia's life in Europe as a child and in this country as a young woman, then a mother, now a famed restaurateur. She was born in Istria, a coastal region of Italy between Venice and Yugoslavia. While Istrian cooking is thoroughly Italian, there are also middle-European touches, which remain evident in her food even today. With recipes for sauerkraut and strudel, this book does a lot to remind us of the very real differences between Italy's regional cuisines. It's also a very good read and a rather brilliant cookbook. (Don't miss the long section on making one's own prosciutto.) Lidia is tireless in her pursuit of "simple, sophisticated food."

CONSIDER: Mussels in Parsley Vinaigrette; Polenta with Fontina and Porcini Mushrooms; Sauerkraut and Bean Soup; Ziti with Broccoli de Rape and Sausage; Butternut Squash Gnocchi; Swordfish in Sweet and Sour Sauce; Roasted Veal Shanks; Calf's Liver with Balsamic Vinegar; Sweet Yogurt Fritters; Ricotta Cheesecake; Peach Tart; Chocolate Zabaglione Cake; and Cherries in Grappa.

Bayless, Rick, with JeanMarie Brownson and Deann Groen Bayless. *Salsas That Cook.* **Paperback: 128 pages with color photographs, over 60 recipes. Fireside, 1998.**

Bayless conceived this book with his sister in mind. A busy mother with a full-time job, she found it difficult to make Mexican dishes as often as she and her chef/author brother wanted her to. His solution: Six varied, lively, and relatively easy salsas that provide the seasoning basis for a number of dishes, some south-of-the-border traditional, some north-of-the-border creative, all quick and yet deeply and authentically flavorful. Fans of Bayless's earlier books will recognize both the idea of a homemade repertoire of concentrated Mexican flavor-makers (condiments, really, similar to teriyaki or barbecue sauce), as well as his use of them in dishes that fit into the way we cook and live today. In this colorful and approachable work, however, the two concepts find their fullest expression, in dishes that taste like they simmered all day in a Mexican kitchen but were actually cooked at your place, after a day at the office. Suppertime, your next dinner party, a zippy brunch for friends—all will be enlivened and simplified when you cook from this fiery little treasure of a book. (The photos sizzle, too.)

CONSIDER: Mellow Red Chile Salsa with Sweet Garlic and Roasted Tomatoes; Sweet-and-Spicy Chilied Pork Empanadas; Emerald Corn Chowder with Roasted Tomatillos and Poblano; Breakfast Enchiladas with Scrambled Eggs, Woodland Mushrooms, and Spicy Roasted Tomatoes; Tomatillo-Baked Chicken Breasts with Roasted Asparagus; Green Chile Crab Cakes; Frontera's Chocolate Pecan Pie

Bars; Mexican Fruit Pops; and Honest-to-Goodness Margaritas for a Crowd.

Brennan, Ella, and Dick Brennan, with Lynne Roberts. *The Commander's Palace New Orleans Cookbook.* **Hardcover: 206 pages, 175 recipes. Clarkson Potter, 1984.**

Commander's Palace is housed in an opulent landmarked mansion in New Orleans's historic Garden District. Operated by Ella Brennan and her brother Dick, two members of the nationally influential Louisiana restaurant family, Commander's Palace, at the writing of this book, featured what the authors called Haute Creole cuisine. This was their attempt to lighten the city's—and Commander's—typically rich and hearty fare, and while it is true that the long-cooked amalgam of oil and flour called a roux is not used in the gumbos, most of the rest of the Big Easy's lush fare remains faithful to its fattening past. The Brennans have always had a sure touch for fine dining and lively times, and, trendy dietary cosmetics aside, deliver the goods here once again.

CONSIDER: Shrimp Remoulade; Crawfish Bisque; Duck Jambalaya; Panéed Veal and Fettuccine; Steak Diane with New Potatoes and Parsley Butter; Creamed Oyster Omelet; Eggs Commander (with ham, sausage, *and* hollandaise); Bananas Foster; Bread Pudding Soufflé with Whiskey Sauce; and Creole Cream Cheese Ice Cream.

Burke, David, and Carmel Berman Reingold. *Cooking with David Burke.* **Hardcover: 241 pages with color photographs, 180 recipes. Alfred A. Knopf, 1994.**

Burke, of Manhattan's Park Avenue Cafe, is one of the country's most highly regarded chefs. Following training at the Culinary Institute of America, he apprenticed in a number of France's finest restaurants. Like many restaurant-derived books, this volume may better serve to illustrate the chef's elaborate creative style than function as a working how-to. For the record, Burke appears to have pioneered the practice of stacking food in perilous towers on the plate; many recipes, in fact, come with a presentation note, titled "Building This Dish." In your own kitchen, of course, much of this can be ignored.

CONSIDER: Preserved Lemon Rings in Tempura Batter; White Bean Puree with Caviar; Artichoke Soup with Bay Scallops; Braised Lamb Shanks with Honey-Baked Turnips and Bacon; Halibut Steamed in Foil with Prosciutto and Lemon; Rabbit, Fennel, and Mustard Pot Pie; Coffee Barbecue Sauce; Riesling-Chive Oil; and Chocolate Whiskey Torte with Chocolate Sauce and Cream-Cheese Caramel.

Cobb, Sally Wright, and Mark Willems. *The Brown Derby Restaurant: A Hollywood Legend*. Hardcover: 160 pages with archival black-and-white photographs and celebrity caricatures, 35 recipes. Rizzoli, 1996.

It could be argued that this book, with one index for the celebrity photos with which it is illustrated, another for the movie star caricatures that appear throughout, but none at all for the limited number of recipes, barely qualifies as a cookbook. In fact, transformed by Robert Cobb from a single struggling eatery to a mini-chain with an international reputation, The Derbies, as they were called, had serious kitchens, and the stars, at least, came to them because the food was very good. Packed with lots of reminiscences (the author is Cobb's widow), and the original Cobb Salad recipe (always served with Old-Fashioned French Dressing and thin, crisp Pumpernickel Cheese Toast), this book is edible showbiz nostalgia.

CONSIDER: Pot Roast Brown Derby, served with Potato Pancakes (a favorite of Gable and Lombard); layered Spaghetti Derby; Beverly Salad Bowl; Catalina Sand Dabs; Filet Mignon Tidbits; Brown Derby Grapefruit Cake with Grapefruit Frosting; and Black Bottom Pie.

English, Todd, and Sally Sampson. *The Figs Table*. Hardcover: 235 pages with color photographs, 110 recipes. Simon & Schuster, 1998.

At Figs, one part of noted chef English's Boston restaurant empire, the specialty is pizza. Impossibly thin-crusted and adventurously topped, this pizza is both showy and delicious. It's also at the heart of English's second cookbook, one dealing almost exclusively with that and other such casual fare as pasta, polenta, sandwiches, salads, and desserts. As in the chef's earlier book, the flavor profile is mainly Mediterranean (with touches of the Deep South and New England), and English again manages to extract intense and layered flavors from relatively simple preparations. Some chefs' books are records of impossibly contrived dishes better dreamed over than actually attempted, but this is food you'll want to make—and eat—right now.

CONSIDER: Roasted Beets with Walnut-Gorgonzola Dressing; Baba Ghanoush with Mint Oil and Lemon Zest;

Mushroom Minestrone; Couscous Carbonara with Country Ham; Fig and Prosciutto Pizza; Portobello Mushroom Burger; White-Chocolate Challah Pudding; and Ginger Peach Crumble.

English, Todd, and Sally Sampson. *The Olives Table.* Hardcover: 367 pages with black-and-white photographs, 160 recipes. Simon & Schuster, 1997.

This book is from one of the country's most acclaimed chefs. At his four Boston restaurants, especially the one called Olives, English serves his personal take on Mediterranean cuisine. Influenced by both his Georgia upbringing and his New England location, English offers a particular type of stylish, modern comfort food that Boston diners line up for. The good news for those of us who can't make it to Beantown is that the authors have managed to capture the flavors, signature dishes, and food philosophy that make Olives unique. The book is personal, enthusiastic, and chatty, and the very accessible recipes are about layered flavor, not show-off techniques.

CONSIDER: Corn Cakes with Whipped Goat Cheese; Gorgonzola-Stuffed Figs with Balsamic Glaze; Parmesan Pudding with Sweet Pea Sauce; Littleneck Clam and Sweet Carrot Bisque; Penne with Lobster and Green Tomato Sauce; BBQ Slow-Roasted Suckling Pig with Ginger-Honey Glaze; Falling Chocolate Cake with Raspberry Sauce; Double Lemon Tart; and Pumpkin Bread Pudding with Caramel Sauce and Whipped Cream.

Fearing, Dean. *The Mansion on Turtle Creek Cookbook.* **Hardcover: 287 pages with color photographs, 160 recipes. Grove/Atlantic, 1987.**

Among the five or six chefs known for remodeling southwestern food into fine restaurant cuisine, Fearing sticks closer to his stove at the elegant Mansion on Turtle Creek than his fellows do. That makes him no less inventive a cook, as this, his only book, illustrates fully. The multiple-step formulas may look daunting, but Fearing urges the reader not to relegate the book to the coffee table. Many "garnishes" are actually side dishes, and completing the recipe yields a delicious and elegantly visual plateful.

CONSIDER: Warm Lobster Taco with Yellow Tomato Salsa and Jicama Salad; Pan-Fried Louisiana Crabcakes with Smoked Bell Pepper Butter Sauce; Roasted Eggplant and Romano Cheese Soup with Basil Cream; Grilled Chicken Breasts with Warm Cucumber Salad and Artichoke-Lime Sauce; Pumpkin Crème Brûlée with Frangelico Sauce; Brown Butter Berry Tart; and Chocolate Carrot Cake.

Flay, Bobby, and Joan Schwartz. *Bobby Flay's From My Kitchen to Your Table.* **Hardcover: 253 pages with color and black-and-white photographs, 125 recipes. Clarkson Potter, 1998.**

This is a book of "casual" party dishes, an exuberant and boldly photographed collection from one of Manhattan's (and of television cookery's) most energetic stars. Multiple international influences are at work, with flavors of the Southwest and Spain predominating. Like most modern restaurant chefs, Flay often composes the big picture, and main courses are frequently accompanied by side recipes that complete the effect. This can look like a lot of work; on the other hand, it shows how to combine unique, big-flavored dishes in a way that doesn't result in chaos on the plate.

CONSIDER: Roasted Wild Mushrooms with Goat Cheese and Chile Oil; Spicy Maple-Glazed Pork Chops with Red Onion Marmalade and Blue Corn-Sweet Potato Tacos; Pan-Roasted Rabbit with Crushed Blackberry-Ancho Sauce; Green Onion Smashed Potatoes; Pomegranate Granita; Catalan Custards with Dried Fruit; and Pistachio-Phyllo Ice Cream Sandwiches with Very Rich Chocolate Sauce.

Flay, Bobby, and Joan Schwartz. *Bobby Flay's Bold American Food*. Hardcover: 214 pages with color photographs, 200 recipes. Warner, 1994.

With wonderful photos by Tom Eckerle and a cutting-edge design that will either entrance or annoy, this book features the food of one of New York City's hottest young chefs. Based upon the menu of Flay's first restaurant, Mesa Grill, this cuisine is from the New Southwestern School. Despite his Manhattan upbringing, Flay wields the regional ingredients with panache, always seeking, he says, food that is "bold and sizzling." Working toward a complex finished product in which the various ingredients remain separate and identifiable, the chef plays mix and match with an array of salsas, savory marmalades, and flavored butters, often used to top a simply grilled, steamed, or pan-fried dish.

CONSIDER: Yellow Tomato Gazpacho; Shrimp Tamale with Roasted Garlic Sauce; Blue Corn-Fried Chicken Salad with Cayenne-Buttermilk Dressing; Chipotle Pork Tenderloin with Green Apple Juice Sauce; Apple-Blackberry Crisp with Cinnamon Ice Cream; Mango Tarte Tatin; and Pecan and White Chocolate Tart.

Flores, Carlotta. *El Charro Café*. Hardcover: 136 pages with color photographs, 110 recipes. Fisher Books, 1998.

Few visitors to Tucson leave without sampling the fare at El Charro. Located in a 100-year-old basalt-stone house, aglow with neon and colorful folk art, the restaurant serves up huge portions of the distinctive cuisine of Sonora, the Mexican state directly across the Arizona border. Based upon beef and utilizing enormous thin flour tortillas, this is earthy and simple food, not as spicy as the more familiar dishes of Texas or New Mexico but still every bit as savory and satisfying. Now Flores, granddaughter of the restaurant's founder, Monica Flinn, has collected the family's legendary recipes in a book as generous and colorful as El Charro itself. This is not new-wave Southwestern (one recipe calls for canned peas because that's how Monica did it), but it does occasionally surprise and it will always satisfy. Chimichangas (oversized, deep-fried burritos) stuffed with shredded carne seca (beef sun-dried in metal cages suspended above the restaurant's roof) and smothered with red chile sauce and guacamole may be best enjoyed at El Charro, while other dishes will be remarkably easy to prepare at home.

CONSIDER: Cheese Fondue with Chiles; Sonoran Flat

Enchiladas with Pickled Vegetables; Green Corn Tamales; Meatball Soup (Albondigas); volcano-shaped Totopo Salad; and Caramel Custard Flan.

Foo, Susanna. *Chinese Cuisine*. Hardcover: 352 pages with color photographs, 130 recipes. Chapters Publishing, 1995.

Though this book, by its title, purports to be about China's cuisine, it is really about something much more unique. Foo, whose Philadelphia restaurant earns consistent raves, uses Chinese cuisine as her starting point, letting her own culinary curiosity, the American marketplace in which she shops, and her sophisticated clientele join in modifying an ancient system of cookery into something fresh, new, and exciting. For Susanna Foo, improvisation only works if the foundations are first understood. This excellent chef's book will help home cooks begin to understand those foundations and make some very good food as well.

CONSIDER: Veal Dumplings in Ancho Chile Sauce; Grilled Chinese Eggplant Salad with Balsamic Vinaigrette; Hundred Corner Crab Cakes with Pineapple Salsa; Prawns with Poached Pears and Curry Sauce; Honey-Grilled Lamb Chops with Jalapeño Pepper Puree; Chinese Risotto with Wild Mushrooms; Peanut Ice Cream; and Frozen Mango Souffle.

Forgione, Larry. *An American Place*. Hardcover: 293 pages with color photographs by the author, 275 recipes. William Morrow, 1996.

CIA-trained Forgione first purveyed his special brand of American cuisine at Brooklyn's River Cafe before opening An American Place. Known for basing his recipes on research into historical fare and for his respect for the freshest ingredients from the finest (frequently smallest) farmers, fishermen, and gatherers, Forgione turns out food that manages to be both freshly exciting and comfortably familiar at the same time. If this big, handsome book lacks anything, it is deeper insights into just what makes this or that impeccable ingredient impeccable.

CONSIDER: New Mexican Corn Mushroom Salad with Sage-Mint Vinaigrette; Deviled Crab and Oyster Fritters; Pasta with Grilled Duck Sausage and Wild Mushrooms; Charred Rib-Eye Steak; Pork with Peppered Apples and Onions; Cheddar Cheese Biscuits; Banana Betty; Apple Pandowdy; Quince and Raspberry Tart; and Pennsylvania Dutch Chocolate Nut Pie.

Franey, Pierre, with Claudia Franey Jensen. *Pierre Franey Cooks with His Friends.* **Hardcover: 214 pages with color photographs, 120 recipes. Artisan, 1997.**

This last book of Franey's, completed just before his death in 1996, was based on a PBS television series. For the program and the book, Franey traveled to Europe, visiting familiar culinary stars like Paul Bocuse and Michel Guerard, along with less well-known kitchen faces such as Italy's Paola and Maurizio Cavazzini and Spain's Ferran Adria. The challenge to all the chefs was to cook with less fat and calories while still delivering three-star flavor. Most of the recipes are Franey's own, though each chef and his specialties serve as creative springboard. The food is indeed light (one rule was "no cream") as well as relatively simple, and the photographs of both the restaurants visited and the finished dishes are luscious, a fitting final tribute to a master.

CONSIDER: Tomato Tart; Quail Leg Appetizers; Marinated Seafood Salad; Grilled Tuna with Capers and Tomato Sauce; Medallions of Lamb with Basil; Tortellini with Ground Turkey and Red Wine Sauce; Poached Pears in Port Wine; Banana Sherbet with Yogurt and Strawberry Sauce; and Passion Fruit Soufflé.

Goldstein, Joyce. *Back to Square One: Old World Food in a New World Kitchen.* **Hardcover: 420 pages, 240 recipes. William Morrow, 1992.**

Among writer-chefs, Goldstein is one of the few who gets equal respect for both endeavors, having a finely tuned palate and an eye for authentic but unexpected flavor combinations that always produce stimulating food for thought or plate. This book, her second, while named after her award-winning San Francisco restaurant, takes its inspiration from the world at large, rather than from Square One's menu—less than good news for deprived regulars now that Goldstein has closed her eatery. The food, nevertheless, is quite dazzling, and the recipes are developed with a light touch when it comes to calories and fat.

CONSIDER: Indonesian Hot and Sweet Fruit Salad; Chinese Chicken Salad Sandwich; Crabmeat, Corn, and Spinach Risotto; Grilled Chicken with Honey and Mustard; Roast Salmon with Spiced Onions and Currants; Portuguese Pork Roast with Cumin, Lemon, and Cilantro; Scotch Crème Brûlée; Persimmon Pudding; and Tiramisù.

Gray, Rose, and Ruth Rogers. *The Cafe Book.* Hardcover: 351 pages with color and black-and-white photographs, 200 recipes. Broadway Books, 1998.

In 1995 Rogers and Gray, chefs at London's very hot River Cafe, published *Rogers Gray Italian Country Cookbook* (Random House). Its cutting-edge design, stunning photography, and simple but mouthwatering Italian cuisine made it a sensation. In the intervening years the cafe has installed a wood-burning oven, and so where that first book made much of grilling, this new, equally attractive one celebrates roasting, both with high heat and done low and slow. Otherwise the successful formula has not been tampered with even slightly. This is our idealized fantasy of light but bold, easy but stylish Italian food made manifest.

CONSIDER: Zucchini Carpaccio; Salt Cod Soup; Crab Salad; Spaghetti with Mussels; Red Snapper with White Wine, Parsley, and Garlic; Pot-Roasted Pheasant Stuffed with Ricotta; Pizza with Taleggio, Artichokes, and Prosciutto; Bitter Chocolate Roasted Hazelnut Torte; Apricot, Nectarine, and Plum Bruschetta; and Panna Cotta with Grappa and Raspberries.

Greaves, Ellen, and Wayne Nish. *Simple Menus for the Bento Box: Seasonal American Meals and Japanese Presentations.* Hardcover: 165 pages with color photographs by Nish, 48 recipes. William Morrow, 1998.

The shokado bento box is a lacquered Japanese individual

serving tray, divided into four ten-inch-square compart-ments, each square meant to hold a single, exquisitely arranged dish. Greaves is chef at Takashimaya's Tea Box Café in Manhattan, and Nish is chef and owner of the restaurant March. In this book they present twelve seasonal menus, each consisting of four recipes, occasionally Japanese-influenced. Individually, the four dishes are quite simple, but when served together in a bento menu, they create, say the authors, a larger and more artful whole.

CONSIDER: Grilled Quail in Soy Sauce and Sake Mari-nade; Salad of Shrimp with Chanterelles and Tomatoes; Fo-caccia with Mozzarella and Anchovy Salad; and Wild Rice with Pine Nuts and Sweet Peas.

Guerithault, Vincent, with John Mariani. *Vincent's Cookbook*. Hardcover: 276 pages with technical illustrations, 200 recipes. Ten Speed Press, 1994.

Among new southwestern chefs, Phoenix-based Gueri-thault stands out by being French-born and classically French trained. With a résumé including such Gallic bastions as Maxim's, Fauchon, and Jean Banchet's Le Français, Guerithault first came to the Southwest pro-nouncing *chile* with a Provençal accent. Over the years (and with the help of an Arizona-born wife), he has subtly, sensibly, and creatively incorporated into his refined cui-sine certain touches from the southwestern larder that give his food a style—and a little kick—that stands out from that of his fellows. With the help of veteran restaurant critic Mariani, the vision has been translated to paper, for all to enjoy.

CONSIDER: Chilled Cucumber Soup with Smoked Salmon and Dill; Grilled Sea Scallop Salad with Papaya Dressing; Lobster and Watercress Tacos; Ratatouille Tamales; Mesquite-Grilled Chicken with Chipotle and Apple Chutney; Wild Mushroom Ragout; Frozen Blackberry Soufflé; Crème Brûlée in Sweet Taco Shells; and Jalapeño and Orange Chutney Tarts.

Hafner, Dorinda. *United Tastes of America: Cultural Origins of Your Favorite Dishes*. Hardcover: 137 pages with color photographs, 128 recipes. Ballantine, 1997.

Based on the PBS cooking series hosted by Hafner, this slim but satisfying book is a journey through America's dominant ethnic roots. Born in Ghana and a naturalized Australian, she may be the perfect guide to the heart of Chinese-American, Cajun-American, Jewish-American, Italian-American, German-American, and African-American foods. Native Americans are also included, and New Mexican food gets its own separate chapter, too unique, apparently, to have an original European source. Hafner makes a voluble host, and her essays on the cultural groups are informative and accurate. She "gets" America in a way that even some Americans don't.

CONSIDER: Phyllis's Jambalaya; Cajun Seafood Salad; Southern-Fried Chicken; Kung Pao Shrimp; Bratwurst in Ale; Cioppino; Veal Parmigiana; Matzo Balls; and New York Cheesecake.

Kagel, Katharine. *Cafe Pasqual's Cookbook: Spirited Recipes from Santa Fe*. Paperback: 159 pages with hand-

tinted color photographs, 65 recipes. Chronicle Books, 1993.

This book's subtitle says it all. Popular with both locals and tourists, Pasqual's, crammed into what was once a corner waffle house, is famed for three things, aside from the lack of space: the length of the lines of hungry people waiting to get in, the size of the portions, and the quality of the food, which is never less than terrific. Though plenty on the menu is southwestern, plenty isn't, for Kagel's interests range far and wide. This colorful and attractive book of her specialties presents some of the vivid, eclectic possibilities.

CONSIDER: Steamed Mussels with Thai Basil and Lemongrass; Hearts of Romaine with Maytag Blue, Toasted Chile Pecans, and Sliced Pear; Mango-Lemon Soup; Breakfast Quesadillas; Grilled Salmon Burrito with Goat Cheese and Cucumber Salsa; Leg of Lamb Redolent of Garlic and Rosemary; Sangria Sorbet; Lemon Tart with Piñon Crust; and Lavender Honey Ice Cream.

Kenney, Matthew, and Sam Gugino. *Matthew Kenney's Mediterranean Cooking.* Hardcover: 167 pages with color photographs, 110 recipes. Chronicle Books, 1997.

Matthew Kenney is a wunderkind of a chef, helming three Manhattan restaurants while retaining the air of a paperboy. Each restaurant has its area of focus—Morocco, Greece, Sicily—but this is more by way of a creative anchor than authenticity. Kenney is a restless spirit who likes to sample the best the Mediterranean has to offer, then run it through the filters of what he and his customers want to eat. He has a sure hand, or else this audacious adapting wouldn't work as well as it does. This attractive book covers what he dubs the "Mediterranean Rim," and gives plenty of space to the foods of Northern Africa, for which he has a particular feel.

CONSIDER: Almond-Crusted Calamari with Mediterranean Dipping Sauce; Spicy Lamb Dumplings; Bitter Greens with Walnut Dressing, Blue Cheese, and Figs; Curried Shellfish Risotto; Moroccan Spiced Squab; Pineapple with Ginger Syrup; Roasted Peaches and Apricots with Cardamom; and Pistachio-Dried Fruit Biscotti.

Killeen, Johanne, and George Germon. *Cucina Simpatica.* **Hardcover: 221 pages with color photographs, 135 recipes. HarperCollins, 1991.**

Derived from the fare at Al Forno, one of two restaurants in Providence, Rhode Island, run by this talented husband and wife team (Lucky's is the other), this food is casual and Italian, impeccably fresh and vibrantly flavored. The soul of the establishment is a huge wood-burning brick oven designed by Germon. Consequently, much of this food is roasted or grilled. Especially distinctive are the baked pastas and grilled pizzas, which are a kick to master at home. Because of the way the recipes are written, giving an entire step over to preheating the oven, for example, some look longer and more complicated than they really are.

CONSIDER: Polenta Lasagne; Spicy Clam Salad with Oven-Cured Tomatoes; Roman Style Pizza with Potatoes and Rosemary; Pasta with Asparagus in a Lemon Cream Sauce; Grilled and Braised Short Ribs of Beef; Tartufo Ice Cream; and the best shortcake biscuit dough we've ever tasted, zipped up with white cornmeal and a touch of ginger.

Kleiman, Evan. *Angeli Caffé's Pizza, Pasta, and Panini.* Hardcover: 245 pages with black-and-white photographs, 130 recipes. William Morrow, 1997.

Angeli Caffé, on Los Angeles' rakish Melrose Avenue, has been serving up its uniquely zesty California-style Italian cuisine for some fifteen years. During that time, Kleiman, the restaurant's owner-chef, has written (or cowritten with Viana La Place) four other cookbooks and established herself as a serious proponent of a certain kind of lighter Italian fare. This book focuses on the menu strengths of the cafe—pizzas, pastas, and sandwiches—which was originally intended to be merely a pizzeria. There are no soups, salads, traditional main dishes, or desserts, but what there is is choice indeed.

CONSIDER: Pizza with Shrimp, Clams, Mussels, and Squid; Fried Calzones with Ricotta, Mozzarella, and Salami; Sicilian Double-Crust Pizza with Fresh Tuna, Herbs, Capers, and Tomato-Basil Sauce; Penne with Meat Sauce, Eggplant, and Fresh Mozzarella; Pasta with Tiny Meatballs, Tomato Sauce, and Garlicky Bread Crumbs; and a panino (sandwich) of balsamic chicken salad and arugula.

Kump, Christopher, and Margaret Fox, with Marina Bear. *Evening Food.* Paperback: 213 pages with black-and-white photographs, 100 recipes. Ten Speed Press, 1998.

This book of rather ambitious "evening" food comes from the famed Mendocino, California, eatery, Cafe Beaujolais. Kump, husband of the cafe's owner, Margaret Fox, is also the son of the late Manhattan cooking school operator Peter Kump, and grew up in the thick of the New York gourmet scene. All of which serves to explain the vivid complexity of a lot of his food, very different fare from the homey morning menu upon which the cafe's original reputation was built. Ingredients from around the world, techniques and dishes from France, Italy, Asia, and Mexico, and ingredients from California's bounty are stirred together with imagination.

CONSIDER: Rosemary Sea Scallop Skewers with a Fig, Fried Polenta, and Shredded Radicchio; Chicken and Goat Cheese Ravioli in Soy Beurre Blanc; Zanzibar Fish Soup; Smoked Pheasant Salad with Poached Pears and Toasted Hazelnuts; Braised Pork Loin with Prunes and Cream Sauce; Simca's Bittersweet Chocolate Raspberry Bavarian; Huckleberry Pie; and Fresh Tarragon Sorbet.

Lagasse, Emeril, and Jessie Tirsch. *Emeril's New New Orleans Cooking.* **Hardcover: 354 pages with black-and-white photographs, 220 recipes. William Morrow, 1993.**

If you find Lagasse's exuberance (on his hit Television Food Network program) a little overwhelming, turn to this book. The food remains every bit as lively and compelling, but the overall experience will be quieter. Despite his name, Lagasse is of Portuguese ancestry and hails from Massachusetts, not New Orleans. He likes to "mix things up," fusing Creole and Cajun flavors with those of the Southwest and Asia. Chef for seven years at Commander's Palace before opening his own restaurants, Lagasse respects the

classics but lightens and enlivens them with showy panache. Fresh ingredients, bold seasonings, and a willingness
to break the rules *are* the rules at Emeril's.

CONSIDER: Crawfish Egg Rolls with Hot Sesame Driz-
zle; Pumpkin Soup with Spicy Roasted Pumpkin Seeds;
Oysta Pasta with Caviar; Tender Roast Chicken with
Chestnut Corn-Bread Stuffing; Herbed Lamb Patties
with Creole Ratatouille and Rosemary Jus; Banana Cream
Pie with Caramel Drizzles; Chocolate Fantasy Cake; Feel-
Good Rice Pudding; and a dazzling Raspberry Chocolate
Cheesecake.

**Lagasse, Emeril, and Marcelle Bienvenu. *Louisiana Real
and Rustic*. Hardcover: 347 pages with black-and-white
photographs, 150 recipes. William Morrow, 1996.**

Away from the slick restaurant fare of his New Orleans
turf, Lagasse finds the same inherent Louisiana passion for
flavor, but on a simpler scale. The result is food that is indeed "real" (also delicious), much of it borrowed from—or
at least inspired by—the good cooking of folks he met along
the way. Louisiana's roots (French, Spanish, African, and
Caribbean) show in the ingredients, techniques, and gutsy
flavors, all given a useful structure by Lagasse's well-honed
kitchen sensibility. Evocative photos of native faces enrich
the book, and allow the reader to overlook some design
mistakes (eye-straining green ink on green paper) that
would harm a lesser book.

CONSIDER: Oyster and Spinach Soup; Eggplant-
Shrimp Beignets with Creole Tartar Sauce; Pan-Fried Cat-

fish with Lemon and Garlic; Chicken-Andouille Hash; cedar-shake-grilled Campfire Steaks; Pork Chops with Sweet Potato Gravy; Peach Upside-Down Cake; Praline Cream Pie; and Blueberry Peach Cobbler.

Lomonaco, Michael, with Donna Forsman. *The '21' Cookbook*. Hardcover: 390 pages with color and black-and-white photographs and archival illustrations, 150 recipes. Doubleday, 1995.

Formerly a Prohibition-era speakeasy, '21' survived long after the return of hard liquor to the United States by putting together a unique mix of homey food, personal service, and occasionally strange decor to become a legendary restaurant. Managing to operate like a home away from home for old-money New Yorkers, it also attracted Hollywood stars, presidents, and the generally famous and/or infamous. Following a recent renovation and reopening, it continues to flourish, serving up food that is an uneasy blend of the old menu and rather newer ideas. Chef Lomonaco has moved on, but this book accurately reflects the traditional and the renewed '21,' and celebrates with yarns, photos, and cartoons the history of a truly fabled eatery.

CONSIDER: Roasted Oysters with Country Bacon; Tequila-Cured Salmon Gravlax; '21' Traditional Cuban Black Bean Soup; '21' Traditional Sunset Salad (tongue, chicken breast, and greens); Quail with Roasted Figs; two versions of the famous '21' Burger; '21' Traditional Rice Pudding; Huckleberry and Pecan Crunch Pie; and Fresh Fruit in a Cool Ginger Broth.

Meyer, Danny, and Michael Romano. *The Union Square Cafe Cookbook.* **Hardcover: 329 pages with black-and-white photographs and color illustrations throughout, 160 recipes. HarperCollins, 1994.**

Fans of Union Square Cafe, voted most popular restaurant in New York City by the Zagat Guide three years in a row, will be delighted with this approachable volume. While in our opinion many chefs' books present dream material—that is, you're better off dreaming about it than trying to make it—these recipes are clearly designed to be cooked at home. More difficult preparations are eased by explanations and tips in the text. The authors, respectively owner and co-owner/chef, are generous with their recipes. An added bonus is the wine suggestions that accompany many of the dishes, not surprising given the superb wine list at the restaurant.

CONSIDER: Porcini Gnocchi with Prosciutto and Parmesan Cream; Pumpkin Risotto; Yellowfin Tuna Burgers with Ginger Mustard Glaze; Grilled Marinated Fillet Mignon of Tuna; Lobster Shepherd's Pie; Mama Romano's Baked Lemon Chicken; and Mashed Yellow Turnips with Crispy Shallots.

Miller, Mark. *Coyote Cafe.* **Hardcover: 192 pages with color photos and illustrations, 150 recipes. Ten Speed Press, 1989.**

The Southwest seems to have more than its share of revisionist chefs, perhaps because so much creativity is required to elevate the region's stark daily fare into fine restaurant cuisine. Miller, both as showman and as chef, leads the pack, and this first work (among many) of his is a fine introduction to the process by which the ordinary becomes extraordinary. Though he's tagged as more entrepreneur than working cook, Miller, formerly an anthropologist, is better grounded than his fellows, with a restless curiosity that informs this book and the recipes in it. Like Santa Fe itself, the lively results are a blend of the Southwest and Mexico, with a plentiful dash of Texas. As we went to press, a revised version of this classic was in the works.

CONSIDER: Green Chile and Oyster Chowder; Carpaccio of Venison; Blue Corn Shrimp Tamale; the cafe's signature Cowboy Steak with Red Chile Onion Rings; Pecan Crust Rack of Lamb; Ibarra Chocolate Cake with Chocolate Glaze; Blackberry Cinnamon Shortcakes; and Mango Raspberry Brûlée.

Milliken, Mary Sue, and Susan Feniger, with Helene Siegel. *Cooking with Too Hot Tamales*. Hardcover: 226 pages with black-and-white photographs, 150 recipes. William Morrow, 1997.

In the food biz, as in showbiz, it's not really possible to be "too" hot, so perhaps that's a misnomer in the title of this spicy little book, the companion volume to the cooking duo's popular TVFN cooking show. It's also a nice pair-up with their previous book, *Mesa Mexicana*. There they dealt with Mexico's cuisines; here they cast the net a little wider, exploring the whole world of Latin flavors. There is plenty of scattershot culinary advice sprinkled around like cilantro on a bowl of guacamole, and as always, the recipes are lively, light, and fresh.

CONSIDER: Tomatillo Guacamole; Quinoa Fritters; Tequila Martini; Fresh Corn Tamales with Roasted Red Peppers; Pork Chops with Prunes and Pine Nuts; Hazelnut Custard Cups; Vanilla Flan; Sweet Tamales; and Pink Grapefruit Sorbet.

O'Connell, Patrick. *The Inn at Little Washington Cookbook.* **Hardcover: 182 pages, over 300 color photographs, 110 recipes. Random House, 1996.**

Listed in the exclusive French-based *Relais & Chateaux*, the Inn at Little Washington has been voted Best Restaurant of the Year by the James Beard Awards, which also named Patrick O'Connell best regional chef of the Mid-Atlantic in 1993. In a word, it's to die for. If you ever dreamed of opening your own restaurant, bed-and-breakfast, or country inn—or even if you haven't—you'll enjoy O'Connell's lively and amusing story of how he and his partner, Reinhardt Lynch, went from catering over a wood cookstove and a secondhand electric skillet to the initial inn, financed on a $5,000 nest egg, to the perfectly exquisite jewel it is today. And if you love to cook or read cookbooks, the innovative ideas, relatively simple recipes, and glorious presentation, as celebrated in Tim Turner's close-enough-to-eat photographs, make browsing a hedonistic experience.

CONSIDER: Chilled Charcoal-Grilled Salmon in a Mustard Seed Crust; Creamy Garlic Polenta; Steamed Lobster with Grapefruit Butter Sauce; Rack of Baby Lamb on New Potatoes with Barley and Wild Mushrooms; Chocolate Bourbon-Pecan Tart; and Double Chocolate Ice Cream Cake.

Ogden, Bradley. *Bradley Ogden's Breakfast, Lunch, and Dinner.* **Paperback: 336 pages, 205 recipes. Random House, 1995.**

Blessed with an impeccable sense-memory of life growing up in Michigan and the Midwest, Ogden cooks elevated California restaurant cuisine with homey heartland flair. The book's inclusion of all three meals signals the home-cooking angle to come. While much of Ogden's food is restaurant-elaborate, much is not, and those seeking comfort and style simultaneously will find plenty worth heading to the kitchen for.

CONSIDER: Shrimp and Corn Fritters; Summer Squash and Lobster Soup; Pan-Fried Catfish with Black Walnut Butter; Old-Fashioned Pot Roast with Herb Dumplings; Grilled Calf's Liver and Bacon with Caramelized Apples and Onions; Sage Butter-Basted Turkey with Giblet Stuffing and Gravy; Baked Cinnamon-Raisin French Toast; Lemon Poppy Seed Waffles; Banana–Sour Cream Hotcakes; Date Muffins with Crumb Topping; Rhubarb Apple Turnover; Peach Dumpling with Warm Caramel Sauce; and Nectarine Tapioca.

Palmer, Charlie, with Judith Choate. *Great American Food.* **Hardcover: 205 pages with color and black-and-white photographs, 100 recipes. Random House, 1996.**

This book is as richly visual as the cuisine Palmer serves at his award-winning Manhattan restaurant, Aureole. It is food, Palmer says, that consists of "rambunctious, intense flavors, unexpected combinations, superb ingredients, substantial portions, and flavors and displays that will make the diner sit up and take notice." For the book, Palmer's brilliantly designed restaurant fare has been home-tested and streamlined (by coauthor Choate). Still, many dishes remain complex, often calling for special ingredients or multiple operations; one dessert has five sub-recipes.

CONSIDER: Sea Scallop Sandwiches with Citrus Juices; Cold Lobster and Sauterne Cream; Wild Mushroom Minestrone with Mascarpone Dumplings; Double Garlic Chicken with Overnight Tomatoes; and Beef Tenderloin with Foie Gras–Stuffed Morels. Crunchy Flourless Chocolate Cake is topped with Chocolate-Bourbon Ice Cream, served with two sauces and garnished with two different cookies.

Peel, Mark, and Nancy Silverton, with Ian Smith. *The Food of Campanile*. Hardcover: 309 pages with black-and-white photographs, 160 recipes. Villard, 1997.

As it approaches its tenth birthday, Campanile has become a California institution, and Peel and Silverton have repeatedly been honored for the quality of their food. This book is a record of that food, which has been called "simple and rustic" and which they describe as being Mediterranean-derived Californian. With a fierce dedication to premium raw ingredients and a uniquely focused philosophy of flavor, Peel and Silverton appear to spend plenty of kitchen time cooking that simple and rustic food (as with most chef's books, there are a lot of sub-recipes). This may or may not be time you want to spend, but you'll surely be impressed that they do, all in service of the final effect on the plate. There are also many simpler dishes or those that sound delicious enough to be worth the extra effort.

CONSIDER: Swiss Chard Stuffed with Grilled Pecorino, Eggplant, and Red Bell Pepper; Tuscan Minestrone; Duck Confit and Cannellini-Bean Ravioli with Port Wine Sauce; Chicken Salad with Belgian Endive, Apples, and Walnuts; Soft-Shell Crabs with Beer Batter; Mom's Apple Pie; and Chocolate Chip Cookies.

Pellegrino, Frank. *Rao's Cookbook*. Hardcover: 182 pages with color and black-and-white photographs, 100 recipes. Random House, 1998.

Rao's is a Manhattan institution. A family-run, hundred-year-old Italian restaurant in remote East Harlem, it serves no lunch, is open only five nights a week, and long ago permanently assigned its ten tables to a group of regular customers. Some famous, some merely loyal, they cherish—and trade—their "table rights" like prized baseball cards, and you and I can fuhgeddabout trying to get a reservation: There aren't any. Which makes this book a real treasure, since the simple, southern-Italian home cooking is a fresh and vibrant joy. Cook this food, and, despite the fact that the governor of New York, the producer of *60 Minutes*, and Regis Philbin are not seated nearby, you'll get a garlicky whiff of eccentric greatness.

CONSIDER: Roasted Peppers, sprinkled with pine nuts and raisins; Seafood Salad; Escarole and Bean Soup; Chicken Scarpariello; Shrimp Francese; Steak Pizzaiola; Tiramisù; and Almond Biscotti.

Pepin, Jacques, and Claudine Pepin. *Cooking with Claudine*. Hardcover: 267 pages with color photographs and

illustrations by Jacques Pepin, 250 recipes. KQED Books, 1996.

Based on the popular television cooking program, this book features Pepin and his daughter and cohost, Claudine. The give-and-take between the two provides a lot of material for recipe and menu development, as he serves as teacher and she the young modern, interested in integrating good food into her busy, sometimes budget-conscious life. Between the two of them, they arrive at a number of attractive, occasionally offbeat menus designed for specific purposes. Particularly useful are several cooking lessons on duck, seafood, pastry, and lamb, which show myriad ways of getting the most out of the main ingredient once you know the necessary techniques.

CONSIDER: "Easy Shortcut Supper" (Greens and Sardines, Shoulder Steak with Herbs, Roasted Potatoes and Onions, and Blueberries "au Citron"); "The Duck Party" (Duck Liver Pâté, Duck and Beans Casserole, Mock Peking Duck, Sautéed Duck in Vinegar Sauce, and Rhubarb with Strawberry Coulis); and "A Family Celebration" (Artichoke and Tomato Stew, Poached Salmon in "Ravigote Sauce," Green Couscous, and Chocolate Paris-Brest).

Pepin, Jacques. *Jacques Pepin's Table.* Hardcover: 518 pages with color photographs, illustrations by the author, 300 recipes. KQED Books, 1995.

This substantial tome contains the recipes from all three seasons of Pepin's acclaimed television series, *Today's Gourmet.* As in other of his reduced-fat books, Pepin seeks a balance between pleasure and health, often using his mastery of techniques to draw maximum flavor out of simpler, leaner—and sometimes humbler—ingredients. The food is "low on drudgery, high on joie de vivre." Themed by menus (including brunch and lunch), the recipes are then given in chapters by courses, making putting your own meal plans together easy. Sidebars provide lots of chatty insight, and the author's illustrations are charming. Nutritional counts for all recipes are given.

CONSIDER: Braised Shiitake Mushrooms on Bitter Salad; Sautéed Soft-Shell Crabs on Asparagus; Red Pepper Pasta with Walnuts; Puerto Rican Pork and Beans; Couscous of Lamb; Red Swiss Chard with Ginger; Soufflé of Mango with Mango Sauce; Blueberry Crumble; and Chocolate-Mint Truffles.

Perrier, Georges, with Aliza Green. *Le Bec-Fin Recipes*. Hardcover: 224 pages with color and black-and-white photographs, 120 recipes. Running Press, 1997.

Le Bec-Fin ("a fine palate"), a Louis XVI–style jewel box of a restaurant in Philadelphia, is arguably one of the best French restaurants in the country. Opulently romantic, aglow with the light of chandeliers, its exquisite food presented under gleaming silver domes by tuxedoed waiters, it is the polished fulfillment of its creator's vision of how fine dining ought to be. Perrier, born near Lyon and trained at Ferdnand Point's legendary La Pyramide, serves classic French cuisine just ever so slightly lightened by the times in which he cooks. Some of these recipes are quite simple, while others can be daunting. A few, which have not been successfully reduced to home size, yield more food than those not feeding a crowd will desire.

CONSIDER: Le Bec-Fin Crab Cakes with Light Mustard Sauce; Mushroom Ravioli with Ivory Sauce; Warm Vichyssoise with Oysters, Chive Cream, and Caviar; Medallions of Veal with Morels; Floating Islands with Caramelized Raspberries; Lemon Tart; and the elaborately ruffled Signature Chocolate Cake.

Ponzek, Debra, and Joan Schwartz. *French Food: American Accent*. Hardcover: 271 pages, 160 recipes. Clarkson Potter, 1996.

"Simple food cooked really well" is the straightforward motto of this Manhattan chef, formerly of Montrachet, now of the gourmet shop Aux Delices. Despite her big-city restaurant training, Ponzek has written a book of French-inspired food that American home cooks can indeed use. Sauce-making has been simplified and butter and cream reduced, while substitutions and improvisations are encouraged. On the other hand, menu-making advice, easy but effective plating suggestions, and an overall stylish simplicity make it possible for the cook to turn out professional-quality food in the home kitchen—no small feat.

CONSIDER: Crab Salad with Citrus-Ginger Vinaigrette; Squash Soup with Pan-Roasted Chestnuts; Pennette with Mushroom Cream, Lobster, and Asparagus; Pumpkin Risotto; Halibut with Tomato-Cumin Broth and Curried Couscous; Seared and Roasted Duck Breasts with Green Peppercorn Sauce; Oxtail Stew; White Chocolate Mousse;

Warm Orange-Lime Pudding; Eggnog Cheesecake; and Peach Tarte Tatin.

Portale, Alfred. *Alfred Portale's Gotham Bar and Grill Cookbook.* **Hardcover: 384 pages with color and black-and-white photographs, over 200 recipes. Doubleday, 1997.**

It's a little disconcerting to read a book in the first person written by a third party. That aside, this magnificent volume from the maestro of the justly acclaimed Greenwich Village restaurant is a book all Portale's fans and most cookbook collectors will want to own. As a driving force behind the current architectural style of food, which involves layering different flavors and textures vertically on the plate, Portale has influenced a whole school of younger chefs. Here he's brought together a talented team to tell his history, give an insider's view on a chef's creative process, and translate his recipes into a form that can be used by home cooks.

CONSIDER: Chicken Breast with Roasted Shiitake Mushrooms and Braised Endive; Grilled Leg of Lamb with Moroccan Spices, Grilled Vegetables, and Basmati Rice; and Braised Short Ribs with Baby Root Vegetables and Mashed Potatoes.

Prudhomme, Paul. *Chef Paul Prudhomme's Louisiana Kitchen.* **Hardcover: 351 pages with color photos, 200 recipes. William Morrow, 1984.**

Prudhomme, who practically created the Cajun craze, has also produced one of the best chef's cookbooks ever written. Although he says his Louisiana cuisine is a blend of Cajun (French country home cooking spiced up in the Louisiana bayous) and Creole (New Orleans city food, with French, Spanish, Italian, African, and Native American accents), it is the former that makes this book work. Deep, "round" flavors and layers of fiery heat, which build on the tongue, are the Prudhomme trademarks. Despite the restaurant presentations, this is hearty bayou home cooking, and the recipes never fail—and never fail to please.

CONSIDER: Creamy Crawfish Enchiladas con Queso; moist and spicy Cajun Meat Loaf; Creole Chicken and Dumplings; Red Beans and Rice with Ham Hocks and Andouille Smoked Sausage; Candied Yams, with a touch of orange, lemon, cinnamon, and vanilla; New Orleans Bread Pudding with Lemon Sauce and Chantilly Cream; Sweet Potato Pecan Pie; and classic Louisiana Pralines.

Puck, Wolfgang. *Adventures in the Kitchen*. Hardcover: 264 pages with color photographs, 175 recipes. Random House, 1991.

Despite his tycoon status, Puck gets the respect of his colleagues, probably on the strength of how well he does all the things he does. This book, while his latest, is not new, yet still manages to be fresh and interesting. Whether at Spago (his Hollywood version of Italian food), the pan-Asian Chinois-On-Main, the pub-style (and now defunct) Eureka Brewing Company, or any number of other eateries, Puck provides the people with what they want—he's the consummate commercial chef. Given the range of restaurants from which these recipes are drawn, expect the unexpected when you cook from this adventurous book.

CONSIDER: Chicken Saté with Mint Vinaigrette; Sizzling Calamari Salad with Potato Strings; Tempura Sashimi with Uni Sauce; Gazpacho with Crabmeat; Stir-Fried Chicken with Cashews and Pine Nuts; Braised Moroccan Lamb; Eureka Duck and Black Bean Chili; Spicy Chicken Pizza; Chocolate Bread Pudding; Cinnamon Ice Cream; Strawberry Shortcake; and Apple and Dried Cherry Turnovers.

Pyles, Stephan. *The New Texas Cuisine*. Hardcover: 428 pages with color and black-and-white photographs, 200 recipes. Doubleday, 1993.

One of five or six important chefs who have redefined the cooking of the West and Southwest, Pyles stands out as being a little earthier than some of his fellows. He also celebrates the vast possibilites of Texas, ranging as it does from New Mexico to Creole country. As an in-demand guest chef and high-powered Dallas restaurateur, he serves up complex and sophisticated food but dips occasionally into a homier vein. Down-home airs aside, many of Pyles's dishes remain restaurant-glamorous, with multiple sub-recipes and complementary side dishes often built in.

CONSIDER: Fermented Pineapple-Rum Daiquiris; Smoked Tomato Salsa; Beer Batter Shrimp with Cayenne Rémoulade; Pork Chops Stuffed with Andouille, Apples, and Cornbread; Roast Chicken in Adobo Sauce with Black Bean–Prosciutto Refrito; Pumpkin Gingerbread; Summer

Berry Buckle with Pecan Ice Cream; Chocolate Pudding Cake with Mocha Sauce; and Peanut Butter–Banana Cream Pie.

Rodriguez, Douglas. *Nuevo Latino: Recipes That Celebrate the New Latin-American Cuisine*. Hardcover: 168 pages with color photographs, 150 recipes. Ten Speed Press, 1995.

One of the leaders in the Miami culinary revolution was Doug Rodriguez. Born in New York City of Cuban heritage, he eventually ended up in South Florida, where along with the other chef-members of the so-called Mango Gang, he pioneered, in a succession of restaurants, an eclectic new style of Latin-influenced cookery that shows no signs of stopping. This free-ranging cuisine sticks to no one country, celebrating pretty much everything south of the border. As the Latin population continues to boom and markets increasingly stock produce and other ingredients needed to cook these dishes (chayote, taro, boniato, yuca, guava, dried shrimp, etc.), Rodriguez's book will only increase in usefulness.

CONSIDER: Lemon-Cayenne Yuca Chips; Plantain, Pineapple, and Serrano Salsa; Avocado Crabwich with Roasted Garlic Aioli; Latino-Style Chicken Fricassee; Guava-Glazed Barbecued Ribs; Chocolate-Rum Flan; and Coconut Ice Milk.

Rosengarten, David, with Joel Dean and Giorgio DeLuca. *The Dean & DeLuca Cookbook*. Hardcover and paperback: 563 pages, 400 recipes. Random House, 1996.

Joel Dean and Giorgio DeLuca raised the purveyance of

groceries to a fine art. Opening their beautiful, minimalist, European-inspired food store in the gallery-studded Manhattan neighborhood of SoHo in 1977, the duo educated the emerging American gourmet on the importance of impeccable ingredients and pioneered a whole new style of lush presentation that was the antithesis of the sterile, prepackaged supermarket approach. Now, supermarkets ape their methods, and as a corporate entity, Dean & DeLuca seems to have gotten away from its creators, but their philosophy remains as important as ever. Rosengarten, a TVFN anchor and *Gourmet* magazine restaurant critic, packs the book with sound but simple ingredient information and recipes shrewdly chosen to fit our modern lives (but, surprisingly, no desserts).

CONSIDER: Buffalo Chicken Wings; Manhattan Clam Chowder; Caesar Salad with Roquefort Dressing and Crispy Walnuts; Italian-American Lasagne with Ricotta and Tomato Sauce; Slow Roast Chicken, Bistro-Style, with Goose Fat; Thai Noodles with Peanut Sauce and Cucumbers; and Mashed Potatoes with Green Olive Oil.

Roux, Michel. *Sauces: Sweet and Savory, Classic and New*. Hardcover: 176 pages with color photographs, 200 recipes. Rizzoli, 1996.

Among sauce books, few are more beautiful than this one, by the renowned chef of the Waterside Inn in Bray, on the Thames River. Blessed with luminous photographs, this is a complete and satisfying work that chefs and home cooks alike will find useful. Most of the sauces are in "stand-alone" recipes, which saves space and promotes flexibility.

In the index, they are matched with appropriate main ingredients: Look up "lamb," for example, and you find lamb-compatible sauces.

CONSIDER: Fresh Goat-Cheese Sauce with Rosemary; Lavender Vinaigrette; Crustacean Oil; Thai Vinaigrette with Lemongrass; Foie Gras Butter; Light Carrot Coulis; Arabica Fig Sauce (nice with wild duck or squab); Vineyard Sauce with Five Spices; Strawberry Coulis with Green Peppercorns; and White Chocolate Sauce with Mint.

Ruggerio, David. *Little Italy Cookbook*. Hardcover: 213 pages with color photographs, 135 recipes. Artisan, 1997.

Ruggerio is Brooklyn-born and the chef/owner of a number of successful New York restaurants. This loving tribute is the companion volume to his PBS series. The focus here is East Coast big-city Italian-American cooking, the kind one still dreams about when on a garlic-scented walking tour of lower Manhattan. Behind the lace-curtained windows of brick row houses or at the red-and-white-checked-tablecloth restaurants with the candles stuck in Chianti bottles, the lively, fresh, and satisfying food is as good as it gets. Although some recipes prove problematic, Ruggerio's book captures this fragrant place, which is increasingly, one suspects, giving way to less tasty "progress." Recipes from friends, relatives, and noted neighborhood cooks enrich the book, as do essays on local purveyors.

CONSIDER: Escarole Soup with Meatballs; Salad of Rice, Tuna, Tomato, and Capers; Spaghetti with Crabs; deep-dish Pizza Rustica; Oxtail Stew; Parmesan Mashed

Potatoes; Prosciutto Bread; Amaretto-Chocolate Cheese-cake; Peaches in Red Wine, Tuscan Style; ice cream-like Chestnut and Ricotta Semifreddo; and a warm, boozy Zabaglione.

Scotto, Marian, and Vincent Scotto. *Fresco: Modern Tuscan Cooking for All Seasons*. Hardcover: 180 pages with color photographs, 125 recipes. Abbeville Press, 1997.

This attractive book is slightly schizophrenic. On one hand it is clearly the product of an ambitious New York City restaurant (trademarks are declared and celebrity clients' names are dropped), while on the other it reads and feels like the memoir of a particularly food-savvy Italian-American family from Brooklyn. Indeed, Fresco the restaurant is the product of several members of the Scotto family of Brooklyn, and while there is no indication that their origins are Tuscan, they and their chef (who trained at Al Forno in Providence) have a nice feel for the kind of rustically sophisticated Italian food we like to think of as Tuscan. The book's seasonal organization creates a muddle but the recipes are fine.

CONSIDER: Chicken Soup with Escarole and Orzo; Beet Salad with Goat Cheese and Walnuts; Roasted Chicken with Lemon, Sage, and Bruschetta Stuffing; Braised Lamb Shanks with Creamy Polenta; Almond Poundcake with Cherry Sauce; and Raspberry-Fig Tart.

Soltner, André, with Seymour Britchky. *The Lutèce Cookbook*. Hardcover: 573 pages with black-and-white photographs, 335 recipes. Alfred A. Knopf, 1995.

For many years, on the short list of "best restaurants in America" the name of Andre Soltner's Lutèce could be counted on to appear, often in first place. Now that Lutèce's longtime chef/proprietor has sold his famed establishment, that evaluation must remain in suspension, a state of affairs that makes the publishing of this book all the more an event. Cowritten with a longtime observer of the New York restaurant scene, the book is as thoroughly civilized and as thoroughly French as Soltner and Lutèce, serving as a fitting record of and tribute to both. The all-in-French recipe titles can give the impression that this is strictly a book of classics, but in fact, Soltner frequently innovates, although always in a classic context.

CONSIDER: Salmon Glazed with Mousse of Mustard; Terrine of Roquefort Cheese; Duck Liver with Caramelized Apples; Endive and Walnut Salad with Black Olives; Preserved Rabbit with Lentils; Boned Saddle of Veal Stuffed with Sweetbreads; Almond Tart; and Frozen Soufflé with Raspberries.

Spilchal, Joachim. *Joachim Spilchal's Patina Cookbook: Spuds, Truffles, and Wild Gnocchi.* **Hardcover: 144 pages with color and black-and-white photographs, 60 recipes. HarperCollins, 1995.**

The first (and apparently the only) book in a projected series of chef-based works, this one celebrates the cuisine of a legendary Los Angeles restaurateur. It takes a writer (Charles Perry), an editor/tester (Brigit Legere Binns), a designer, and two photographers to capture Patina on paper, but the results are so successful that one laments the other books that never got written. Following the chef through his day, from pre-dawn marketing to weary clockout, the book serves up Spilchal's whimsical, imaginative, and complex food (potatoes are a particular passion) much of which will appeal to ambitious home cooks.

CONSIDER: Layer Cake of Odd Potato Chips and Smoked Sturgeon with Horseradish Sauce; Roasted Chicken Wings with Unorthodox Chopped Liver; Potato and Forest Mushroom Lasagna; Sweetbreads Club Sandwich; Quartet of Crème Brûlées; Strawberry Rhubarb Pie with Strawberry Sorbet; and Chocolate Croissant Pudding.

Tower, Jeremiah. *Jeremiah Tower's New American Classics.* **Hardcover: 233 pages with color photographs, 250 recipes. Harper & Row, 1986.**

Among the chefs who transformed American cooking in the 1980s, few had a greater effect than Tower, who remains less a household word than some of his fellows. A partner in and a chef of Chez Panisse, later creator of the remarkable San Francisco restaurant Stars, Tower uses American ingredients, applies classic French techniques, and creates neoclassic food—never gimmicky, always elegant and delicious. This book features brilliant essays on techniques, dishes, and food memories, plus over 125 evocative photos. Despite the chef's prodigious intellect (he earned a master's in architecture from Harvard), the food is sensual, even voluptuous.

CONSIDER: Truffled Sweetbread Ravioli; Cream of

Corn Soup with Crayfish Butter; Warm Pasta Salad with Smoked Duck and Radicchio; Grilled Calamari with Lobster Mayonnaise; Rabbit Chili; Ham with Black Beans, Oranges, and Lime Cream; Lamb Stew with Artichokes; Pears in Red Wine with Basil; White Peaches with Raspberry and Blackberry Sauces; and Mango Mousse with Coconut Sauce.

Tropp, Barbara. *China Moon Cookbook*. Hardcover and paperback: 518 pages, 250 recipes. Workman, 1992.

China Moon was a San Francisco restaurant created by Tropp, a noted Chinese cooking teacher and author. Dubbed a "bistro," to indicate that it was not a traditional Chinese restaurant, China Moon served what Tropp called California-Chinese cooking. Influenced by that state's multiple cultures and abundant and varied produce, and intended to combine casual San Francisco cafe style with authentic Asian flavors, China Moon's food, as represented in this prizewinning book, was flavorful and fun. Relying on a pantry of homemade condiments, infused oils, and other flavor-makers, it can also be a lot of work, although for the dedicated project cook, the results will always reward the effort.

CONSIDER: Crab and Corn Won-Ton with Green Chili Sauce; sweet and smoky Strange Flavor Eggplant; Chicken and Coconut Soup with Crispy Almonds; Casserole of Spicy Sparerib Nuggets with Garlic; Sesame–Brown Sugar Shortbreads; Black Fig Streusel Tart; and Fresh Ginger Ice Cream with Bittersweet Chocolate Sauce.

Trotter, Charlie. *Charlie Trotter's Seafood.* **Hardcover: 240 pages with color and black-and-white photographs, 75 recipes. Ten Speed Press, 1997.**

Legendarily fussy about ingredients, and known for complex and multiple flavors and intricate and beautiful plate presentations, Charlie Trotter has nevertheless managed to transfer his restaurant vision to paper. In this opulently produced book, his subject is seafood, a particular passion of the chef's. He finds it "sensual," and of course it is a challenge to locate seafood of the best quality, a daily battle he obviously enjoys. There is no general seafood information, just a parade of recipes grouped in chapters by the wines that best suit them—as good a way as any of organizing recipes for which there is no real precedent. The recipes themselves are serious and hard going, but just when you think the author must be completely humorless, you find a photo of him in his chef's whites awash in the Hawaiian surf.

CONSIDER: Rainbow Trout with Shellfish Eggdrop Soup; Sea Urchin and Osetra Caviar with Vodka Crème Fraîche and Daikon; Mahimahi with Wilted Greens, Chinese Longbeans, Fried Hawaiian Ginger, and Star Anise Vinaigrette; and Frog Legs with Roasted Eggplant Puree and Saffron-Yellow Squash Coulis.

Van Aken, Norman, with John Harrisson. *Norman's New World Cuisine.* **Hardcover: 312 pages with color and black-and-white photographs, 160 recipes. Random House, 1997.**

The descriptor "rock and roll" might be used on any number of our best-known culinary superstars, but it seems most aptly applied to Van Aken. A former short-order cook and carnival worker, he is self-taught; yet it's not out of the question to find him addressing the graduating class of a culinary academy. With Hawaii, Key West, and the entire Caribbean making up his kitchen palette, he serves up food as complex and ambitious as any in the country, yet does it with a kind of beach-bum bonhomie that adds to, rather than detracts from, the culinary seriousness. Except that a good many tropical ingredients are not fully explained, the book offers a colorful trip through Van Aken's vividly flavored and layered food—and life.

CONSIDER: Voodoo Beer–Steamed Shrimp with a West Indian Cocktail Salsa; Little Havana Chicken and Plantain Sopa; Mongolian Pork Brochettes with a Confit of Cayenne-Dusted Carambola; and Toasted Pecan Caramel Tart with Jamaican Blue Mountain Coffee Bean Crema.

Vongerichten, Jean-Georges, and Mark Bittman. *Jean-Georges: Cooking at Home with a Four-Star Chef.* Hardcover: 288 pages with color and black-and-white photographs, over 150 recipes. Broadway Books, 1998.

Minimalist is the buzzword for this book, dedicated to showcasing the unique, French-Asian style that the chef/owner of restaurants Jean-Georges, Jo Jo, and Vong has taken to high art and at the same time proved that his extraordinary food can be reproduced in a home kitchen. Vongerichten has streamlined his recipes, using as few ingredients as possible and foods largely available in better supermarkets. Coauthor Mark Bittman, who not coinciden-tally writes a "Minimalist" cooking column for *The New York Times*, has done a masterful job of writing those recipes in a style that is original, approachable, exacting, and for-giving, answering questions before you can ask them.

While the book is not for complete novices or budget watchers—one recipe recommends truffle oil if you do not have the harder-to-come-by truffle juice—even complex preparations are broken down into easy-to-follow steps, and designed to cook any night of the week.

CONSIDER: Leek and Potato Tart; Sautéed Chicken with Prunes; Lamb Chops with Root Vegetables and Horse-radish; Shrimp and Noodle Salad with Grapefruit and Peanuts; Sautéed Chicken with Licorice and Ginger; Tuna Skewered with Lemongrass; Scallops and Cauliflower with Caper-Raisin Sauce; Warm, Soft Chocolate Cake; Pear Clafoutis with Star Anise; and Lemongrass Pots de Crème.

White, Jasper. *Jasper White's Cooking from New England.* Hardcover: 367 pages, 300 recipes. Biscuit Books, 1998.

New England has many fine chefs, but none cook with the same sense of place and history as Jasper White. The award-winning chef for many years of Jasper's, on the Boston waterfront, he now consults for the Legal Sea Foods restaurant chain. Born in New Jersey, into an Italian-Irish family, White learned from his grandmothers to disdain any ingredient but the best, that the best was linked directly to the land, and to always be thankful for that bounty. Mar-riage to a New Englander brought him to that part of the country he seemed destined to find. With both wild and

farmed abundance, dramatic seasons, and a rich ethnic
heritage (there's more to New England than Pilgrims), this
was a region made to be explored and exploited by someone
with White's exuberance, technical expertise, and thoughtful creativity. Especially adept with products from the sea
(he has also written a book on cooking lobster at home), his
skills extend to both traditional and contemporary dishes
that manage to be both hearty and sophisticated. This is a
very fine chef's book, indeed, for both reading and cooking from.

CONSIDER: New England Clam Chowder; Warm Salad
with Lobster, Papaya, and Foie Gras; Medallions of Tuna
Wrapped in Bacon with Red Wine Sauce; beer-battered
Fish and Chips with Cole Slaw and Tartar Sauce; Roast
Vermont Turkey with Giblet Gravy and Sausage and Sage
Dressing; Crispy Fried Rabbit; Sweet Corn and Bread Pud-
ding; Cranberry-Streusel Tart; and Maple Sugar Crème
Caramel.

**Wicks, Judy, and Kevin von Klause, with Elizabeth
Fitzgerald. White Dog Cafe Cookbook. Paperback: 335
pages with black-and-white photographs, 250 recipes.
Running Press, 1998.**
The White Dog Cafe is a Philadelphia institution, a
homey place known for comforting but brilliantly conceived food and a social conscience that involves it in
many charitable good works. The kitchen's style is American with an international cast, and Wicks (the owner) and
von Klause (the chef) dish up a generous helping in this attractive, oversized book. Anecdotal and chatty, it's an ap-

pealing work that even those who have never eaten at The White Dog will want to cook from.

CONSIDER: Roasted Beets and Gorgonzola with Orange-Rosemary Vinaigrette; Baked Shrimp and Pork Spring Rolls with Apricot-Pickled Ginger Dipping Sauce; Chili- and Corn-Crusted Calamari with Tangy Citrus Aioli; Vietnamese Chicken Salad; Jamaican Curried Lamb Stew; Tomato and Sweet Corn Risotto; Shepherd's Hash with Baked Eggs; Six-Grain Pecan Pancakes with Apple Cider Syrup; Harvest Fruit Crisp; Cappuccino Crème Brûlée; and Havana Banana Cake with Pineapple-Rum Compote.

Wolf, Burt. *Gatherings & Celebrations*. Hardcover: 353 pages with color photographs, 105 recipes. Doubleday, 1996.

More than just an entertaining book (which is what the title might lead you to believe), this work of special occasions goes behind the scenes at events around the world, giving the history and explaining the rituals and folklore that make these celebrations indelibly unique. Wolf is the host of a number of highly regarded and award-winning television series, including the one upon which this book is based. Packed with pictures and insights both large and small, the book was researched by the inimitable Margaret Visser and is written in the same dry, witty, and enthusiastic voice with which Wolf does his hosting. Ranging from Chinese New Year in Taiwan to A Barbecue in Puerto Rico to A Birthday Party at Walt Disney World, the gatherings run the gamut. Along the way we learn the meaning of red and green at Christmas, why there are chocolate rabbits at Easter, and the reason we stuff the Christmas turkey. Often set in wine-producing regions, the book is also knowledgeable about the beverages with which we toast each other at our gatherings. This book is a wry, smart, and classy party, with food that is no less wonderful.

CONSIDER: Wild Rice Pancakes with Salmon Roe; Mini Crab Cakes with Remoulade Sauce; Gravlax; Grilled Shrimp with Mango Salsa; Chicken and Sausage Gumbo; Portuguese Seafood Stew; Beef with Ginger and Bell Peppers; Stuffed Acorn Squash with Apple, Onion, and Spinach; Chocolate-Coated Almonds; Cheesecake with Orange Honey Sauce; and Cranachan (Scottish Raspberry Cream) with Petticoat Tail Shortbread Cookies.

Yamaguchi, Roy, and John Harrisson. *Roy's Feasts from Hawaii.* **Hardcover: 232 pages with color photographs, 150 recipes. Ten Speed Press, 1995.**

This is contemporary Euro-Asian restaurant cuisine, in strong contrast to the simple Hawaiian street fare known as "local food." A member of the pioneering Regional Cuisine Movement, Yamaguchi celebrates Hawaii's bounty while acknowledging that much of what is being cooked has only been grown on the islands for the past few years. In the context of climate, though, that which grows well wherever one is usually also tastes good eaten there. That said, Yamaguchi, of Japanese descent, was trained at the CIA and worked in a number of mainland restaurants before opening his string of island eateries. The ingredients may be local, but the food is international restaurant overkill of the very best kind.

CONSIDER: Roy's Kalua Pork Quesadillas with Smoked Mozzarella, Avocado, and Lomilomi Salmon; Thai Hot and Sour Miso Soup with Shrimp Dumplings; Maui Onions and Kula Tomatoes with Pancetta and Basil Balsamic Vinaigrette; Lanai Venison in Red Currant–Cabernet Sauce with Pesto Potatoes; Island Cheesecake with Coconut Crust and Macadamia Nut Praline; and Caramelized Pineapple Tart.

Cookbooks Featuring Grilling and Other Techniques and Equipment

Grilling

Chesman, Andrea. *The Vegetarian Grill.* **Hardcover and paperback: 296 pages, 200 recipes. Harvard Common Press, 1998.**

Designed for vegetarians, this book is nevertheless a fine recipe and technique resource for all grillers, regardless of their attitudes toward eating meat. Following a brief but thorough rundown on equipment and techniques, Chesman, a prolific writer of cookbooks, gets things going with a strong chapter on simply grilled vegetables. She then moves on to what many cooks (particularly nonvegetarians) will think of as more interesting fare, including appetizers, soups, salads, sandwiches, veggie burgers, wraps, pizzas, pastas, kebabs, and even desserts—all getting a welcome touch of smoky grill flavor.

CONSIDER: Charred Corn Salsa; Grape Leaves Stuffed with Brie; Vietnamese Noodle Salad with Grilled Vegetables; Mushroom Steak Sandwiches with Blue Cheese Dressing;

Vegetable Fajitas with Chipotle Sour Cream; Sesame-Grilled Tofu; Foil-Wrapped Apple Brown Betty; Pears Stuffed with Hazelnut Cream; Basic Grilled Pineapple; and Campfire Cinnamon Toast Treats.

Hearon, Reed. *La Parilla: The Mexican Grill*. Paperback: 131 pages with color photographs, 95 recipes. Chronicle Books, 1996.

Given the number of blissful vacation days Americans spend on Mexican beaches, it's no wonder that the sizzle of garlicky shrimp on an open grill is so happily associated with life south of the border. Of course, it's not only at the beach where Mexicans shine at the art of the grill (*parilla* or *parrilla*). From the tender baby goat of northern Mexico to the fragrant banana-leaf-wrapped, pit-roasted chicken of the Yucatan, a whole repertoire of grilled dishes exists, often overlooked by traditional Mexican cookbooks. Hearon, a noted restaurant chef, begins with a number of recados (seasoning pastes or rubs) and salsas, which bring explosive flavor to the food before and after it is grilled.

CONSIDER: Seared Spiced Tuna; Grilled Salmon in Corn Husks; Spicy Quail with Green Chorizo; Duck and Pomegranate Tacos; and Pork Ribs with Tamarind Recado.

Jamison, Cheryl Alters, and Bill Jamison. *Smoke and Spice*. Hardcover: 414 pages, 300 recipes. Harvard Common Press, 1994.

Food cooked low and slow with smoke is barbecued, while food sizzled quickly over an open flame is grilled. The distinction is made because this large and useful book concentrates on the former. Once the province of professional pit-masters, smoking can now be accomplished at home, using one of several types of newly available equipment. Choosing a smoker is just the beginning of the adventure, say the Jamisons, veteran cookbook writers to whom real barbecue is "bragging food." Fuels, tools, and regional barbecue distinctions are discussed; tips and trucs shared; and chatty sidebars scattered around like so much pepper on a slab of ribs.

CONSIDER: Bragging Rights Brisket; Apple City Back Ribs; gin-mopped Martini Lamb; Hot Times Jalapeño Turkey Breast; Jamaican Jerked Salmon; San Antonio Cactus Corn Salad; Kansas City Baked Beans; Wild Huckleberry Pie with Coconut Crumble; Texas Peach Cobbler; Candy Bar Cheesecake; and Sweet Potato Pudding.

Jamison, Cheryl Alters, and Bill Jamison. *Born to Grill*. Hardcover: 500 pages, 310 recipes. Harvard Common Press, 1998.

By now the Jamisons' award-winning format is well established: pack as many vividly titled, down-home recipes as possible into a single volume; support the many recipes with an abundance of factoidal sidebars; and maintain a folksy expertise through friendly, readable headnotes. This book begins, as does any grill book worth its salt, with plenty of technique and equipment advice. While not dogmatic, the Jamisons are advocates of uncovered grilling, consider smoking chips an affectation, and seem to prefer natural charcoal over propane, while adding that the fuel isn't anywhere near as important as the grill cook's skills.

CONSIDER: Southern Ham and Shrimp Skewers; Charred Eggplant Spread; Green Chile and Chicken Mexican Pizza; Devilish Horseradish Burger; Crunchy Kraut Dog; Red-Hot Bayou-Blackened Strip Steak; Vietnamese Fajitas Salad; Grilled Green Tomatoes; Campfire Classic S'Mores; Bourbon Caramel Apples; and Grilled Banana Split with Chocolate-Toffee Melt.

Kerr, Park, and Michael McLaughlin. *The El Paso Chile Company's Burning Desires: Salsa, Smoke, and Sizzle from Down by the Rio Grande.* Hardcover: 269 pages, 160 recipes. William Morrow, 1994.

Grilling and smoking both get their southwestern-style due in this funny, readable, idea-packed work. Kerr, whose Texas-based company manufactures gourmet salsas and other condiments, manages to keep the promotional nature of the book in the background, going instead for creative new ways to apply the smoky kiss of the fire to a wide range of edibles. With a main title and a cover that, at the very least, do not quite convey what the book is about, this tasty resource may have been overlooked by serious grillers and smokers.

CONSIDER: Thunder and Lightning Salsa; Dark Secrets Mole Barbecue Sauce; Roasted Garlic Rosemarynade; Skillet-Smoked Shrimp Cakes; Fiery Lemon Chicken; Grilled Spareribs with Pineapple-Mustard Glaze; Chicken Fajitas Salad; Grilled Pizza with Eggplant and Roasted Red Peppers; Smoked Loin of Tuna; Chopped Smoked Pork on a Bun with Oink Ointment; Pink Margarita Sorbet; Lemon Ice Cream Pie with Raspberry Sauce; and Chocolate Whiskey Pudding.

McLaughlin, Michael. *All on the Grill*. Hardcover: 221 pages, 170 recipes. HarperCollins, 1997.

With his usual virtuoso combination of hearty flavors, impeccable technique, and some of the best food writing around, McLaughlin makes you want to eat the page. Here he offers complete menus, all kissed with smoke. As both the title and the subtitle—"170 Recipes for the Complete Meal, from Savory Starters to Delectable Desserts"—imply, he tackles just about everything you might want to do on a grill.

In addition to standard selections—meats, poultry, seafood, vegetables—are chapters on "Especially Spicy Grill Meals" and "Grill Meals for Entertaining." With each menu McLaughlin includes a list of what to do in advance and then, when you're ready to grill, the order of steps to take to complete the meal.

CONSIDER: Grilled Red Snapper Veracruz with Olive and Roasted Chile Relish; Grilled Baby Back Ribs with Molasses-Mustard Glaze; Rosemary-Smoked New Potatoes; Spicy Slaw with Smoky Grilled Carrots; Lime Caesar Salad with Grilled Chile-Rubbed Shrimp; Teriyaki Turkey T-Bones; and Grilled Pineapple and Pound Cake with Kahlúa Fudge Sauce.

Raichlen, Steven. *The Barbecue! Bible*. Hardcover and paperback: 556 pages with black-and-white photographs, 500 recipes. Workman, 1998.

For this veritable tome, Raichlen visited over twenty-five countries and spent three years shaping their grilling traditions and recipes for the American cook. The basic messages are not new, but the global depth of coverage is. From cultures as diverse as those of Greece, Japan, Australia, South Africa, and Argentina, the author has collected recipes that will transform what you toss on the barbie. Since the publisher is Workman, it should come as no surprise that sidebars abound; there's also a separate chapter on vegetarian grilling.

CONSIDER: Vietnamese Grilled Beef and Basil Rolls; Australian Beer-Barbecued Wings; Pancetta-Grilled Figs; Grilled Corn Chowder; Grilled Chicken Salad with Indian Spices; Salmon Grilled in Grape Leaves; and Balinese Grilled Bananas in Coconut Milk Caramel.

Schlesinger, Chris, and John Willoughby. *License to Grill*. Hardcover: 400 pages with color photographs, 200 recipes. William Morrow, 1997.

As generously packed with ideas and recipes as its predecessor (see below), this work, by one of America's most popular restaurant chefs and his longtime collaborator, seems more evenhanded and less eager to shock or impress. The result is a very attractive and desirable grill book, one that will take backyard cooks ready for a challenge to new heights. As usual, the authors ignore gas-fired grills, but their general information is sound, and anyone with propane expertise will have no trouble re-creating these smoky delights on their own equipment. Not missing are Schlesinger's trademark guy-with-a-beer style and informative sidebars, plus a remarkable number of boldly desirable recipes.

CONSIDER: Lime Soup with Grilled Cumin Chicken; Grilled Shrimp and Black Bean Salad with Papaya-Chile

Dressing; Korean-Style Grilled Chicken Wings; Grilled Veal Chops with Expensive Mushrooms; Grilled Pineapple with Sweet Lime–Black Pepper Sauce; Gingered Mango Mousse; and Malaysian-Style Coconut Pudding.

Schlesinger, Chris, and John Willoughby. *The Thrill of the Grill: Techniques, Recipes, and Down-Home Barbecue.* Hardcover: 395 pages with color photographs and technical drawings, 200 recipes. William Morrow, 1990.

Among chefs who have earned national acclaim, Schlesinger may be alone in the casual, even rustic quality of both his restaurants and the food he serves. Centered around the charcoal grill and the smoker, this book is personal, imaginative, highly seasoned, and presented with the slightly loopy air of a man who has had perhaps one beer too many while waiting for the fire to burn down to perfection. In other words, except for his rather pointed failure to even mention propane grilling, this book is the perfect union of author and subject.

CONSIDER: Chilled Grilled Tomato Soup with Fresh Basil; Grilled Chicken Thighs with Peach, Black Olive, and Red Onion Relish; Grilled Pork Loin with Indonesian Chile-Coconut Sauce; Grilled Salmon with Watercress; Doc's Cheddar Biscuits; Chocolate Pudding Cake; Peach Cobbler; and Sweet Potato–Peanut Pie.

Voltz, Jeanne. *Barbecued Ribs, Smoked Butts, and Other Great Feeds.* Paperback: 272 pages with archival black-and-white photographs, 260 recipes. Alfred A. Knopf, 1995.

This lively and rather mouthwatering book was revised for the Knopf Cooks American Series. Voltz, a noted food writer and editor of a certain age, remarks that grilling was big in the fifties and then caught on again in the eighties. As we prepare to depart the nineties, grilling shows no signs of slowing down, and books that share well-seasoned tips, techniques, and abundant recipes—as this one does—are always in demand. Born in Alabama, Voltz has also grilled in Florida, North Carolina, California, and on various fire escapes in New York City. With a funny, no-nonsense approach, she leads the reader through a world of casual outdoor cookery—great "feeds" of all sorts.

CONSIDER: Pig Pickin's, Home-Style; Key West Roast Pig; Oriental Short-Rib Barbecue; Greek Lamb Kebabs; Chicken Thighs with Pesto; Whole Salmon in Foil; Smoked Capon; Bone-Broth Basting Sauce; Tallahassee Hushpuppies; Texas Coleslaw; Peaches with Buttered Almonds; Flaming Bananas; and Toasted Marshmallow Sundaes.

Wright, Clifford. *Grill Italian*. Hardcover: 214 pages with color photographs, 100 recipes. Macmillan, 1996.

Of the many world cuisines in which grilling plays a part, Italian cooking, with its emphasis on premium ingredients, simply prepared, would seem the likeliest natural match. Based upon this appealing book, it is, indeed, and whether the recipes are for classic Italian grilled dishes or more modern, Italian-inspired flights of fancy, the food is never less than enticing. Wright, who has also written about the foods of Sicily and about lasagne, takes the typical grill-book approach and begins by discussing fuels (including propane), equipment, and techniques in a brief but thorough way. There is also a nice pantry section on authentic ingredients.

CONSIDER: Grilled Skewered Pork with Prosciutto and Sage; Grilled T-Bone Steak from Florence; Calabrian-Style Grilled Skewered Meatballs; Spit-Roasted Cornish Hens with Juniper and Bay; Grilled Chicken Oregano; Grilled Tuna in Rosemary and Garlic, Palermo-Style; and Grilled Eggplant Roll-Ups.

Miscellaneous

Brody, Lora. *Lora Brody Plugged In—The Definitive Guide to the 20 Best Kitchen Appliances.* **Ringbound hardcover: 388 pages, 375 recipes. William Morrow, 1998.**

Brody (who has written several books on bread-machine baking) obviously celebrates electric appliances. In this work, she picks the top 20 of the 80 or so machine types found on the market and tells how to select, operate, and get the most out of them, sometimes in unconventional ways. From blenders to deep fryers, and from the microwave oven to the electric water smoker, the design flaws (or pluses), desirable power levels and capacities, and other technical information on the gadgets is very thorough. Each appliance profile is followed by recipes that illustrate what Brody thinks the appliance does best.

CONSIDER: Smoky Joe Bloody Mary; Curried Pumpkin Soup; Grilled Lamb and Green Tomatoes; Lasagne (in the slow cooker!); Electric Skillet Pizza; Black Bean Tortillas;

Crème Brûlée with Dried Cherries and Kirsch; Blender Gingerbread; and Key Lime Ice Cream.

Carpenter, Hugh, and Teri Sandison. *Hot Wok*. Paperback: 105 pages with color photographs, 50 recipes. Ten Speed Press, 1995.

Carpenter's expertise in Asian cookery is broad, and, given his skill as a cooking teacher and his penchant for fusion food blended from several cuisines (not all Asian), this stir-fry book, though not specifically technique oriented, contains a very complete guide to nearly everything your wok can do for you (steaming is not covered). The food is zestily flavored, though not necessarily with chiles, and gentle guidance toward improvising your own recipes in the wok is spread throughout. Much of the food may be on the modern and creative side, but that doesn't mean you won't find some old Chinese restaurant favorites.

CONSIDER: Spicy Shrimp in Hunan Black Bean Sauce; Kung Pow with Fresh Bay Scallops; Squid with Hawaiian Mango Salsa; Spicy Tangerine Chicken; Thai Lobster with Mint, Ginger, Chiles, and Lime; Classic Mu Shu Pork; Mongolian Lamb with Shredded Scallions; and Hot Southwest Pasta with Chipotle Chiles.

Downard, Georgia Chan, and Eva Righter. *Reasons to Roast*. Paperback: 256 pages, 100 recipes. Chapters Publishing, 1997.

What's old is new again, say the authors of this modest book, pointing out that roasting is back in style and still producing the kind of richly browned and flavorful foods we've always craved. They celebrate other roasting pluses, too, including ease and speed of preparation, relatively unattended cooking, and reduced fat. Although not as revolutionary as Barbara Kafka's seminal work on roasting, this is nevertheless an engaging and well-thought-out book loaded with stylish recipes.

CONSIDER: Asian Honey-Roasted Peanuts; Roasted Potato Skins with Monterey Jack Cheese and Chipotle Chiles; Roasted Eggplant and Red Pepper Soup; Roasted Sea Bass with Bread Stuffing; Prime Rib of Beef with Shiitake Mushroom Sauce; Pork Sausages Roasted with Onions and Apples; Roasted Sweet Potatoes with Garlic and Rosemary; Roasted Pear and Bacon Salad with Blue Cheese; Roasted Bananas with Caramel Sauce; Roasted Gingered Nectarines with Pecan Topping; and Roasted Figs with Mascarpone.

Kafka, Barbara. *Microwave Gourmet*. Paperback: 575 pages with technical drawings, 450 recipes. William Morrow, 1997.

This groundbreaking book was originally published in 1987, and it set the microwave world on its ear. Both a stickler for quality and a radical realist, Kafka was the perfect person to reinvent the microwave oven, freeing it from snobbish oblivion and elevating it into an essential piece of fine culinary equipment. Along the way she broke many of the rules that microwave manufacturers (scientists, obviously, not cooks) had established long ago.

Thrilled with the newly discovered things "the oven" can do, she remains brutal about those things at which it fails miserably. Variations follow many recipes, while a dictionary of foods at the end gives precise timings for dozens of ingredients.

CONSIDER: Veal and Ham Pâté; Clams Casino; Cold Curried Tomato Soup with Yogurt; Szechuan Shrimp with Chili Paste; Heart of the Home Beef Stew; Barbecued Spareribs; Sweet and Sour Red Cabbage; Bourbon Peaches; Key Lime Pie; Butterscotch Pudding; American Chocolate Layer Cake; Ginger Lace Cookies; and Peanut Brittle.

Kafka, Barbara. *Roasting: A Simple Art.* Hardcover: 452 pages with black-and-white and color photographs, 370 recipes. William Morrow, 1995.

Opinionated and willing to break rules in the quest of something good to eat, Kafka is always working to refine our kitchen ways. Here it is roasting that gets the treatment, her entire premise for which can pretty much be summed up thusly: "Roast at 500 degrees until done." From easy roast chicken to a festive venison party, these dishes are all simple. Of course you will need to open a window, turn on the exhaust fan, and disconnect the smoke detector, and it helps to have a self-cleaning oven, but, as Kafka asserts, the results are worth it.

CONSIDER: Tarragon Roast Chicken; Roast Quail with Fresh Sage and Bacon; Wholesome Brisket with Roasted Vegetables; Roast Fresh Ham with Onion-Rhubarb Sauce; Roasted Cod with Pacific Rim Glaze; Roasted Baby

Artichokes with Garlic; Pears with Honey Glaze; and Whole Roasted Peaches with Ginger Syrup.

Rodgers, Rick. *The Slow-Cooker Ready and Waiting Cookbook*. Paperback: 256 pages, 160 recipes. William Morrow, 1998.

This book will revolutionize how you use your slow-cooker. To clear up any confusion, Crockpot is a trademarked brand name while *slow-cooker* is the awkward generic term that other manufacturers—and publishers—must use. Rodgers celebrates the slow-cooker's good qualities—unattended cooking, cheaper cuts of meat simmered to tenderness, no scorched pot bottoms, the oven freed for other purposes—while offsetting its weaknesses. The results are head and shoulders above the bland and stringy food typical slow-cooker recipes produce, and there finally seems to be a reason to own this appliance.

CONSIDER: Ricardo's Chile con Queso; Castroville Artichoke Dip; Farmer's Market Lobster and Corn Chowder; Slow-Cooked Meat Loaf; Chinese Country Ribs; Very Nice Red Beans and Rice; Erna's Sauerbraten; Southern-Style Smothered Green Beans; Gingered Apple Butter; Back Bay Indian Pudding; and Hot Fudge Spoon Cake.

Rodgers, Rick. *Fondue: Great Food to Dip, Dunk, Savor, and Swirl*. Hardcover: 152 pages, 50 recipes. William Morrow, 1998.

The message here: Fondue is back! Who better to ring the creative changes on this casual, communal style of cooking and eating than Rodgers? Taking the process about as far as it can go, he celebrates in this attractive little book cheese-based fondues, Asian hot-pot–style fondues that involve simmering, an international array of deep-fried fondues based upon the classic fondue Bourguignon, and dessert fondues. To many readers, who grew up after fondue originally faded from the scene, this will be new and adventurous; older eaters will feel a sense of nostalgia. Either sort will appreciate the sound advice on selecting cheeses, setting up a fondue pot, and getting it hot and ready to go.

CONSIDER: Classic Three-Cheese Swiss Fondue; Classic Beef Fondue with Sour Cream and Horseradish Sauce; Mongolian Lamb Hot Pot with Spicy Dipping Sauce; Chocolate Coconut Almond Fondue; and Peach Caramel Fondue.

Taylor, Hoppin' John Martin. *The Fearless Frying Cookbook.* **Paperback: 201 pages, 125 recipes. Workman, 1997.**

Fried foods, says Taylor, are not to blame for the broadened backsides and hardened arteries of our times. A little exercise is all it takes to make up for a sedentary existence, and anyway, properly prepared fried food is not heavy, greasy, or fattening. An unreconstructed southerner (he is the author of two books on southern cooking and operates a cookbook store in Charleston), Taylor set out to champion crisp, light, and greaseless fried food and discovered an appreciation of the cooking method that is international in scope. Not all his food is deep-fried, by the way; sautéing, pan-frying, and stir-frying also appear here. A few simple techniques and a bit of essential but affordable equipment will yield maximum eating pleasure, says Taylor.

CONSIDER: Chiles Rellenos; Southern-Fried Fish and Hush Puppies; Chicken Kiev; Fried Rice; Stir-Fried Vegetables; Apple Fritters; Fried Peach Pies; French Toast; and Sweet Fried Ricotta.

Ziedrich, Linda. *The Joy of Pickling*. Paperback: 382 pages with technical drawings, 200 recipes. Harvard Common Press, 1998.

The smells of pickle-making are inescapable, and if you grew up in the right sort of household, you may have fond memories of the fragrance and the flavors of a big, tangy batch. Or you may still, as generations before you have done, put up your own pickles as summer reaches its peak. Like a lot of the home arts, pickle-making these days is done not because we don't have year-round produce or more efficient ways of preserving it, but because the process itself creates a new food, transforming a raw ingredient into something different and wonderful. We pickle for its own sake. Now comes this book, packed with pickles and sure to have another generation of cooks heading for the salt, the jars, and the dill. Except, of course, that many of these pickles are not canned, merely refrigerated, and many of them take no jars or dill at all, much less cucumbers. It's a big pickle world out there, and Linda Ziedrich has pretty much covered the bases in this mouthwatering book. The technical pickling and food safety information sections seem first-rate (they're certainly thorough), and the recipes range the world—not to mention the garden. If you think you don't like pickles, you're a rare bird whose mind will probably be changed by a trip through these pages.

CONSIDER: Half-Sours, by the Quart; Spicy Crock Pickles; Russian Dill Pickles; Cabbage and Radish Kimchi; Cornichons à Cru; Old-Fashioned Bread-and-Butters; Marinated Artichoke Hearts; Polish Pickled Mushrooms; Japanese Pickled Ginger; Moroccan Preserved Lemons; Sauerkraut with Juniper Berries; Chowchow; Cherry Relish; Mango-Apple Chutney; Tomato Salsa; and Spiced Blueberries.

Breads

Alford, Jeffrey, and Naomi Duguid. *Flatbreads and Flavors: A Baker's Atlas.* **Hardcover: 441 pages with color and black-and-white photographs, 210 recipes. William Morrow, 1995.**

Alford and Duguid operate a stock photo library that specializes in agricultural and culinary images. Traveling the world in the grip of their mutual wanderlust and under the spells of their twin passions for travel photography and culinary research, they became particularly enamored of flatbreads. Simple, often to the point of being unleavened, flatbreads in one form or another are common to most regions of the world. In this award-winning book, the authors paired an international collection of 60 flatbreads with 150 recipes for the main dishes, condiments, or other toppings with which they are typically served. The result is an exotic, culturally rich cookbook.

CONSIDER: Pebbled Persian Bread paired with Pomegranate and Meatball Soup; Malaysian Flung and Folded Griddle Breads teamed with Egg Curry with Tomato; Papaya and Peanut Salad accompanied with Chickpea Flour Country Bread; Chicken Tagine with Olives and Onions served with Moroccan Anise Bread; and Anna's Cured Salmon alongside Norwegian Crispbread.

Beard, James. *Beard on Bread*. Paperback: 230 pages with technical drawings, 100 recipes. Alfred A. Knopf, 1995.

Commercial bakeries producing high-quality, European-style breads are fairly common these days, as are serious home bread bakers and books written for them. Twenty-five years ago, however, when this book was new, the bread scene was much less encouraging, and Beard was campaigning hard to get Americans interested in good bread. Signs of the times include frequent apologies for recipes that produce more than one loaf of bread, as well as Beard's use of more sugar and yeast than today's sophisticated bakers will want. The medium-sized book remains a thorough resource, though, with good ingredient, equipment, and technique information as well as a wide variety of recipes; and it surely deserves some of the credit for the modern bread revolution. Chapters on griddle breads and batter breads are nice to see, as is the generous number of Scandinavian loaves.

CONSIDER: Buttermilk White Bread; Walnut Bread from Southern Burgundy; Finnish Sour Rye Bread; Italian Feather Bread; Saffron Bread; Rich Sour-Cream Coffee Cake; Challah; Dill-Seed Batter Bread; Persimmon Bread;

Sweet Potato Rolls; Armenian Thin Bread; Raised Dough-nuts; Potato Scones; and Crumpets.

Clayton, Bernard. *Bernard Clayton's New Complete Book of Breads*. Hardcover: 748 pages with technique drawings, 300 recipes. Simon & Schuster, 1987.

This is a legendary book, thoroughly revised after a long shelf life to be even more useful and information packed. It is doubtful that any bread book, even at 300 recipes, could be considered truly "complete," but Clayton certainly comes close, as a couple of generations of home cooks and professional bakers can testify. The recipes are clearly written, with special equipment needs and a timetable of the various preparation stages given in side-bars. A trouble-shooting section will help in the rare event something goes wrong. Clayton, a dog lover, also gives his recipe for dog biscuits, and even includes drawings for building an adobe bread oven. Trust that all the classics—ryes, pumpernickels, sourdoughs, baguettes—are here in full force, as well as some more unusual recipes.

CONSIDER: Old Milwaukee Rye; Finnish Barley Bread; Swiss Cheese Potato Bread; Minted Yogurt Bread; North African Coriander Bread; Coconut Banana Quick Bread; Raisin Coffee Cake; Syrian Salted Sesame Bagels; Lithuanian Bacon Buns; Black Walnut Bread; and Petit Pain (little rolls) from the S.S. *France*.

Clayton, Bernard. *Bernard Clayton's Complete Book of Small Breads*. Hardcover: 287 pages, 100 recipes. Simon & Schuster, 1998.

A new bread book from this grandfatherly icon of baking is always welcome. The concept here is small breads, and the book contains an international collection of buns, biscuits, bagels, crackers, croissants, flatbreads, muffins, rolls, and more. In some ways this would make a nice first baking book, since the recipes are thorough and clear, the technical information reassuringly brief, and the notion of putting together small breads somehow less daunting than that of wrestling with whole loaves. The book also runs the gamut of leavenings, from baking powder to yeast to sourdough. All of which is not to say seasoned bakers won't also welcome a work just packed with enticements.

CONSIDER: Pecan Sticky Buns; Chinese Steamed Buns with Pork; Greek Feta Biscuits; Petit Pain au Chocolat (Chocolate-Filled Brioches); Bialys; Swedish Oatmeal Crackers; Lemon-Zucchini Muffins; Parker House Rolls; and Cherry-Studded Scones.

Eckhardt, Linda West, and Diana Collingwood Butts. *Rustic European Breads from Your Bread Machine.* Hardcover: 325 pages with 100 recipes. Doubleday, 1995.

This book was written for those bakers who love the speed of the bread machine but hate the flabby supermarket-style loaves they seem designed to produce. The authors (award-winners for their *Bread in Half the Time*) have pretty much reinvented the bread machine, breaking some manufacturers' recommendations, redefining its purpose, and coaxing rustic, crunchy, crusty big-holed

European loaves from it. The main revision? Don't bake in the bread machine, but do let it knead the soft and sticky European-style doughs that produce rustic breads. The bread machine is also great for rising doughs, but come baking time, they get turned out, shaped by hand, and baked in a conventional oven, often on clay tiles and with generous spritzings of water, emulating the brick ovens professional bakers have used for centuries.

CONSIDER: Pain au Levain with Sun-Dried Tomatoes and Herbs; Sweet Butter Loaves from the South of France; Whole Wheat–Walnut Bread; Monogrammed Wheat and Rye Bread; Rosemary-Raisin Focaccia with Pine Nuts; and Golden Raisin Lemon Buns with Saffron.

Esposito, Mary Ann. *What You Knead*. Hardcover: 151 pages with color photographs, 50 recipes. William Morrow, 1998.

This book is not typical of others by this popular public television cooking teacher. Based upon three simple yeast doughs—a "straight" dough, a sponge-based one, and a sweet dough—the book's recipes run the gamut from plain to fancy, from savory to sweet. Blessed by both useful technique photos and some rather luscious "beauty" shots of the finished breads, pastries, pizzas, and other dough-based dishes, the book is as engaging as its author, and the recipes are doable indeed. There are also chapters on using up leftover bread and on making your own bread flavorings and go-withs. The number of recipes isn't overwhelming—it's a slim volume—but there are many keepers.

CONSIDER: Sausage- and sweet pepper-filled Double-Crusted Focaccia; Italian Country Chicken Pie; Tuscan Rosemary and Currant Rolls; Spring Spinach, Prosciutto, and Fontina Tart; Grilled Pizza; Almost Apple Charlotte; Poppy Seed Pretzels; Fat Tuesday Donuts (oozing a luscious chocolate cream); and Mango and Dried Cherry Pie.

Greenstein, George. *Secrets of a Jewish Baker: Authentic Jewish Rye and Other Breads*. Paperback: 368 pages with technique drawings, 120 recipes. The Crossing Press, 1993.

Though the baker is Jewish, the breads run the gamut, and this book is simply packed with attractive recipes and seasoned bread-making know-how. Greenstein owned and operated a bakery on Long Island for years. Now retired, he has assembled a collection of breads that are outstanding, and done so with the astuteness of a real professional. Sidebars (labeled "Baker's Secret") are sprinkled around like poppy seeds; the clear, concise recipes are written for kneading by both food processors and stand mixers; and recipe variations broaden the scope of an already expansive book. From a publisher not widely known for cookbooks, this was the surprise winner of the James Beard Award for Best Baking and Dessert Cookbooks in 1994.

CONSIDER: Potato Rye Bread with Onion and Caraway; the molasses-cornmeal bread called Anadama; classic Challah; the crisp Provençal bread known as Fougasse; Semolina Bread; Bavarian Pumpernickel; and Tuscan Sourdough.

Herbst, Sharon Tyler. *Breads* (revised). Paperback: 276 pages with technical drawings, 190 recipes. HP Books, 1994.

This friendly, approachable book, originally published in 1983, admirably succeeds at demystifying bread-making. With jolly confidence, Herbst covers the necessary ingredients, techniques, and tips with professional skill. In addition to advice on high-altitude baking and a good chart laying out the causes for various common bread problems, there is a short section on adapting your favorite recipes for the bread machine. Her heart is not entirely into this appliance, it seems, since the recipes themselves have not been reworked, leaving that task up to the reader. Because the majority of the breads are not the sort one makes in a machine anyway, this lapse is forgivable, and indeed, it is the batter breads, quick breads, muffins, coffee cakes, and so on that seem to capture the largest part of Herbst's attention and imagination.

CONSIDER: Peppered Walnut Bread; Blue Cheese Baguettes; Swedish Limpa; Marzipan Coffee Ring; Old-Fashioned Cinnamon Rolls; Peanutty Branana Muffins; Caramel Apple Twist; and Cranberry Stollen.

Leader, Daniel, and Judith Blahnik. *Bread Alone: Bold Fresh Loaves from Your Own Hands.* Hardcover: 332 pages with color photographs, 70 recipes. William Morrow, 1993.

The quest for quintessential bread reaches near fulfillment in this single-minded book. The founder of a renowned bakery in upstate New York, Leader is a passionate perfectionist when it comes to producing crusty, European-style loaves. Organic, high-protein flours, pure water, and sea salt are preferred and slow, natural starters the norm. Multi-page recipes and techniques that take place over several days are also given in succinct charts, which will be all that seasoned bakers need to get started (this is *not* a book for beginners). Some glaring typos and organizational snafus can cause confusion, but Leader's quest for ideal breads is infectious.

CONSIDER: Country-Style Hearth Loaf with Dried Figs, Cognac, and Hazelnuts; Dark Pumpernickel with Raisins; Lemon Dill Rye; Pain au Levain (a type of sourdough) with Olives and Rosemary; and a chocolate-apricot version of the coffee cake called Kugelhopf.

Miller, Mark, and Andrew MacLauchlan, with John Harrisson. *Flavored Breads.* **Hardcover and paperback: 216 pages with color photographs, 100 recipes. Ten Speed Press, 1996.**

At Mark Miller's Coyote Cafe, flavor is packed into every possible thing to eat. This includes the basket of house-made breads that lands on every table. Despite the generous size of the entrées to follow, few can resist digging into the baked offerings, and diners often pass nibbles back and forth, analyzing the tasty creations. Now Miller and his executive pastry chef MacLauchlan (with longtime collaborator Harrisson) have turned that bounty into a book. Though the flavors tend toward the southwestern pantry, breads from around the world are considered fair game for embellishment. Some recipes are designed with optional slow-rise steps for those who have the time to let the extra flavor develop; conversely, most recipes come with bread machine directions for bakers in a rush.

CONSIDER: Open-Fire Cowboy Cornbread; Apple-Cinnamon-Walnut Muffins; Killarney Irish Oatmeal Bread; Fennel–Black Olive Bread; Mushroom Flatbread; Potato Focaccia; Sesame-Peanut Breadsticks; and Chocolate Cherry Sourdough.

Ortiz, Joe. *The Village Baker: Classic Regional Breads from Europe and America.* Paperback: 306 pages with color photographs and technique drawings, 50 recipes. Ten Speed Press, 1998.

Now that hand-shaped, crusty, artisanal, mostly sourdough European-style breads are taking over from the flabby, mass-produced kind, the number of books designed to let bakers make the same sorts of loaves at home is also on the rise. Among them, this passionate work stands out. A professional bread-maker, Ortiz visits bakeries wherever he goes. That there are only fifty recipes is a measure of how much painstaking attention Ortiz gives each of his breads, as well as a clue to the amount of supporting human and professional detail he goes into with each of his bakery visits. A final chapter includes commercial-sized versions of the recipes, designed for professional use.

CONSIDER: Country-Style French Bread; Raisin-Nut Rye Rolls; Brioche; Italian Olive Oil Bread; Prosciutto Bread; and Jewish Rye.

Rosenberg, Madge. *The Best Bread Machine Cookbook Ever.* **Paper-over-board, spiral bound: 216 pages, 150 recipes. HarperCollins, 1992.**

Maybe the reason this bestselling bread-machine book—over 100,000 copies and still going strong—is so popular is that the recipes are so good. Author Rosenberg is owner of a highly rated New York bake shop, Bakery Soutine, and her ideas are inventive and appealing. This small, square volume details everything you need to know to use your bread machine with confidence of success. The assortment of breads includes all the basics, but the fun is in the interesting ingredients and flavorings she adds. There's even a final chapter that takes doughs prepared in the machine a step further by shaping them, filling them, topping them, and baking them in the oven. If this book appeals to you, look also for Rosenberg's other two titles in the same series: *Ethnic Breads* and *Low-Fat, No-Sugar Breads*.

CONSIDER: Corn and Cheddar Bread; Ratatouille Bread; Prosciutto and Black Pepper Bread; Welsh Raisin Bread; Provençal Olive and Thyme Bread; Bananas and Cream Bread; and Blueberry and Oat Bread.

Scherber, Amy, and Toy Kim Dupree. *Amy's Bread.* **Hardcover: 196 pages with color and black-and-white photographs, 40 recipes. William Morrow, 1996.**

New York is a city with many fine, serious bakeries, both established and recent. Among the newcomers, Amy's ranks very high, especially famed for attractively shaped breads with added, flavor-boosting ingredients. Scherber worked at Bouley and Montrachet restaurants and studied in France before striking out with partner Dupree to found her own shop. There are not a lot of recipes here, but the ones offered are fresh and distinctive. The information on producing slow-rise European-style doughs and the photographs that illustrate how to shape them are clear and first rate. Somehow, while saying many of the same things other recent bread books have said, this one manages to be simpler and more approachable. Not quite a beginner's book, perhaps, but a remarkably lucid bread-baking volume.

CONSIDER: Cinnamon Raisin Bread; Semolina Bread with Apricots and Sage; Rich Focaccia with Basil Oil; Chewy Olive and Thyme Sticks; Pecan Sticky Buns; and Buttermilk Oatmeal Scones.

Silverton, Nancy, with Laurie Ochoa. *Nancy Silverton's Breads from the LaBrea Bakery: Breads for the Connoisseur*. Hardcover: 260 pages with black-and-white photos and color photo endpapers, 60 recipes. Villard, 1996.

The subtitle says it all: Silverton is a perfectionist, perhaps even more so now that she operates one of the best bread bakeries in the country. This is European-style artisanal bread, leavened with a natural sourdough starter. The process is slow but not arduous, and Silverton's specific directions on tools, ingredients, and techniques leave as little to chance as is possible when baking bread at home. She also advises the reader to keep a journal, noting successes and failures; like gardening, bread-making is a constant learning process. She also explains how to fit this kind of baking into your busy, modern schedule. There aren't a lot of recipes here, but they are choice.

CONSIDER: Walnut Bread; Rosemary–Olive Oil Bread; Potato-Dill Bread; Mushroom Bread; Grape Focaccia; Fig-Anise Bread; Italian Bread Sticks; Izzy's New York Rye; Sourdough Onion Rings; Sourdough Waffles; and Warm Sourdough Chocolate Cake.

Van Over, Charles. *The Best Bread Ever: Great Home-made Bread Using Your Food Processor*. Hardcover: 272 pages with color and black-and-white photographs, 60 recipes. Broadway Books, 1997.

Van Over, a professional baker, has been employing his food processor and an extraordinarily easy method for kneading bread dough with it for years. Since most bread books these days celebrate the slow, artisanal, European-style method of making bread by hand, a system using cold water, no proofing of the yeast, and a 45-second machine kneading that apparently turns out flavorful, crusty, open-textured bread every time is revolutionary. This is the kind of breakthrough that rapid-rising yeast was supposed to be but wasn't, and it seems to be applicable to a wide range of possible loaves.

CONSIDER: Semolina Bread; Anise-Scented Moroccan Bread; Crunchy Wheat Rolls; Swiss Twist with Ham and Gruyère; Four-Cheese Pizza with Garlic; Feta and Herb Focaccia; Ciabatta; Whole Wheat Pita Pockets; Holiday Stollen; Babas au Rhum; Poppyseed Danish Bread; Tunisian Bread Soup; Chocolate Bread Pudding with Caramel Sauce; and Raspberry French Toast with Ricotta Lemon Cream.

Baking and Desserts

Alston, Elizabeth. *Tea Breads and Coffeecakes.* Hardcover: 87 pages, 36 recipes. HarperCollins, 1991.

The best small cookbooks take a narrow subject and explore it in some depth; kitchen creativity is stimulated and good recipes find their way into the hands of good cooks. Alston, the food editor of *Woman's Day* magazine, is the author of a number of successful small books, including this sweet, cozy, and inspiring one. Covering its subjects from morning to evening, the book's recipes are simple, imaginative, and clearly written. Initial information on basic baking is lucid and sound; in fact, this would be a good first baking book. Frozen pastries or store-bought doughnuts pale beside such fresh, warm possibilities.

CONSIDER: Whole-Wheat Carrot-Apple Honey Cake; Nutmeg Plum Cobbler Cake; Lots-of-Blueberries Coffeecake; Chocolate-Marbled Sour Cream Cake with Cinnamon-

Almond Topping; Rhubarb Upside-Down Cake; Intense Chocolate Tea Bread; Peaches and Cream Kuchen; Spicy Upside-Down Sausage Corn Bread; and Sweet Marsala-Rosemary Corn Meal Cake.

Baggett, Nancy. *The International Cookie Cookbook*. Paperback: 256 pages with color photographs, 150 recipes. Stewart, Tabori, and Chang, 1996.

This book is organized in a different and rather insightful way: by country. Page through the recipes herein, and the universal appeal of a well-made cookie is readily apparent. Except for Africa, where there does not seem to be much baking, and Antarctica, where there is not sufficient heat, all continents are represented. (If you are curious as to what constitutes an Australian cookie, look no further than the ANZAC, a wartime favorite using coconut and oats.) Aside from the breadth of its tasty recipes, this book's other major plus is its photographs by Dennis Gottlieb. Just try to resist heading for the kitchen after looking at his picture of Peanut Butter Sandies.

CONSIDER: Chunky Macadamia Nut–White Chocolate Cookies (U.S.); Brown Sugar Peanut Bars (Colombia); Jam-Filled Almond Shorties (Scotland); Lemon-Filled Sandwich Cookies (England); Embossed Cardamom Wafers (Norway); Holiday Prune-Filled Pinwheels (Finland); Cinnamon Stars (Germany); Sesame Seed Biscotti (Italy); Cinnamon-Walnut Rugelach (Israel); and Chinese Almond Cookies (Hong Kong).

Beranbaum, Rose Levy. *The Cake Bible*. Hardcover: 556 pages with color photographs, charts, and technical drawings, 200 recipes. William Morrow, 1988.

This book, from the last-word-on-the-subject school of cookbook production, was an instant classic upon publication over ten years ago. Given its size, attention to detail, and overwhelming amount of information, it's easy to be afraid of this book or to think it was written only for professionals. Yes, there is a nice section dedicated to the more arcane aspects of baking (the whys as well as the hows), and there are recipes that serve hundreds, but much of this book is about simple cakes and other sweet, easy things, all of them rendered a little less mysterious by Beranbaum's relentless quest for perfection. From waffles to wedding cakes, they're all here.

CONSIDER: Buttermilk Country Cake; Down-Home Chocolate Mayonnaise Cake; Less Fruity Fruitcake; Zucchini Cupcakes; Chocolate Oblivion Truffle Torte; Sticky Buns; Crepes Suzette; and Bittersweet Cocoa Almond Génoise.

Beranbaum, Rose Levy. *The Pie and Pastry Bible*. Hardcover: 692 pages with color photographs and technical drawings, over 300 recipes. Scribner, 1998.

Ten years in the making, this book, the hefty twin to Beranbaum's award-winning *Cake Bible*, is every bit as scientifically painstaking, organized, and, well, hefty. Covering far more than pies (quiches, biscuits, strudel, filo, puff pastry, Danish pastry, brioche, and cream puff pastry, to name many), this latest entry in the dessert-making steeplechase belongs on the kitchen shelf of any serious baker. Even if, as some have said of Beranbaum's earlier work, a few of the recipes themselves are not ultimately seductive in the mouth, the insights into ingredients, techniques, and equipment make it indispensable. One anecdote says it all: When Beranbaum, a newlywed and a pie novice, prepared her husband's favorite Thanksgiving dessert with nothing but unsweetened pumpkin puree by way of filling, she headed back to the kitchen the following week, determined to get it right. These recipes are tirelessly tested, retested, and analyzed to produce flawless results every time. Charts summarize each formula, giving ingredients by volume as well as in ounces and grams. Drawings of essential equipment accompany each recipe. Extensive sections on fillings, toppings, sauces, glazes, and embellishments supplement the main body of the book and will leave few of your pastry-making needs unfilled.

CONSIDER: Open-Faced Designer Apple Pie; Raspberry Chiffon Pie; Perfect Peach Pie; Tahitian Vanilla Cheesecake Tart; Kiwi Tart with Lime Curd; Savory Spinach Quiche; Hungarian Poppy Seed Strudel; Marionberry and Passion Cream Napoleon; Bear Claws; Sticky Buns; and Chocolate-Glazed Cream Puffs filled with Vanilla Lover's Ice Cream.

Beranbaum, Rose Levy. *Rose's Christmas Cookies*. Hardcover: 255 pages with color photographs, technical drawings, and design templates, 60 recipes. William Morrow, 1990.

Christmastime may be cookie time, but cookies know no real season, and those in this imaginative, impeccably written, and mouthwatering book really deserves to be cooked the year-round. Begin at Christmas, though, to get the full effect of Beranbaum's thoroughly tested recipes and to take advantage of the sound advice on everything from baking cookies for decorating the tree to packing a batch to ship off to loved ones away from home. As usual, charts give ingredients by both weights and measures and directions are given for both food processor and electric mixer steps where appropriate. Each cookie has its own photo, which will guide you even further toward Christmas cookie perfection.

CONSIDER: Gingerbread People; Stained-Glass Cookies; Spritz Butter Cookies; Peanut Butter and Jelly Jewels; Mom's Coconut Kisses; Meringue Mushrooms; Maple Macadamia Bars; Moravian Spice Crisps; and for the family pooch, crunchy and nutritious Bone à Fidos.

Bergin, Mary, and Judy Gethers. *Spago Desserts*. Hardcover: 273 pages with color photographs, 140 recipes. Random House, 1994.

Wolfgang Puck has always understood that despite the light, California style of his cooking, his customers love desserts. Previously the brilliant Nancy Silverton functioned to provide the sweets; now it is Mary Bergin. Spago operates as a kind of private Hollywood club, with regulars coddled and treated to their favorites, so the desserts run the gamut from high style to homey. More than just an eclectic collection of good recipes, the book aims to function as a teaching work as well and is based around essential techniques, which then get enlarged upon in subsequent, spin-off recipes. If the resulting desserts are not quite as single-mindedly focused as those of Silverton, they are nevertheless well worth the kitchen time.

CONSIDER: Chocolate-Chiffon Cake; Buttermilk Layer Cake with Strawberry Bavarian Cream; Caramelized Lemon Chiffon Cake with Fresh Berries and Crème Brûlée; Chocolate Tiramisù; Old-Fashioned Apple Pie; Autumn Brown Butter Apple Tart; Pear Cherry Napoleons; Marbled Brownies; and Peanut Butter Cookies.

Bloom, Carole. *International Dictionary of Desserts.* Paperback: 356 pages, 85 recipes. Hearst Books, 1995.

A dictionary of over 800 international dessert terms might sound like something only a professional would want (and indeed, pros should buy this book). So packed with interesting information is it, however, that even home bakers—armchair or actual—will gain hours of browsing pleasure. And with listings such as *awwam, zerde,* and *stroopwafel,* cut-throat Scrabble players will have a new reference work. Bloom, a noted pastry and confectionary teacher and writer who has studied extensively in Europe, seems the ideal author for this useful book. In addition to the brief but thorough A-to-Z listings, nearly ninety recipes round out the big dessert picture.

CONSIDER: Classic Chocolate Truffles; Hazelnut White Chocolate Cheesecake; Lemon Spice Chiffon Cake; Linzertorte; Madeleines; Banana Walnut Muffins; Pound Cake; Classic Puff Pastry; Cream Scones; Rice Pudding; Shortbread; Blueberry Sorbet; and English Toffee.

Bluestein, Barry, and Kevin Morrissey. *The Complete Cookie.* **Hardcover: 322 pages with color photographs, 100 recipes. Doubleday, 1996.**

When it comes to a cookbook on a subject about which you are obsessed, the word *complete* is very much a matter of opinion. So whether a hundred cookie recipes is anywhere near sufficient is strictly up to you. Regardless, this is a very good cookie book, indeed—one of the best. The popular and prolific authors, former owners of a Chicago area cookbook store, have a fine knack for mixing traditional favorites with creative updatings, producing a collection that should please everyone. The technical information is brief but thorough, and the photography engagingly fresh.

CONSIDER: Viennese Raspberry Sandwiches; Ginger Pear Biscotti; Snickerdoodles; Chocolate Grouchos; Scottish Shortbreads; Nutty Blue Cheese Wedges; Fig Port Bars; New England Farmhouse Cookies; Apricot Hamantaschen; Gingersnaps; Lemon Poppyseed Wafers; and Peanut Butter Jack-o'-Lanterns.

Boyle, Tish, and Timothy Moriarty. *Grand Finales: The Art of the Plated Dessert.* **Hardcover: 348 pages with color photographs and technical drawings, 50 recipes. Van Nostrand Reinhold, 1997.**

Produced by editors of *Chocolatier* and *Pastry Art & Design* magazines, this expensive coffee-table book is devoted to the new breed of fantastic restaurant desserts— conceived, constructed, plated, and presented by the new breed of pastry chef. The recipes come from fifty of the country's most renowned dessert designers, and each is meticulously rendered in photographs and, where necessary, drawings, in order that the home baker might reproduce them. The photos are dazzling, while the recipes sometimes sound fabulous and other times appear too intricate to touch, let alone eat. Interviews with the chefs (Hubert Keller, Andrew MacLauchlan, and Emily Luchetti among them) set out their philosophies.

CONSIDER: Banana Buttercrunch Cake; Mocha Panna Cottas with Caramel Rum Sauce; and Pear Bavarian.

Braker, Flo. *The Simple Art of Perfect Baking.* **Paperback: 399 pages with color photographs and technique drawings, 170 recipes. Chapters Publishing, 1992.**

Perfection in baking is rather Zenlike: always approaching, never quite reaching. There will always be too many variables for a collection of baking recipes (or any recipes, really) to be completely foolproof. That said, Braker, among only a handful of writers on and teachers of pastry making, comes close. The intelligent reader who studies the systems of baking (rather than just plucking a recipe out of the middle of the book), stands a good chance of getting it right every time. In addition, Braker is a friendly voice on the page—understanding, unflappable, and seasoned from thirty years of baking experience. This revised version of a highly regarded hardback also contains many foundation recipes—mousses, fillings, glazes—that will let confident bakers construct their own works of art.

CONSIDER: Cornmeal Pound Cake; Yogurt Bundt Cake; Lemon Parfait Cake; St. Lily Peach Cake; Boston Trifle; Classic Banana Chiffon Cake; Cranberry Chocolate

Eistorte; Flag-Raising Apple Pie; Lemon Tart with Blueberries; Chocolate Eclairs; and Raspberry Cream Torte.

Desaulniers, Marcel. *Death by Chocolate: The Last Word
on a Consuming Passion.* **Hardcover: 143 pages with
color photographs and technical drawings, 60 recipes.
Rizzoli, 1992.**

Desaulniers apparently wanted to be a mortician before
he found his culinary calling, which perhaps explains this
book and its successors, *Desserts to Die For* and *Death by
Chocolate Cookies.* Those for whom chocolate is a problem
requiring a twelve-step solution may relate to the fatal attraction concept; others, for whom chocolate is just one of
a number of seductive dessert choices, can easily ignore the
overheated prose and enjoy the sexy photographs and opulent recipes. Though the author is a noted chef, not all the
recipes are complex affairs. In fact, the book proceeds from
the simple to the truly ornate, with plenty of chocolate information and dessert-making advice along the way.

CONSIDER: Bittersweet Chocolate Sauce; Chocolate
Honey Almond Crunch; Deep Dark Chocolate Fudge
Cookies; cayenne-spiked "Hot" Chocolate Cake; White
Chocolate Cheesecake; and the truffly (and presumably
lethal) Chocolate Demise.

Desaulniers, Marcel. *Death by Chocolate Cookies.* **Hardcover: 144 pages with color photographs and technique
drawings, 75 recipes. Simon & Schuster, 1997.**

Despite the title, this book is more likely to sweeten
your life than end it. Among Desaulniers's various "deadly"

works, it stands out as containing the largest number of easier recipes. There is good basic information on working with chocolate and on cookie-making in general before the recipes begin. Practical advice, in the form of "The Chef's Touch," lets even amateurs turn out cookies a pro would be proud of, but not all the recipes are simple. For those who just can't leave well enough alone, there is a final chapter of multi-step, restaurant-style, plated cookie creations that will challenge the most ambitious baker.

CONSIDER: Road Trip Cookies; Cocoa Coffee Toffee Cookies; Buttermilk Pecan Brownies with Brown Butter Icing; Chocolate Peanut Butter Bengal Cookies; Black Magic Cookies with Blackstrap Icing; Chocolate Almond Truffle Bars; Chocolate Lemon Biscotti; and Chocolate Mango Ambush.

Desaulniers, Marcel. *Desserts to Die For*. Hardcover: 144 pages with color photographs and technical drawings, 60 recipes. Simon & Schuster, 1995.

Calling himself the "guru of ganache," Desaulniers, the executive chef and co-owner of the famed Trellis restaurant, celebrates in this book sheer, unabashed, dessert-time hedonism. The recipes range from the simplest of sweet nothings to the kind of baroque fantasies only a professional pastry chef (or an obsessed home baker) would have the patience to construct. Every dessert gets opulently photographed, and many require technical drawings to explain their construction complexities. Either you will want to make these desserts immediately or you will want someone else to immediately make them for you.

CONSIDER: Butterscotch Walnut Pumpkin Cake; Lemon Blueberry Cheesecake; Fallen Angel Cake with Golden Halos and Sinful Cream; Oven-Roasted Peaches with Very Berry Yogurt; Sweet Dreams Ice Cream Sandwiches; Whiskey-Soaked Raisin Bread Pudding with Jack's Honey Raisin Sauce; Connie's Sticky Buns; Chocolate Madonna; and Sambucca Almond Biscotti.

Dodge, Jim. *The American Baker*. Hardcover: 350 pages with color photographs and line drawings, 212 recipes. Simon & Schuster, 1987.

This is an American dessert classic that we believe belongs on every serious baker's shelf. Dodge grew up in a family of New England innkeepers, and he found his métier in baking. After studying and apprenticing with a top Swiss pastry chef and refining his native talents, Dodge was recruited by hotelier James Nassikas as pastry chef for the Stanford Court Hotel in San Francisco. There he developed his distinctive style: a simplicity and clarity of taste that is classical, using ingredients and forms that are unmistakably American. He excels at cobblers and crisps, creating twists on flavors that make them seem fresh. Besides baked desserts, the book also includes puddings, ice creams and sorbets, and poached fruit. Both the full-page color photos, which show presentation, and the line drawings, which illustrate technique, are very helpful.

CONSIDER: Fig and Lemon Tart; Orange-Zested Chocolate Cake; Praline Ice Cream Pie; Blackberry-Lime Cobbler; Gingered Rhubarb Crisp; and Peach Crisp with White Chocolate and Brandy Sauce.

Durst, Carol G. *I Knew You Were Coming, So I Baked a Cake.* **Hardcover: 224 pages, 140 recipes. Simon & Schuster, 1997.**

Despite the title, there are relatively few cakes in this modest, approachable book. The premise of the author (a New York City caterer and cooking teacher) is that a well-organized pantry and a few efficient touches can let even the busiest person produce a warm-from-the-oven dessert in short order. Given the time restraints, the cakes that do appear are very simple indeed. Building-block recipes for alternate fillings and icings broaden the repertoire, but if towering, multilayered constructions are your desire, look elsewhere. There are plenty of noncake desserts, however, that really are fairly quick and simple on their own. Durst then streamlines things even more, and it's easy to imagine, several years down the line, butter-spotted copies of this useful book in kitchens across the land.

CONSIDER: Boston Cream Pie; Mango-Molasses Upside-Down Cake; Apple Kuchen; Blondies in a Pot; Peanut Butter Truffles; Tapioca Pudding; and Tiramisù.

Fobel, Jim. *Jim Fobel's Old-Fashioned Baking Book.* **Paperback: 207 pages with black-and-white archival photographs, 155 recipes. Lake Isle Press, 1996.**

Though this terrific baking book is based upon the recipes of the author's Ohio-based Finnish family, it will surely become an heirloom in your house as well. Whether you had a grandmother like his, who baked seven days a week, or unfortunately grew up in a home where Pop Tarts were considered a warm dessert, these simple, homespun, yet exactingly written recipes will provide you with enough genuine sweet memories for a lifetime. Fobel has meticulously tested and retested this collection of heritage treats and has had to occasionally call up his sense memory to compensate for an ingredient omitted (no doubt by accident) or a measurement made too casually for modern replication. Originally published in hardcover in 1987, this classic's paperback version is worth seeking out.

CONSIDER: Raspberry-Cheese Danish; Boston Cream Pie; Banana Pineapple Cake; Grandma's Gingerbread; Burnt Butter Cupcakes; Mom's Sour Cream Peach Muffins; Sticky Caramel Pecan Rolls; Cardamom Cookies; and Buttered Bread Pudding.

Gonzalez, Elaine. *The Art of Chocolate*. Paperback: 165 pages with color photographs, 60 recipes. Chronicle Books, 1998.

A quick glance at this work might lead you to believe it's only for professional bakers, candy makers, and other obsessive types. And, in fact, much of the book covers exactly the kind of breathtakingly manipulative chocolate artistry that seems designed more to admire than eat. But persevere. Gonzalez is one of the country's best cooking teachers and a knowledgeable chocolate specialist who regularly leads chocolate tours to Mexico. She is also very funny (her single best piece of advice on working with chocolate: "Wear brown.") and she understands that chocolate, however beautifully transformed, must ultimately taste great. To that end, there are among the dazzling showpieces lots of terrific recipes for desserts any of us can make and serve with pride. There are also long sections on tempering chocolate and using specialized chocolate-working tools, and technique sections covering truffle-dipping, forming chocolate roses, leaves, and ribbons, making chocolate dessert cups (use an inflated balloon for a mold, then pop it), and much, much more. One dense chocolate cheesecake is topped with a hole-punched wedge of white chocolate "Swiss cheese" and accompanied by truffles in the shape of tiny mice. In Gonzalez's able hands, chocolate is both a pliable medium for high art and the ultimate comfort food.

CONSIDER: Chocolate Butter-Pecan Toffee; Marbleized Dipped Strawberries; Death by Truffles; Chocolate Woven Heart Basket with Sculpted Chocolate Roses; Chocolate Banana Cream Cake; All-American Chocolate Layer Cake; Chocolate Date-Nut Cake; and Chocolate Fondue Birdbaths with Chocolate Birds.

Greenspan, Dorie. *Baking with Julia.* Hardcover: 481 pages with illustrations and 100 color photographs throughout, over 190 recipes. William Morrow, 1996.

Forget that diet! Just preheat the oven and start baking. If these truly mouthwatering, in-your-face photos of delectable goodies don't grab you, the tantalizing recipes will. From the simple to the complex, these samplings are irresistible. The book covers both sweet and savory baking, with extensive attention given to "artisanal" breads and the currently popular flatbreads, such as pizza and focaccia.

It's not often that a book based on a television series, as this one is, emerges with this sort of quality. But then, everything Julia Child touches is magic, and here she is assisted by a phenomenal team of culinary professionals, including author Dorie Greenspan, a European-trained baker and food writer whose work is filled with attention to detail. While these are a collation of recipes from twenty-seven different chefs, cooking teachers, and cookbook authors, they've been deftly woven together into a dream book for bakers.

CONSIDER: Blueberry-Nectarine Pie; Buttermilk Crumb Muffins; Summer Vegetable Tart (with mushrooms and goat cheese); Chocolate Ruffle Cake; Homemade Bagels; and Miniature Florentine Squares.

Greenspan, Dorie. *Desserts by Pierre Herme*. Hardcover: 287 pages with color photographs, 80 recipes. Little, Brown, 1998.

Pierre Herme is the most famous pastry chef in France, a wunderkind and a superstar. His dessert creations and career moves are tracked in the popular press, and he earns awards apparently at the rate the rest of us earn frequent-flier miles. At Fauchon for many years, he now operates a new outpost of the venerable tea and pastry salon, Laudree, on the Champs-Elysées. He has been called The Picasso of Pastry and The Dior of Desserts. Teamed with the (also award-winning) American author and baking expert Dorie Greenspan, he has now compiled his second dessert book in English. Hardly a household word here (except among fellow patissiers), he has been accorded a large, glossy, and very beautiful book. It is his refinements in taste and texture and his brilliant flavor marriages that make his creations unique, says Greenspan, although her description of the sheer happiness baking one of his recipes gave her hints at what may actually make him a star on this side of the Atlantic. The book is spaciously laid out, with an excellent section of fundamental recipes, and ranges from utterly simple sweets (fresh raspberries buried in a bowl of chocolate cream) to a multitiered, orange-scented wedding cake.

CONSIDER: French Toast with Blueberry Sauce; Strawberry-Rhubarb Soup; Earl Grey Tea-Flavored Crème Brulee; Pineapple Carpaccio (seasoned with salt, pepper, and sugar) topped with Lime Sorbet; Lemon Crepes; Mascarpone and Blueberry Cake; and Crispy and Creamy Rice Treat, combining ladyfingers, Nestle's Crunch Bar, and basmati rice.

Heatter, Maida. *Maida Heatter's Cakes* (338 pages), *Pies and Tarts* (276 pages), and *Cookies* (308 pages). Andrews McMeel, 1997.

Maida Heatter has reigned as the Queen of Desserts since before many of today's cooks were born. Her recipes have always been renowned for being absolutely surefire, and since baking can be tricky, she is the perfect choice for the beginning cook. Because her recipes are so excellent, her books are the perfect choice for advanced bakers.

Someone very smart—actually agent Janis Donnaud and Michael Cador of Cador Books—realized that a number of Heatter's recipes had fallen out of print, and he did all of us a favor by reissuing them in these three volumes. Testimony that nothing is out-of-date is given in forewords by Wolfgang Puck, Jacques Pepin, and Nancy Silverton. Heatter has tremendous knowledge and a great sense of humor, both of which come through loud and clear in the copy that precedes each recipe. Instructions are crystal clear and include tips such as this one for Dione's Chocolate Roll, a classic fallen soufflé filled with whipped cream: "There will be a few cracks on the surface of the cake—it is to be expected." Before a Walnut Tart from Saint-Paul-de-Vence, she writes: "Just a note to give an idea of how special I consider this dessert: When I was invited to dinner at Julia and Paul Child's, this is the dessert I brought." If you love to bake, you must own these books.

CONSIDER: Key West Rum Cake; Triple-Threat Cheesecake; Raisin Cake with Apples; Individual Maple Pecan Tarts; and Palm Beach Brownies, one of Heatter's signature desserts.

Klivans, Elinor. *Bake and Freeze Chocolate Desserts.* Hardcover: 306 pages with color photographs, 120 recipes. Broadway Books, 1997.

Klivans, a frequent contributor to *Bon Appétit,* is the champion of a particular type of dessert-making. Once the one-person pastry department of a busy restaurant, she began tucking everything from fundamental components to completed desserts into her freezer. The frozen assets let her manage her time better, and she learned that a remarkable number of dessert preparations were not harmed—were sometimes even improved—by being frozen. Home cooks may not need to turn out the same quantity of desserts, but can still benefit from the convenience of a well-stocked freezer. Her first book (*Bake and Freeze Desserts*) was nominated for an IACP Award but has headed rather rapidly for the remainder tables; grab one if you get the chance. This attractive sequel takes the same efficient approach, but exclusively celebrates chocolate desserts, and the results are amazing.

CONSIDER: Chocolate Cream Pie; White Chocolate Brownies with Chocolate Cherries; Winter White Yule Log; Mochaccino Cheesecake; Chocolate Chestnut Satin Torte; and Macadamia Praline Ice Cream Loaf.

Luchetti, Emily. *Stars Desserts*. Hardcover: 267 pages with color photographs, 150 recipes. HarperCollins, 1991.

As the food at Jeremiah Tower's Stars restaurant balances classicism and sensuality, so too do the desserts created by his former pastry chef. In this remarkable book, Luchetti balances tradition with innovation, always working to produce desserts that are meticulously planned and precisely executed to look spontaneous and taste ravishing. From simple notions to warm, last-minute desserts to big-deal cakes and tortes, Luchetti covers the bases, always keeping in mind that the treat's the thing. For home cooks who find many professionally derived baking books to be overly complex, this one's for you.

CONSIDER: Hazelnut Crème Caramel; Lemon Blueberry Trifle; Pear Cornmeal Bread Pudding; Raspberry Pistachio Crepes; Plum Soufflé with Orange Custard Sauce; Peach Boysenberry Cobbler; Blackberry Napoleons with Tangerine Sabayon; Frozen Sour Cherry Mousse; Cranberry

Linzertorte; Drunken Chocolate Cake; and Brown Butter Madeleines.

MacLauchlan, Andrew, with Donna K. Flynn. *Tropical Desserts*. Hardcover: 164 pages with color photographs, 150 recipes. Macmillan, 1997.

Given the increasing interest in Asian and Latin foods, the accessibility of ingredients from those regions at the market, and the generally happy, sunny, and laid-back image conjured by the word *tropical*, this attractive book is a natural winner. MacLauchlan, originally pastry chef at Charlie Trotter's before becoming executive pastry chef for Mark Miller's Coyote Cafés, and Flynn, his wife, have lived and worked in the tropics and find the fruits, nuts, and spices from those regions inspiring as dessert ingredients. Despite his restaurant background, many of the recipes are simple; others emphatically aren't. Recipe yields are occasionally a little large for home cooks, but the results are very appealing.

CONSIDER: Papaya-Ginger Soup with Kiwi Granita; Tequila Ice Cream; Chocolate-Kumquat Bombe; Three-Spice Cake with Figs and Oranges; Guava Crème Brûlée; Green Mango–Green Apple Pie; Jasmine Rice Pudding with Honey, Tamarind, and Almonds; Cashew-Banana Baklava; and Macadamia Dark Rum Muffins.

Malgieri, Nick. *How to Bake*. Hardcover: 457 pages with color photographs and black-and-white technical line drawings, over 230 recipes. HarperCollins, 1995.

Author Malgieri, a food writer, cooking teacher, and

professional baker, puts his finger on it when he sets bakers in a class by themselves. "What unifies all of us," he writes, "from the home baker to the professional, is love of baking." Malgieri is a masterful baker, and the same style and deftness he exhibits in his classes are here transformed into a text eminently usable and filled with all manner of "cakes, cookies, pies, tarts, breads, pizzas, muffins, sweet and savory." He is meticulously specific about ingredients and techniques, which takes out any guesswork. Every recipe contains storage information, a valuable extra bit, and serving suggestions as well as "hints for success" wherever appropriate.

CONSIDER: Sourdough Bread and Peach Cobbler with Buttermilk Biscuit Crust; Chocolate Pecan Dacquoise; Swedish Rye; Pissaladière Niçoise; Swiss Chocolate Truffle Cake; and Irish Currant Cake.

Malgieri, Nick. *Chocolate*. Hardcover: 464 pages with color photographs, 380 recipes. HarperCollins, 1998.

Nick Malgieri is to desserts what George Balanchine was to dance. He choreographs each step of a recipe so gracefully and cleanly that there is no way to trip up. In his latest book he turns his attention to chocolate, and we're all lucky he did. A protégé of famed former White House pastry chef and CIA teacher Alfred Kumin, Malgieri apprenticed in Switzerland, produced desserts at Windows on the World, and is currently director of the baking department at Peter Kump's New York Cooking School. Here he offers a dual approach to everyone's favorite flavor. Included are both extraordinary, professional-looking creations such as the Chocolate Flowers Wreath Cake, which looks like a brown Della Robbia pretty enough to hang on your wall, and the simple, homey recipes, such as the best dark Hot Fudge Sauce—the kind that hardens as soon as it hits ice cream. This is a book both for the advanced cook who treats baking as hobby and art as well as for the average home cook, who just happens to love chocolate.

CONSIDER: Chocolate Chunk Pecan Crunch Cake; Vermont Farmhouse Devil's Food Cake; Chocolate Banana Layer Cake; Chocolate Walnut Biscotti; Bittersweet Chocolate Crème Brûlée; Frozen Chocolate Bourbon Soufflé; White Chocolate Coconut Cream Pie with Chocolate Cookie Crust; and Chocolate Marzipan Wedding Cake (which serves fifty).

Malgieri, Nick. *Great Italian Desserts*. Hardcover: 276 pages, 125 recipes. Little, Brown, 1990.

There are only a handful of Italian dessert books, perhaps because Italian cooking experts always seem to be stressing that, with the exception of a few ornate and impossibly sweet holiday confections, fresh fruit is the country's sweet finale of choice. For Malgieri, this has proven not to be the case. His "glorious odyssey" through the desserts of Italy began with his first visit in 1973. Traditional, modern, and regional specialties alike caught—and still catch—Malgieri's fancy. The result is a larger, more colorful, and more interesting array of Italian desserts than ever before assembled.

CONSIDER: Fennel, Raisin, and Pine Nut Bread from Genoa; Fried Ravioli with Sweet Ricotta Filling; Savory

Carnival Pastry with Pecorino, Mozzarella, and Dried Sausage; Lattice Tart of Roman Sour Cherries; Napoleon Cake with Apricots; Zuppa Inglese; Tiramisù; Honey-Almond-Cinnamon Biscotti; and Chocolate-Hazelnut Gelato.

Malgieri, Nick. *Nick Malgieri's Perfect Pastry.* **Paperback: 352 pages with black-and-white how-to photographs and technical drawings, 200 recipes. Macmillan, 1998.**

This is the paperback edition of a book originally published nearly ten years ago. Among the most knowledgeable and popular of baking teachers, Malgieri graduated from the Culinary Institute of America and was formerly the executive pastry chef of Windows on the World in New York. This book is designed around basic techniques and fundamental recipes (berry puree, cream puff dough, praline paste), which, once mastered, can be combined and recombined into a larger number of classic desserts. There are useful (if grainy) photos illustrating crucial stages of various pastries, and there is, as always, Malgieri's sound and sane advice.

CONSIDER: Chocolate Eclairs; Golden Lemon Tart; Ultimate Apple Pie; Strawberry Puff; Pastry Shortcakes with Vanilla Sauce; Hazelnut Mocha Roll; Bûche de Nöel; Quadruple Chocolate Cake; Peach Meringue Cake; and Strawberry Trifle.

Marin, Mindy. *The Secret of Tender Pie: American Grandmothers Share Their Favorite Recipes.* **Hardcover:**

163 pages with black-and-white photographs, 77 recipes. Ballantine, 1997.

It may take some doing to locate this small, nostalgia-packed book (the lovely but misleading title often results in its being stocked in the dessert section), but persevere: It's worth the hunt. Containing plenty of desserts (including pie), it has savory recipes as well, all contributed, along with reminiscences and snapshots, by grandmothers of all sorts. Some are famous (Lady Bird Johnson, Liz Carpenter), some glamorous (one svelte California granny poses on a motorcycle and confides that she likes to serve her famous artichoke soup on Christmas Eve, accompanied by cracked Dungeness crab and melted Brie with almonds), and all have something worth making, even the grandmother who offers her lye soap recipe.

CONSIDER: Apple Cider French Toast; Cheese Blintzes; Ruby Begonia's Chicken and Dumpling Soup; Shrimp Gumbo; Madame Wong's Crispy Duck; Deviled Short Ribs; Pepper Relish; Grape Jelly; Green Tomato Pie; Grandma Pheney's Passover Sponge Cake; Peanut Brittle; and Abuelita's Flan.

Medrich, Alice. *Cocolat: Extraordinary Chocolate Desserts*. Hardcover: 205 pages, glossy paper with technical line drawings and full-page color photographs throughout. Warner, 1990.

Cocolat is to chocolate desserts what Givenchy is to fashion. High style, uncluttered design, elegant lines, and rich taste distinguish these spectacular presentations. Self-taught and LeNotre-trained, Medrich was shaped by a year in France. It was there that she learned what "grown-up" desserts should taste like: simple, less sweet, intense in flavor. While this volume looks like a coffee-table book, it is written to be used. Techniques are clearly explained in words as well as illustrations. Some of the methods, especially for forming decorations and special icing effects, are not for the beginning cook—chocolate can be tricky to work with—but devoted bakers and dessert lovers will embrace the challenge with pleasure. The food styling here is gorgeous, as are the photographs; each picture presents a dessert so sumptuous, it looks as if it could be served right off the page.

Medrich, Alice. *Chocolate and the Art of Low-Fat Desserts*. Hardcover: 192 pages with color photographs, 120 recipes. Warner, 1994.

Who better than Medrich, founder of the legendary Berkeley sweet shop called Cocolat and a noted author and teacher, to produce a book of fabulous-looking, wonderful-tasting, low- (or at least lower) fat desserts? First, a warning: not all are chocolate. Second, while some are remarkably lean, Medrich's goals were recipes weighing in at 300 calories or less per serving, with less than 30 percent of those calories coming from fat. Each recipe comes with basic nutritional information, which makes clear that this is not a weight-loss book, but rather one of well-designed treats that can be easily fit into an otherwise sensible diet. Watch out for sub-recipes, which can lengthen kitchen time considerably, and don't miss the low-fat theory and practice section that concludes the book—it's invaluable.

CONSIDER: Kahlúa Fudge Ring; Spicy New Orleans Gingerbread; Fallen Chocolate Soufflé Torte; White Chocolate Charlotte with Strawberries; Coconut Rice Pudding; Lemon Mousse Cake; Black Bottom Banana Napoleons; Apple Rose Tartlets; and Chocolate Chip Biscotti.

The Moosewood Collective. *The Moosewood Restaurant Book of Desserts*. Hardcover and paperback: 398 pages, 250 recipes. Clarkson Potter, 1997.

A book of desserts from a vegetarian restaurant may seem a dopey concept, unless, of course, it's the legendary Moosewood Restaurant. Known for hearty, imaginative, internationally influenced, mostly meatless comfort fare, prepared in rotating assignment by the nearly twenty members of the collective who own and operate it, Moosewood's desserts are every bit as terrific as the rest of its food. Noting that desserts are not "necessary, but we celebrate the impulse to make a meal, a daily ritual, finer by topping it with something sweet," the collective serves up a wide array, often prepared with fresh fruit or with the minimum of fat. Refined sugar is used and the word *carob* never appears.

CONSIDER: Triple Ginger Apple Crisp; Lime Tart; Plum Strudel; Chocolate Cherry Angel Food Cake; Tropical Tofu "Cheesecake"; Peanut Butter Ice Cream Pie; and such longtime Moosewood favorites as Amaretto Peach Parfait and Tiramisù di Ithaca.

Neal, Bill. *Biscuits, Spoonbread, and Sweet Potato Pie.* **Paperback: 334 pages with archival black-and-white photographs, 300 recipes. Alfred A. Knopf, 1990.**

The late Bill Neal was a rising southern culinary star who might have given us many worthwhile books. Instead, we must content ourselves with this lovely volume of recipes and historical insights. No part of the country bakes with more regularity, variety, and plain old skill than the South. It is that sweet diversity, a mixed bag of influences ranging from Scotland to Spain to Africa, with other global stops along the way, that Neal captures so well in a book literally packed with sweet—and fairly simple—things to make. The historical insights are always interesting and frequently charming, if that's your bent. On the other hand, if you just want to get baking, open it at any page and begin—you can hardly go wrong.

CONSIDER: Blueberry Corn Cake; Sweet Potato Crackers; Green Bean Dumplings; brioche-like Sally Lunn; Carolina Rice and Wheat Bread; Peach Cobbler with Clabber Biscuits; Brown Sugar Shortbread; Strawberry Ice Cream; Lemon Chess Pie; Pomegranate Ice; and Saturday Night Chocolate Cake.

Ortiz, Gayle, and Joe Ortiz. *The Village Baker's Wife.* **Hardcover: 327 pages with color photographs and technical drawings, 150 recipes. Ten Speed Press, 1997.**

This book celebrates the pastries of Gayle's, a legendary Capitola, California, bakery. (The breads from Gayle's were the basis for the book *The Village Baker*, page 349.) Together Gayle and husband Joe run the store, which has grown over the years from a tiny bakery to a large operation. Though Gayle's now uses two and a half tons of butter a month, the handmade, no chemicals, no freezer, small bakery approach is still followed. Packed with recipes, technical information, charts, and drawings, this book gives readers the sense of what it's like to lovingly operate a quality bakery that daily sweetens the lives of thousands of people. It's literally inspiring, even if you never head to the kitchen to whip up a batch of one of Gayle's specialties.

CONSIDER: Blueberry and Pastry Cream Snails; Chocolate-Apricot Torte; Cherry Pie; Prune-Armagnac Gingerbread; Fresh Berry Génoise Cakes; Daiquiri Cheesecake; and Irish Soda Bread.

Pappas, Lou Seibert. *Biscotti*. Hardcover: 61 pages, 26 recipes. Chronicle Books, 1991.

"Bravo, biscotti," says Pappas, before setting off to celebrate these wildly popular little Italian cookies in depth. Twice-baked and crunchy, biscotti can be enjoyed from breakfast to midnight, an all-day cookie plan that the author fully endorses. A brief examination of the double-baked cookie around the world is followed by biscotti-baking tips and serving suggestions. Organized into four chapters, the book includes traditional recipes, nut-and-chocolate recipes, regional variations, and healthful recipes. Aside from a few chocolate-dipped biscotti, these cookies are low-tech indeed. Whether you're munching your biscotti with morning coffee, crunching it alongside an afternoon espresso, or dipping it, Italian style, into the sweet wine known as Vin Santo, this book has a recipe for you.

CONSIDER: Pignoli Biscotti; Chocolate Ribboned Biscotti; White Chocolate Macadamia Biscotti; and Triple Ginger Lover's Biscotti.

Purdy, Susan G. *Let Them Eat Cake*. Hardcover: 389 pages with color and black-and-white photographs and technical drawings, 140 recipes. William Morrow, 1997.

Noted for masterful works on cakes and pies, Purdy found herself needing to explore low-fat baking in order to accommodate a family member with some health concerns. Two years of research led to this low-fat masterwork, a book that will let many people enjoy reduced-fat, lower-cholesterol baked goods guilt-free. Her process was painstaking, shaving fat grams while insisting that the desserts taste great on their own. So successful was the search that Purdy says her family now finds most conventional baked goods too rich and heavy for any except the most self-indulgent moments. All this happily healthful baking advice is now packed between the covers of a large and handsome book, one that belongs in the collection of any baker who wants to eat well and live longer.

CONSIDER: Peanut Butter Cookies; Fudge Brownies; Vermont Blueberry Pie; Sour Cream Coffee Cake with Chocolate-Almond Streusel; Pumpkin Cream Bombe; New Year's Honey Cake; and Swedish Cardamom Braids.

Purdy, Susan G. *As Easy As Pie*. Paperback: 426 pages with technical drawings, 350 recipes. Collier Books, 1984.

Pie-making is a timeless activity, which means that

while this book is not new, it remains vital. If you like pies, you need this book. Purdy, who has lately been writing thoroughly about cakes, here leaves no pie possibility unexplored—there are over thirty crust recipes, for example. Techniques are discussed before recipes; advance preparation advice and specialized equipment needs are spelled out, and technical drawings illustrate trickier assembly points. Variations following most recipes further broaden the scope of a book that already includes such pie relatives as turnovers, cobblers, crisps, dumplings, quiches, and timbales.

CONSIDER: Currant Cream Pie; French Apple Tart; Two-Berry Orange Cream Tart; Vermont Maple Sugar Pumpkin Pie; Baked Alaska Pie; Hungarian Plum Kuchen; Cherry Strudel; Apple-Plum Pandowdy; Quiche Lorraine; Tomato-Pesto Tart; Cornish Pasties; and English Veal and Ham Pie.

Sands, Brinna. *The King Arthur Flour 200th Anniversary Cookbook.* Paperback: 616 pages with black-and-white illustrations, over 500 recipes. Countryman Press, 1992.

While product cookbooks are often merely pedestrian vehicles designed to peddle their namesake, this generous baking cookbook is an exception. If you skip the first 28 pages, which document the history of the company and the legend of King Arthur, you come to a warm, recipe-packed book chockful of American home baking recipes gleaned from the company's huge files, friends, employees, and relatives. The author is married to the head of the company, but she is also an expert baker in her own right, a member of the International Association of Culinary Professionals, the American Institute of Food and Wine, and the Culinary Historians of Boston. The baking information is authoritative and very clearly put forth, with many helpful tips. The sourdough section is especially thorough, and if you don't want to make your own starter, King Arthur sells an excellent one through mail order.

CONSIDER: Scottish Scones; Banana Pecan Muffins; No-Knead Dinner Rolls; Onion Rye Bread; Gorgonzola and Scallion Pizza; Italian Panettone; Strawberry Shortcake Jelly Roll; Peanut Butter–Chocolate Chip Cookies; Cornmeal Cheddar Crackers; and Lemon Curd Tart.

Sax, Richard. *Classic Home Desserts*. Hardcover: 688 pages with color photographs, 350 recipes. Chapters Publishing, 1994.

What makes this exceptionally attractive, hefty volume really stand out is the mix of desserts. While the subtitle, "A treasury of heirloom and contemporary recipes from around the world," suggests the book is comprehensive, the overall effect is one of tradition and homey goodness. Besides baked sweets, there is a large proportion of fruit desserts, custards, and puddings. The text is both highly informative and deeply entertaining. Along with a tremendous amount of helpful technical information, presented in a most accessible fashion, the side margins contain a number of amusing heirloom writings on food, including an apocryphal recipe for "Favorite Fruitcake," which includes glue and hairspray. For real eating, the late writer's recipes are as usual top-notch, appealing, and dependable. Despite a sprinkling of fine new recipes, including Thomas Keller's Molten Hot Chocolate, this is probably the best single volume of traditional desserts you can own.

CONSIDER: Cranberry Crumble with Fall Fruits; Mexican Chocolate Flan with Kahlua; Buttermilk Corn Bread Pudding; Coconut Jumbles; Boston Cream Pie; Austrian Walnut Torte with Coffee Whipped Cream; Orleans Sweet Potato-Pecan Pie; and Hazelnut Semifreddo.

Sax, Richard. *The Cookie Lover's Cookie Book.* **Paperback: 144 pages, 60 recipes. Harper & Row, 1986.**

Many larger cookie books have come down the road since this little volume was published, but none are better written or more useful. The secret to a great cookie is simple, says Sax: You have to bake them at home. The quality, care, and lingering warmth of the oven are all there—indelible signs that the perfect sweet treat is at hand. Sax's user-friendly advice on baking techniques and ingredients nicely supports the recipes. And since cookies are simple things, it's good to know it doesn't take an encyclopedia-sized work to cover the bases. From basic cookie-jar cookies to cookies for those with aristocratic tastes, this small ode runs the gamut.

CONSIDER: Butterscotch Crunch Cookies; Old-Time Coconut Jumbles; Happy Face Sugar Cookies; Chocolate-Dipped Peanut Brittle Fingers; Baby Fruitcakes; Chunky White Chocolate–Macadamia Cookies; Whole-Grain Lemon Cream Sandwiches; Espresso Bars; and Portuguese Almond Macaroons.

Scholss, Andrew, with Ken Bookman. *One-Pot Cakes*. Hardcover: 105 pages, 60 recipes. William Morrow, 1995.

The authors' goal for this book was simple: Create recipes for cakes made from scratch using only a pot, a spoon, and a pan. No sifting was allowed, and if it took more than ten minutes to put together, it probably wasn't worth it. Certain examples of the high baker's art are necessarily eliminated by these conditions, but as the authors point out, the book still contains more recipes than you'll probably need in your average cake-baking lifetime, so it's unlikely that you'll feel deprived. Of necessity, these are home-style cakes, exactly the sort you'll want to put together on the spur of the moment. Presumably that gnashing sound is the teeth of frustrated cake-mix manufacturers who find their dubious products now rendered obsolete.

CONSIDER: Chocolate Raspberry Cake; Chocolate Bourbon Pecan Loaf; Lemon Poppyseed Cake; Traditional Sour Cream Coffee Cake; Orange Buttermilk Cupcakes; Cognac Pumpkin Cheesecake; Black Coffee Torte; Cherry Yogurt Cake; and Dark, Dark Fruit Cake.

Scicolone, Michele. *La Dolce Vita*. Hardcover: 272 pages with color photographs, 170 recipes. William Morrow, 1993.

Those who loved Scicolone's book on antipasti but regretted its lack of a dessert chapter can rejoice at this collection. Though the party line has it that Italians chiefly prefer fruit for dessert, the author brings enough sweet evidence to the table to suggest otherwise. Most of these treats may be between-meal snacks or grand holiday finales, but they are desserts nonetheless, and those who bake from this book will be living la dolce vita indeed. The recipes run a nice gamut, and include both warhorse sweets (familiar from any trip to Little Italy) and startlingly fresh—but still authentic—recipes that are real discoveries.

CONSIDER: Chocolate-Glazed Chocolate Biscotti; Glazed Lemon Cookies; Pine Nut Macaroons; Upside-Down Peach Poppy Seed Cake; Skillet Cheesecake; Zabaglione with Balsamic Vinegar and Raspberries; Panna Cotta with Chocolate and Raspberry Sauces; Tiramisù; and Almond Semifreddo with Hot Chocolate Sauce.

Shere, Lindsey Remolif. *Chez Panisse Desserts*. Hardcover: 341 pages, 320 recipes. Random House, 1985.

Shere, who was for many years the pastry chef at Alice Waters's groundbreaking California restaurant Chez Panisse, has a food style to match Alice's: subtle, seasonal, and derived from premium ingredients. Many of these desserts were developed to complement specific menus at the restaurant and can, at least on paper, seem almost austere. The recipe format (similar to other Chez Panisse books) is not user friendly, and hard-to-locate ingredients such as Meyer lemons, fresh boysenberries, and black walnuts are called for, frequently without substitutions. This is a rigorous book, not for the beginner or the faint of heart, but a must for the dedicated baker and anyone who wants a sweet taste of a seminal American restaurant.

CONSIDER: Gravenstein Apple Tart with Cinnamon Ice Cream; Baked Caramel Pears with Pecans; Meyer Lemon Soufflé; Passion Fruit Mousse; Rose Geranium

Pound Cake; Sour Cherry Pie; Steamed Fig Pudding; White Chocolate Truffles; and Linda's Olive Oil and Sauternes Cake.

Silverton, Nancy, with Heidi Yorkshire. *Desserts*. Hardcover: 365 pages with technical drawings, 200 recipes. Harper & Row, 1986.

Before Silverton and husband Mark Peel opened Campanile and its companion LaBrea Bakery, she was pastry chef for Wolfgang Puck's Spago and Chinois on Main. Silverton's trademark (endorsed by Puck in his foreword to the book) is making desserts better, not more complicated. Often this comes down to a matter of intensity; flavor, closely followed by texture, is her guiding light. At Puck's restaurants, the dessert selection was always large and guests preferred a tasting plate in order to sample as many of Silverton's treats as possible. This book is the ultimate tasting plate, not to mention one of the best restaurant dessert books written. Passionate bakers will want to own it and work from it often.

CONSIDER: Orange-Espresso Checkerboard Cookies; Cassis Truffles; Cherry Tart with Buttermilk Custard; Huckleberry Pie; Fig Napoleon; Peppermint Tea Ice Cream; Chocolate-Raspberry Mousse Cake; Banana Pecan Layer Cake; and Spago's signature trio of crèmes brûlées—Ginger, Orange, and Mint—served in tiny sake cups.

Teubner, Christian. *The Chocolate Bible*. Hardcover: 240 pages with color photographs and archival illustrations, 150 recipes. Penguin Studio, 1997.

If you are susceptible to chocolate and prefer your cookbooks profusely illustrated, be prepared to be ravished by this volume, perhaps the most seductive work on the subject ever assembled. The product of a European team headed by Teubner, a chef-turned-baker-turned-photographer, this book takes you deep into the heart of darkest chocolate country. Much information on chocolate in history and on how chocolate is produced is followed by step-by-step advice on tempering, making chocolate ornaments, and working with chocolate molds. Unlike a lot of chocolate books, this one covers candy-making as deeply as it does cakes, pies, cookies, mousses, petits fours, and all the other chocolate possibilities.

CONSIDER: Flaky Meringue Torte; Chocolate Layer Cake; Sachertorte; Sweet Chestnut Squares; Marble Cake with Ganache Icing; Chocolate Macaroons; Dates with Pistachio Almond Paste Centers; Amaretto Truffle Squares; Chocolate Cherry Charlotte; Cranberry Cream with Chocolate and Rum Sauce; and even Wild Hare in Chocolate Sauce and Mexican Mole Poblano.

Torres, Jacques, with Christina Wright and Kris Kruid. *Dessert Circus*. Hardcover: 336 pages with color and black-and-white photographs, 100 recipes. William Morrow, 1998.

Torres is the executive pastry chef of the famed New York City restaurant, Le Cirque 2000, as well as the host of a lively public television program upon which this book is based. Intended to be more than a collection of recipes, the book is designed to teach. Given Le Cirque's price range and circus motif, it's no wonder that many of these desserts are complex and playful, resembling ladybugs, pianos, snowmen, or clowns and incorporating multiple sub-recipes. There are many techniques and recipes for ambitious chocolate, spun sugar, and cookie constructions. Given their clarity, following them to success should be no problem for the reasonably experienced baker. The color photographs are dazzling, but the black-and-white technique photos, taken from the television program, are often too muddy to be of use.

CONSIDER: Elegantly free-form Napoleons; doughnut-like Bombolini, filled with jam; Old-Fashioned Macaroons; Peanut Butter Cups; Individual Raspberry Soufflés; and Chocolate-Dipped Biscotti.

Trotter, Charlie, with Michelle Gayer. *Charlie Trotter's Desserts*. Hardcover: 239 pages with color and black-and-white photographs, 150 recipes. Ten Speed Press, 1998.

Based upon the desserts of Trotter's eponymous Chicago restaurant (Gayer works there), this large and beautiful book is at the cutting edge of pastry-making. Complex, textural presentations, rare ingredients, and unusual—even startling—flavor combinations are the norm. These are precisely the kinds of desserts best suited to follow one of Trotter's meticulously planned and executed meals, although accomplished and ambitious bakers will also enjoy preparing them at home. (And professionals seeking inspiration will be exhilarated.) Organized into chapters mostly by ingredient (there is one on Vegetables and Grains, which should give you some idea of how adventurous things get), these recipes may be sensual and satisfying but will also require a certain amount of intellectual appreciation. Among the daring flavors and ingredients are lemongrass, tarragon, tequila, jalapeños, basil, primrose, pink peppercorn, black pepper, green tea, goat cheese, oatmeal, corn, kaffir lime, chickpeas, and black truffles. The chocolate desserts look especially devastating, and one chapter consists of sweets designed to pair well with Chateau d'Yquem.

CONSIDER: Tea Sorbets with Persimmon Chips and Fortune Cookie Tuiles; Blood Orange Soufflé with Chocolate Sorbet; Warm Fig Turnovers with Strawberries and Strawberry-Chartreuse Ice Cream; Poached Pears Wrapped in Brioche with Armagnac-Prune Ice Cream and Prune Sauce; Pecan Pie with Blackstrap Molasses and Sweet Curry Crust; and Chocolate-Bing Cherry Cake with Bing Cherry Sauce.

Walter, Carole. *Great Cakes*. Hardcover: 558 pages, 8 pages of color photography. Clarkson Potter, 1997.

This edition is a reissue of the original Ballantine Books edition, which was published in 1991 and won the James Beard Award for best dessert book. It is a lovely volume, similar to Rose Beranbaum's *The Cake Bible*, but in our opinion much more usable. Walter presents clear, straightforward directions for how to bake a cake, along with all the tips and personal encouragement of a first-class baker and cooking teacher that you need for success. Every recipe features both "At a Glance" detailed information about serving size, pan size, preparation, oven temperature, rack level, baking time, and method—that is, electric mixer, food processor, or, occasionally, by hand. Before you even begin, over 80 pages chockful of information teach you all you need to know about ingredients and technique. Detailed instructions on decorating special-occasion cakes promise professional-looking as well as delectable results.

CONSIDER: Oat Bran Apple Cake; Chocolate Pear Upside-Down Cake; Flourless Chocolate Roulade with Whipped Apricot Soufflé; Black Forest Cherry Cake; and Filbert Gâteau with Praline Buttercream.

Walter, Carole. *Great Pies and Tarts*. Hardcover: 488 pages with color photographs and black-and-white line drawings, over 160 recipes. Clarkson Potter, 1998.

What's immediately striking about this book is how homemade the desserts in the pictures look. Glorious and good enough to eat, but real: crusts crumble when they're cut, crimps are attractive but not perfect, an edge of one puff pastry crust is a little too dark. A companion to Walter's award-winning *Great Cakes*, this is a book designed to be used. Walter is a highly trained baker, but she is first and foremost a teacher, which comes through in the fact-filled primer that gets you started and the easy-to-follow recipes. Little extras, such as storage information with each dessert and "At a Glance" information, which includes degree of difficulty, distinguish the work. If you have any fear of pastry crusts, this book will dispel them.

CONSIDER: Banana Cream Pie with Pecan Brittle; Black Forest Cherry Tart; Pear Tarte Tatin; frozen Fudge

Walnut Sundae Pie; and Lemon Tea Tarts Smothered with Berries.

Willard, Pat. *Pie Every Day: Recipes and Slices of Life*. Hardcover and paperback: 267 pages, 150 recipes. Algonquin Books and Berkeley, respectively, 1997 and 1998.

This congenial little book quickly appeared in paperback, perhaps ensuring it the larger audience it deserves. Willard's goal is to get the homemade pie back into American life. Arguing that the flaky desserts are not scary and need not be picture perfect, Willard makes the claim that "pies, like life, are meant to be enjoyed—and not unduly labored over." Though there are plenty of recipes—thirty for crusts alone—and sound baking information, it is Willard's philosophy and her evocative writing that make the book really special. Bake a pie, pour a cup of coffee, then settle back to work your way through this gem as you would any piece of good literature. There are breakfast pies, company pies, pies for children, and "sitting around gabbing" pies.

CONSIDER: Cheese, Leek, and Ham Pie; Crabmeat Tartlets; Phyllo with Smoked Eggplant Filling; Italian Sausage and Spinach Pie; Double Crust Chicken Pie; Cherry Pie; A Common Apple Pie; Shaker Lemon Pie; Hershey Bar Pie; Miss Glover's Coconut Custard Pie; and Peach Melba Ice Cream Pie.

Yockelson, Lisa. *Country Pies*. Hardcover: 143 pages with technical drawings, 60 recipes. Harper & Row, 1988.

Pies must be easier to make than cakes, since cake books outnumber pie books by a considerable margin—a mixed blessing for pie lovers, it seems, who are expected to succeed with minimal guidance. Fortunately there is this little book, which is well-written and thorough enough to give reassurance to pie beginners, but creative enough to inspire experienced pie bakers to new heights. Among Yockelson's several country baking books, this may be the most drool-inspiring. The technical pie information is sound as well (lots of decorative crusts are illustrated) but it is the simple charm of country pies and the terrific-sounding recipes that make this book so appealing.

CONSIDER: Peach Streusel Pie; Spiced Red Plum Pie; Late Season Green Tomato Pie; Apple-Pear Pie with Apple Cider Syrup; Pumpkin Crunch Pie; Apricot-Yam Pie; Maple Cream Pie; Spicy Sweet Potato Pie; Buttermilk Pie; Glazed Strawberry Pie; Lemon Slice Pie; and Orange-Rhubarb Pie.

Yockelson, Lisa. *Layer Cakes and Sheet Cakes.* **Hardcover: 116 pages, 40 recipes. HarperCollins, 1996.**

This is the latest in a series of small baking books by Yockelson. With a knack for homey desserts of all sorts, she is the perfect author for this collection, featuring the kinds of simple cakes that most often conclude big family meals or show up at bake sales and community suppers. This is casual home baking (as opposed to the overly ambitious pastry chef sort), and the book will be welcome on many a kitchen shelf. Yockelson thoroughly covers the necessary ingredients, technique, and equipment information before setting out her favorite light, tender cakes and creamy frostings (and these do seem to mostly be the kinds of cakes that are *frosted*).

CONSIDER: Old-Fashioned Light Chocolate Cake with Wellesley Fudge Frosting; Banana Cake with Brown Sugar Butter Frosting; Spiced Carrot Sheet Cake with Cream Cheese Frosting; Apple Cake with Walnuts and Raisins; Blueberry Spice Cake with Cinnamon-Butter Crumb Topping; and Lemon Cake with Fluffy White Frosting.

Yosses, Bill, and Bryan Miller. *Desserts for Dummies*. Paperback: 372 pages with cartoons, technical drawings, charts, and color photographs, 130 recipes. IDG Books, 1997.

Given the modest number of desserts in Miller's *Cooking for Dummies*, this book seemed inevitable. As the culinary wing of this popular series of how-to books has taken off, some increased production dollars have been freed up, adorning this volume (as well as *Gourmet Cooking for Dummies*) with welcome, if merely serviceable, color photographs. As usual, there is a breezy, chatty, "this is how things *really* work in the kitchen" attitude that will inspire the novice with confidence. Topics covered include professional pastry chef–type know-how such as "cosmetic surgery," storing extra ingredients, and using up leftovers, as well as more fundamental information on basic equipment and techniques.

CONSIDER: Sour Cherry Pie; Lemon Crepes with Warm Raspberries; Tapioca Pudding; Christmas Cookies; Baked Alaska with Orange Grand Marnier Flambé Sauce; Napoleon with Strawberries; and a tiered wedding cake with apricot-blueberry filling and buttercream icing.

Good Reads, References, and Cookbook Series

Bear, Marina, and John Bear, with Tanya Zeryck. *How to Repair Food.* **Paperback: 140 pages, 50 recipes. Ten Speed Press, 1998.**

Funny, friendly, and packed with advice, this popular little book of kitchen assistance was recently revised. Designed to help fix food that is "overcooked, undercooked, stale, burned, lumpy, salty, bland, too spicy, frozen, mushy, too dry, too wet, flat, tough, too thick, too thin, wilted, fatty, collapsed, curdled, or stuck together," it can get many a cook out of a tight kitchen spot, and do so with a welcome smile. Zucchini overcooked? "There's no going back," say the Bears, "you can only go further," explaining how to turn your former side dish into a cream soup. Organized alphabetically and studded with an eclectic collection of recipes that loosely apply to the various problems at hand, the book concludes with an emergency no-fail substitute pantry dinner menu that takes about twenty-five minutes "from the time your regular dinner is ruined until you sit down at the table."

CONSIDER: Asparagus Risotto; Banana Eggnog à la Mariah; Bears' Bread Pudding; Café Brûlot; Fresh Corn Soup; Farewell Zucchini Bread; and Gail's Southern Fried Tomatoes.

Colwin, Laurie. *Home Cooking.* **Paperback: 193 pages, 40 recipes. HarperCollins, 1993.**

The late Laurie Colwin, a novelist and short-story writer, produced, as a sub-specialty, food writing of a very unique and wonderful sort. For Colwin the subject may have been food, but the real message was human frailty in all its funny and sometimes horrible forms. Though she understood good food, the best of her writing is about bad food—brutally bad food, actually, about which she is brutally funny. The very fine writing will make you laugh and may make you cry (and you will surely mourn the author's untimely death). Because she was an opinionated person, the recipes (which are not really why you want to own this book anyway) are an eclectic lot, and are frequently peppered throughout the text without title or structure.

CONSIDER: Chicken with Chicken Glaze; Estelle Colwin Snellenberg's Potato Pancakes; Yam Cakes with Hot Pepper and Fermented Black Beans; Shepherd's Pie (a recipe serving 150 people); Pepper Chicken with Polenta and Broccoli di Rape; Cornbread and Prosciutto Stuffing; Old-Fashioned Steamed Chocolate Pudding; Gingerbread with Chocolate Icing; and Orange Ambrosia.

David, Elizabeth. *Elizabeth David Classics*. Hard-cover: 665 pages, decorative drawings. Biscuit Books, 1998.

It would not be an exaggeration to say Elizabeth David is to cookbooks what Shakespeare is to plays. She had an amazing breadth of range, an unerring palate, and depth of comprehension. She was erudite and often made surprising connections and allusions. Whatever there is to be said about French and Mediterranean cookery, she found it first and said it better. Many a contemporary food writer has thought he "discovered" a new dish in his travels, only to find it described somewhere in David's pages. How lucky we are to have this reprint of the new American edition of Elizabeth David, which was published in 1970. David Strymish of the mail-order catalog Jessica's Biscuit—a man who knows cookbooks—has dedicated himself to resurrecting classic titles he believes deserve to remain in print. Here we have three of David's great surveys of French and Mediterranean cooking: *Mediterranean Food, French Country Cooking,* and *Summer Cooking.* (Missing are *Italian Cooking* and *French Provincial Cooking.*)

While she wrote prolifically in the 1950s, urging her fellow British back to a gracious table after the strict rations of World War II, her unerring sense of taste is startlingly modern. David is never short of opinions, nor does she lack a sense of humor.

David, a former dancer with the Ballet Russe de Monte Carlo, traveled extensively, and must have read voraciously, because in addition to her own recipes and classics, she cites from Eliza Acton, Mrs. Beeton, and numerous nineteenth-century travel, journal, and literary writers. Her essays on such topics as composing menus and seasonal dining and extended headnotes where warranted on dishes such as cassoulet and bouillabaise are as delightful as they are informative. While the style of recipe writing (no ingredient lists, understanding of certain basic techniques assumed) may be a bit more than the beginner can always manage, Elizabeth David is sure to inspire and inform and should not be missed. She sets the standards for us all.

DeGroot, Roy Andries. *The Auberge of the Flowering Hearth.* Hardcover: 444 pages, 100 recipes. Bobbs-Merrill, 1973.

Ask a food professional, particularly one who takes writing about food as seriously as actually cooking it, what inspired his or her career choice, and you are likely to hear the title of this legendary work. Food writer DeGroot, one of the grand old men of the genre, stumbled across the *auberge*—or country inn—of the title in a remote French Alpine valley, while he was researching an article on the powerful herbal liqueur, Chartreuse. Charmed by the two women who ran the inn—and by the extraordinary food they prepared—DeGroot turned their story into this remarkable book about living the cooking life. Always in the context of the region and the seasons, augmented by the remarkable wines and cheeses of the valley, the French country food is presented in brilliantly designed menus whose savory power is haunting. (Always on one's mind is the hermetic monastery of silent men up the mountain who still produce Chartreuse according to a secret centuries-old formula.) Reading this remarkable work will be enough for some; others will want to taste for themselves such menus as Soufflé of Alpine Cheeses, followed by Ragout of Wild Hare in Red Wine, a Salad of Belgian Endive with Crisped Bacon Dressing, and Homemade Walnut Ice Cream for dessert.

Elfers, Joost. *Play with Your Food.* **Hardcover: 112 pages with full-color photographs throughout. Stewart, Tabori, and Chang, 1997.**

You could easily make the argument that this colorful volume is more of an art or craft book than a cookbook. After all, a Lemon Pig, Cucumber Lizard, Green Pepper Goblin, and Pear Mouse require no cooking. These simple cut and/or assemble projects, however, afford a fresh look at the raw materials we work with in the kitchen every day. They are guaranteed to encourage creativity and delight in young cooks of a wide variety of ages—I'd say three and up . . . all the way up.

Since the success, or quirkiness, of many of these food creatures depends upon choosing the "right" sweet potato, pea pod, pepper, or pineapple to begin with, besides being enormous fun in the kitchen, this book offers a great way to get kids interested in what to look for when shopping for fresh produce. What Elfers can do with a single brussels sprout is not to be believed. And his revolutionary take on the Halloween jack-o'-lantern—using the stem for the nose—alone is worth the price of admission.

Fussell, Betty. *The Story of Corn*. Hardcover: 356 pages with black-and-white photographs and archival illustrations. Alfred A. Knopf, 1992.

Corn is sexy, says Fussell, it has hidden powers, and in her writing of this large book of very readable scholarship, she went a little "corn mad." Corn is so deeply woven into human culture, and particularly the culture of the Americas, that its power is undeniable. A native of the Western Hemisphere, corn has developed in conjunction with man, who has crossbred it from what was essentially a wild grass into a plant that can no longer propagate itself without his help. Packed with delicious historical quirks and link-ups, peopled with fascinating characters, and written with poetic skill, this book is lively, accessible, personal scholarship at its best. Don't read this handsomely designed but dauntingly sized book as if it were homework and there was a quiz tomorrow. Rather dip into it happily and often, as you would into a big bowl of just-popped corn, looking for the tastiest kernels.

Goldstein, Joyce. *Kitchen Conversations*. Hardcover: 378 pages, 160 recipes. William Morrow, 1996.

Former restaurateur, food writer, and noted cooking teacher Goldstein tackles a formidable subject in this book. Attempting to teach principles of taste, this book's robust, imaginative, mostly Mediterranean-derived recipes come with her analysis of why each dish works, as well as a discussion of the flavor ramifications of changes made in the recipe due to market forces or creative choice. These "conversations" are more recipe-specific than general, meaning an overall philosophy of taste needs to be assembled from the many examples. Some readers will make this effort, while others will merely be content to cook and enjoy the vivid, earthy, and often very simple recipes.

CONSIDER: Beet and Arugula Salad with Warm Pancetta Vinaigrette; Persian-Inspired Chicken Salad Sandwich; White Bean Soup with Shellfish and Pesto; Greek Lamb Ragout with Greens, Egg, and Lemon; Milanese Rum and Mascarpone Mousse with Bitter Chocolate Sauce; Turkish Bread Pudding with Cherries; and Custard-Filled Phyllo Pie.

Herbst, Sharon Tyler. *Food Lover's Companion.* **Paperback: 582 pages. Barron's, 1990.**

A must-have reference for the inquisitive amateur as well as any professional chef or food writer, this extremely helpful little book features "comprehensive definitions of over 3,000 food, wine and culinary terms." Want to know the preferred spelling for that popular Middle Eastern chickpea spread? *Hummus.* Unless, that is, you add tahini (sesame seed paste), in which case it becomes *hummus bi tahini.* Want to know how to pronounce it? "Hoom-uhs." Confused about the different types of olive oil you see on your supermarket shelf—light, pure, extra virgin? Read about it here. Which flowers are edible? Why is an egg cream called an egg cream even though it contains no egg? How do you convert Celsius temperatures to Fahrenheit? Every listing is alphabetical, so it's easy to find anything you're looking for. The wine listings are not as authoritative or comprehensive as the food and culinary terms. (For more of that information, see *The Wine Lover's Companion*, written by Herbst and her husband, Ron.) And no one can be right 100 percent of the time (we're dubious about the crisp bacon in the definition of Red Flannel Hash), but Herbst comes awfully close.

Jacobs, Jay. *The Eaten Word*. Hardcover: 254 pages. Birch Lane Press, 1995.

While there are no recipes in this book, it's hard to imagine any good cook who wouldn't enjoy owning it, if nothing else for the sheer pleasure of the read. Jacobs, former restaurant critic for *Gourmet* magazine and a superlative writer, possesses an encyclopedic mind and a keen wit. You can tell he loves his subject matter. Here he explores the use of food words in our history, our language, and our mores as well as in our kitchens. Through those connections, we learn a lot about the foods we cook and eat. It's a book you can read straight through or glance at for an amusing tidbit. Almost anywhere you look it is packed with fascinating information delivered in wry but affectionate style. The first half contains several long essays, the second a glossary of food terms. One example of Jacobs's irreverence: "Ladyfinger. So called for its putative resemblance to the digit it commemorates. The lady in question may have been an ancestor of Minnie Mouse."

Jenkins, Steve. *Cheese Primer*. Paperback: 549 pages with black-and-white photographs and many sidebars. Workman, 1996.

Touted as a "passionate guide" by "America's most opinionated authority," this is the ultimate book for cheese lovers. As New York City's premier cheese monger, Jenkins has designed or revamped the cheese departments of such emporia as Dean & DeLuca, Balducci's, and the Fairway Market. In the beginning he was smuggling raw milk cheeses back from Europe in his luggage; today he is the first American to be awarded France's prestigious Chevalier du Taste-Fromage. Brutally honest or eloquent to the point of poetry, his advice is always readable and reliable, exactly the sort of information you want from your neighborhood cheese man. The only drawback here may be that the book is so thoroughly packed with rare and wondrous-sounding cheeses that only those who live in a neighborhood near one of Jenkins's big-city clients can get full use of it. If that lucky cheese lover is you, the "Ready Reference" section in the back of the book sums up the longer reviews in a concise format; don't hesitate to take it shopping.

Jones, Evan, and Judith Jones. *American Food: The Gastronomic Story.* Hardcover: 516 pages, 450 recipes. Random House, 1981.

Though nearly twenty years have passed since it was published—long enough to justify adding another chapter or two—this second edition of a classic work remains the single best short history of American cookery written. Evan Jones, an historian, food writer, and husband of the famed cookbook editor Judith Jones, tells a good and thorough tale of how American food got to where it is. Lively and detailed, it's a mouthwatering read, one any American cook with aspirations to be taken seriously should undertake. After the two hundred pages of history come three hundred of recipes, produced as a collaboration between the Joneses. Occasional headnotes enlarge the scope of the book, and given the writing skill involved, more would have been welcome.

CONSIDER: Coach House Crab with Prosciutto; Hominy Muffins; Corn Sautéed with Walnuts; Tennessee Country Sausage Stuffing for Turkey; Creole Shrimps; Green Goddess Dressing; Durgin Park Blueberry Cake; Peanut Butter Cookies; and Bananas Baked with Guava Jelly.

Kurlansky, Mark. *Cod: A Biography of the Fish That Changed the World*. Hardcover: 294 pages with 25 black-and-white etchings and photos, 48 recipes. Walker, 1997.

Part history, part biology, and part ecology, this beautifully produced book is of particular interest to any cook who enjoys either fresh cod or salt cod. Kurlansky is a professional journalist and food historian who as a youth worked as a commercial fisherman. By the time you're through with Kurlansky's lively, cogent, and intelligently written volume, you may be torn whether to head for the kitchen or the open seas.

Kurlansky argues that this ideal fish, once so prolific and profitable that it influenced the economic fate of nations, is now verging on extinction. Along the way, you learn everything there is to know about the fishing, preparation, and cooking of the highly edible fish. Some recipes, such as how to make your own Lutefisk, Salted Cod Rounds, and an Icelandic gruel produced from cod bones, are clearly included for their historical or entertainment value. Kurlansky's stylish way with words received the 1998 James Beard Award for food writing.

Lang, George. *Nobody Knows the Truffles I've Seen.* Hardcover: 384 pages with black-and-white archival photographs and drawings by the author, 22 recipes. Alfred A. Knopf, 1998.

"Brilliant" is the word most often applied to legendary restaurateur and storyteller Lang. After reading this remarkable autobiography, you'll agree. At survival, be it in Hungarian forced labor camps during World War II or in Manhattan, in the toughest business imaginable, he has indeed performed with brilliance. This funny, fascinating, and occasionally heartbreaking book is a genuine American success story, except here Horatio Alger was born Gyuri Deutsch, only becoming George Lang upon emigration to the United States. Lang eventually gave up a less-than-promising career as a classical violinist to create some of the world's greatest restaurants, including Café des Artistes in New York and Gundel in Budapest, Hungary. There are priceless anecdotes here (don't miss those about Claudette Colbert's lobster, Colonel Sanders, or Michelangelo's *Pietà*), and recipes, most notable among them the famed Ilona Torte—rich chocolate-walnut layers with a chocolate-espresso frosting.

Mayes, Frances. *Under the Tuscan Sun.* **Hardcover and paperback: 280 pages, over 50 recipes. Chronicle Books and Broadway Books, respectively, 1996 and 1998.**

While the author, a California poet and professor of creative writing, would never describe her memoir as a cookbook, it does contain two chapters of recipes and enough lyrical descriptions of markets, food preparation, and meals to send food lovers everywhere scrambling either to their kitchens or to their travel agents to book a flight to Tuscany. Mayes studied with Simone Beck in France and she's a fine cook and recipe writer, very much in the vein of Elizabeth David, whom she cites more than once and whose form—no ingredient lists, casual but precise descriptions— she follows. The two recipe chapters, "Summer Notes" (Cold Garlic Soup, Risotto with Red Chard, Basil and Lemon Chicken, Hazelnut Gelato) and "Winter Notes" (Wild Mushroom Lasagna, Rabbit with Tomatoes and Balsamic Vinegar, Chestnuts in Red Wine), present recipes that are simple and dependent upon fresh seasonal ingredients, as most good Italian cooking is. If you're tired of cooking, just sit back and enjoy the read; writing doesn't get much better than this.

Naj, Amal. *Peppers: A Story of Hot Pursuits.* **Paperback: 245 pages. Alfred A. Knopf, 1992.**

Lovers of hot food will have to supply their own fiery snacks as they speed through this entertaining but recipe-free read. A tale of personal conversion, the book begins with Naj's childhood in India, where, contrary to everyone else in the family, he abhorred spicy food. It was only later, when he was a college student in Ireland (world head-quarters for mild cuisine), that the insatiable craving for chiles gradually overtook him. The book charts his journey to understand his—and our—compulsion. Ranging from the botany of the potent pods themselves to the reasons we endure their painful pleasure to the quest to breed a more stuffable green chile to the battle over the Tabasco trademark, each step of the journey takes Naj and the reader ever closer to the ultimate chile, the incomparably incendiary habanero, which deservedly has its own chapter. This is a fine and fascinating read for chile lovers and indeed, for anyone interested in man and his relationship to what he eats.

O'Neill, Molly. *A Well-Seasoned Appetite: Recipes for Eating Well with the Seasons, the Senses, and the Soul*. Hardcover: 464 pages, 200 recipes. Viking, 1997.

As the subtitle indicates, O'Neill sets herself an ambitious program with this collection of recipes and essays, yet she mostly succeeds, while keeping the hyperbole to a minimum. Writing about the connection between seasonality at the marketplace and the seasonal hungers that arise within us, she celebrates ingredients that still arrive with the turning of the calendar (morels, soft-shell crabs) and techniques (steaming, barbecuing) that seem geared, however tenuously, to the weather outside. If modern life occasionally rears its necessary head (one summer recipe calls for frozen corn), the point is mostly well made, the essays compelling to read, and the recipes imaginative without being freaky.

CONSIDER: Moroccan Orange, Red Onion, and Black

Olive Salsa; Thai Beef Salad; Smoked Tomato and Chicken Pasta; Flounder Sauté with Asparagus and Crab Vinaigrette; Rack of Lamb with Feta-Garlic Crust; Rabbit Mole; Rosemary-Orange Oven-Dried Tomatoes; Peach Butter; Cranberry-Pear Bread Pudding; Lemon Curd Tart with Candied Almond Topping; and Rich Hazelnut Chocolate Cake.

Reichl, Ruth. *Tender at the Bone: Growing Up at the Table*. Hardcover: 282 pages, 20 recipes. Random House, 1998.

This putative autobiography tells the story of how Reichl grew up to become a sensualist and the restaurant critic of *The New York Times*. It is fashionable, these days, for biographers to hedge their bets, and so Reichl asserts at the beginning of the book that "everything here is true but it may not be entirely factual." Those who have felt for years that her restaurant reviews appeared to be the work of a frustrated screenwriter will not be surprised by this. Rather than split hairs about the truth, it is perhaps better to say this is a funny, moving, and fascinating read about the passage from youth to adulthood, from girl to woman, from the daughter of the Queen of Mold (her mother frequently poisoned guests by serving food long past its prime, or so she says) to the most powerful restaurant critic on the planet. Along the way are such indelible characters as the spoiled rich girl who had never tasted an egg roll and such seminal food-life moments as one's first bite of perfectly ripe Brie. There are recipes and they appear cookable, but seem intended to illustrate a particular story point rather than to actually be prepared.

Rozin, Elizabeth. *Blue Corn and Chocolate.* **Hardcover: 297 pages with black-and-white photographs and archival illustrations, 175 recipes. Alfred A. Knopf, 1992.**

Corn, chocolate, chilies, turkey, potatoes, tomatoes, vanilla, peanuts—the list of foods that originated in the New World before becoming essential everywhere is long and significant. In this book Rozin, a specialist in comparative and historic cuisine, discusses these foods and then illustrates their goodness through recipes historic and modern. This is not a weighty tome, but a book of lively and readable scholarship, which just happens to include a lot of very tasty—and necessarily eclectic—recipes. Early on, Rozin confesses to being "mildly wary" of pinches and sprigs, preferring to season boldly, a philosophy to be heartily endorsed.

CONSIDER: Roast Chicken with Tortilla Stuffing; Corn and Shrimp Fritters Thai Style; Caribbean Seafood Pie in Sweet Potato Crust; Creole Spaghetti Sauce; Hickory Grilled Breast of Turkey; Peanut Beef Kebabs with Spicy Peanut Dipping Sauce; Raspberry Chocolate Pie; Chocolate Chunk Bread Pudding; Hot Fudge Sauce; Praline Brownies; New World Golden Fruit Cake; and Brazil Nut Banana Cake.

Sheraton, Mimi. *From My Mother's Kitchen: Recipes and Reminiscences* **(revised). Hardcover: 321 pages, 200 recipes. HarperCollins, 1991.**

Noted restaurant critic Mimi (Solomon) Sheraton's food memoir of growing up in a Jewish household in 1940s Flatbush, Brooklyn, is a revealing window into a slightly eccentric family, a fascinating city, and a gentler time gone by. The Solomons were the sort of people who ate one meal while planning and discussing the next—fertile ground for a developing food writer. Though her grandfather was a rabbi, Sheraton's mother did not keep a kosher kitchen. This is food from the Jewish-European tradition, liberally mixed with American specialties of the time. Despite her familiarity with the world's finest restaurants, Sheraton has a real feel for simple, homey fare. Fried egg sandwiches, for example, are best on Pepperidge Farm white bread, and "marvelous with champagne, coffee, or beer, in that order."

CONSIDER: Manhattan Clam Chowder; Chicken à la King; Pot-Roasted Brisket of Beef; Glazed Sweet and Sour Stuffed Cabbage; Egg Foo Young; Garlic Dill Pickles; Corned Beef Hash Nests; Rugelach; Passover Almond Macaroons; and Chocolate Layer Cake.

Steingarten, Jeffrey. *The Man Who Ate Everything—and Other Gastronomic Feats, Disputes, and Pleasurable Pursuits*. Paperback: 514 pages, 45 recipes. Vintage, 1998.

Steingarten, formerly a lawyer, now writes regularly on food for a number of publications, chiefly *Vogue*, and is one of the legal profession's great contributions to the writing game. In the course of his monthly investigations into a wide range of foods, collected here, he has apparently come close to eating "everything." While claiming at one point to have no food prejudices, Steingarten then admits to certain food phobias, mostly rated by how long he would have

to be stranded on a desert island, or how hungry his strand-
ing would have to render him before such foods could be
considered edible. This list includes kimchi, dill, sea ur-
chins, falafel, and pretty much the entire cuisine of Greece.
The rest of the food on the planet is fair game, so to speak,
and in these forty or so essays the author eats, analyzes, and
writes very amusingly about everything from the artificial
fat called olestra, to the ultra-tender Japanese beef known
as Wagyu, to the fantastic seafood of Venice, which he enjoyed in the company of Marcella and Victor Hazan. He
goes on diets, goes behind the scenes at barbecue cook-offs,
taste-tests recipes from the back of the box, deep-fries potatoes in horse fat, and reviews the best unpretentious new
bistros of Paris. Steingarten is never less than interesting,
often annoyingly opinionated, and frequently hilarious.

CONSIDER: Olde-Thyme Homemade Ketchup; Salt-
and-Pepper Shrimp; Choucroute Garnie à l'Alsacienne;
Couscous with Fennel Greens; Trader Vic's Mai Tai; Lemon
Granita; and Smith Family White Fruit Cake.

**Thorne, John, with Matt Lewis Thorne. *Outlaw Cook.*
Hardcover: 378 pages with 90 recipes. Farrar Straus
Giroux, 1992.**

John Thorne writes *Simple Food*, a quarterly newsletter
of essays and recipes. In full collaboration with his wife,
Matt Lewis Thorne, also knowledgeable about food, literature, and cookbooks, he enters into meditations on any
number of interesting subjects (and if they weren't interesting to you before, they will be after you've read his

words). This collection is somewhat autobiographical, linking ruminations on everything from artisanal breads to potato pancakes to Chinese noodles to Martha Stewart with seminal moments from his early days as a thoughtful eater. With titles like *The Discovery of Slowness*, *Meatball Metaphysics*, and *On Not Being a Good Cook*, these essays are obviously heading in a different direction from most of today's food writing—outlaw, indeed. Terrific as the Thornes' recipes are, don't cook from this book out of context. In other words, read every word first, then head for the kitchen.

CONSIDER: Welsh Rabbit; Garlic and Walnut Soup with Fresh Goat Cheese; Lamb with Forty Cloves of Garlic; Black Beans and Rice with Ham Hocks and Deviled Eggs Baked in Curry Sauce; Spaghetti with Capers and Black Olives; Oven-Baked Potato and Buttermilk Pancake; Lemon Ice Cream; Raspberry Crumble; and Maple Walnut Pie.

Weaver, William Woys. *Pennsylvania Dutch Country Cooking*. Hardcover: 204 pages with color photographs, 100 recipes. Abbeville, 1993.

The Pennsylvania Dutch are not originally from Holland, of course, but from Germany and Switzerland, particularly the region known as Alsace. Though many settled originally in Pennsylvania, over the years they have spread to Ohio, Virginia, and beyond. Linked by a common language and a cuisine drawn from the land (they are almost exclusively farmers), even today they prepare dishes that are as exotic as the ornate hex symbols painted on their bright red barns. There are identifiable European touches in Pennsylvania Dutch food, but much is also made of Caribbean ingredients like saffron, molasses, and cayenne. Weaver is a noted historian and descendant of these people, and as much as a cookbook, he has written a treatise on a fantastically interesting culture.

CONSIDER: Limburger Dumplings; Smoked Eel Soup with Hominy; Chicken Corn Soup; Braised Pork with Vinegar Cherries; Pheasant Sausage; Chocolate Gingerbread; Apple Butter Pie; and Moravian Sugar Cake.

HarperCollins 365 Ways to Cook Series. Titles include: *365 Ways to Cook Chicken; 365 Ways to Cook Pasta; 365 Quick & Easy Microwave Recipes; 365 Easy Italian Recipes; 365 Quick & Easy One-Dish Meals; 365 Ways to Cook Hamburger; 365 Ways to Cook Fish & Shellfish; 365 Delicious Low-Calorie Recipes; 365 Great Chocolate Desserts; 365 Ways to Wok; 365 Great Cookies & Brownies; 365 Quick & Easy Mexican Recipes; 365 Great Soups & Stews; 365 Snacks, Appetizers, & Hors d'Oeuvres; 365 Ways to Cook Chinese; 365 Great Cakes & Pies; 365 Great 20-Minute Recipes; 365 Ways to Cook Vegetarian; 365 Ways to Cook Eggs; 365 Great Low-Fat Recipes; 365 All-American Classics; 365 More Ways to Cook Chicken; 365 Main-Course Salads.*

For a decade, these hardcover spiral-bound cookbooks (with colorful, washable Kevlar covers) dominated the mass marketplace. About a dozen remain in print, but copies of most are readily available in warehouse-type outlets and through mail order. While they are not glamorous to look at, these practical volumes gained a distinctive reputation for quality and reliability. Each title is written by a different established food authority, and while the books share a common style, the food sensibility of each individual author comes through. Each recipe lists preparation as well as cooking time and the number of servings up front. Recipes were designed to reflect contemporary tastes but respect the modern lack of time. Most are quick and relatively easy, and all use supermarket ingredients. Having sold over 2 million copies, *365 Ways to Cook Chicken* is something of a legend. Its mate—produced ten years later—*365 More Ways to Cook Chicken*, written by Melanie Barnard, is much more up to date. *Mexican* is a cult classic, with an assortment of easy dips, spreads, and snacks that are addicting. *365 Ways to Cook Pasta*, by Marie Simmons, *365 Great One-Dish Meals* by Natalie Haughton, and *365 All-American Classics* by Sarah Reynolds are other stand-outs.

The James McNair Series. Titles (all preceded by the author's name) include *Beans and Grains*; *Beef Cookbook*; *Breakfast* (revised); *Burgers*; *Cheese Cookbook*; *Chicken*; *Cold Pasta*; *Corn Cookbook*; *Custards, Mousses, and Puddings*; *Fish Cookbook*; *Grill Cookbook*; *Pasta Cookbook*; *Pie Cookbook*; *Pizza*; *Potato Cookbook*; *Rice Cookbook*; *Salads*; *Salmon Cookbook*; *Soups, Squash, Stews, and Casseroles*; and *Vegetarian Pizza*; plus *James McNair Cooks Italian* and *James McNair Cooks Southeast Asian*. All except the last two are in paperback; all have color photographs throughout. Chronicle Books.

McNair functions as a packager, not only writing but doing photography for the books in this popular illustrated series, thus ensuring that they most closely reflect his attitude toward the various subjects. Fresh, simple, and stylish, each work is a short but rich trip into dishes we love or ingredients we want (or need) to cook often. Among the most popular books in the series are those on chicken, cold pasta, grilling, pizza, and salmon.

Steven Raichlen's High-Flavor, Low-Fat Series. Titles include *High-Flavor, Low-Fat Cooking; High-Flavor, Low-Fat Italian Cooking; High-Flavor, Low-Fat Chicken; High-Flavor, Low-Fat Pasta; High-Flavor, Low-Fat Vegetarian; High-Flavor, Low-Fat Appetizers;* and *High-Flavor, Low-Fat Desserts.* Hardcover: Various page counts with color photographs, various trim sizes and recipe counts. Viking.

This highly successful series makes utterly clear that the best low-fat cookery comes from writers who are cooks first and calorie-trimmers second. Raichlen's particular skill is to treat low-fat cooking like any other fresh, serious, pleasure-producing cookery, keeping the gimmicks and artificial products to an absolute minimum. All recipes come with nutritional information; as the series has evolved, estimates of preparation time have appeared, and with the Italian book (particularly successful), an ingredient range ("1 to 2 tablespoons olive oil") is given to allow cooks the choice of a little splurge. Good color photos add to the food appeal.

Martha Stewart. While the books that carry Martha Stewart's name as author are not technically a series, she has so many titles in print, we thought this the best place to list the most popular of them.

Titles (of varying length, all with color photographs): *Entertaining* (hardcover and paperback); *Martha Stewart's Hors D'Oeuvres: The Creation and Presentation of Fabulous Finger Foods* (hardcover and paperback); *Martha Stewart's Pies & Tarts* (hardcover and paperback); *Weddings* (hardcover); *Martha Stewart's Menus for Entertaining* (hardcover); *Martha Stewart's Quick Cook* (hardcover and paperback); *Martha Stewart's Heathy Quick Cook* (hardcover); *Martha Stewart's Quick Cook Menus: 52 Meals You Can Make in Under an Hour* (paperback); *The Martha Stewart Cookbook: Collected Recipes for Every Day* (hardcover); and *Martha Stewart's Secrets for Entertaining: A Holiday Feast for Thanksgiving and Other Occasions.*

From her magazine *Martha Stewart Living*, the queen of style regularly turns out "best of" titles in paperback, including: *The Best of Martha Stewart Living; Perfect Gatherings; Desserts; Special Occasions; Christmas with Martha Stewart Living; Decorating for the Holidays; Recipes, Gifts, Decorations, Entertaining Ideas for the Holidays; Good Things; Great Parties; Holidays: Recipes, Gifts, and Decorations—Thanksgiving and Christmas;* and *What to Have for Dinner.*

Martha Stewart was an institution unto herself long before she established the magazine *Martha Stewart Living* and started churning out books as editor. Whatever barbs she may have caught along the way—a few justified, many perhaps poisoned with jealousy—there is no doubt that this woman had much to do with the evolution of style in America. The glorious color photos in *Pies & Tarts*, the clever ideas for presentations in *Hors D'Oeuvres*, the inventiveness and resourcefulness all overlaid with a sheen of impeccable taste, created a new icon of the modern home-maker/cook, light-years above the Betty Crocker ideal.

The Vegetarian Table Series. Titles (all preceded by *The Vegetarian Table*) and authors include: *America* (Deborah Madison); *France* (Georganne Brennan); *Italy* (Julia della Croce); *India* (Yamuna Devi); *Japan* (Victoria Wise); *Mexico* (Victoria Wise); *North Africa* (Kitty Morse); and *Thailand* (Jackie Passmore). Chronicle Books.

This series is as good an argument as any that vegetarian cooking has gone glamorous and mainstream. The publisher has rounded up a solid crowd of food writers and invested a lot of production dollars in a group of hardcover books richly endowed with color photography. Both those countries with a traditional vegetarian culture and those to which the meatless formula has been merely applied are well-served by the imaginative, sometimes authentic, sometimes more fanciful recipes. Vegetarians looking for a creative boost and anyone craving something a little lighter will find plenty of satisfaction here.

The Williams-Sonoma Kitchen Library. Titles (each 108 pages with color photographs) include: *Beans and Rice; Beef; Breads; Breakfasts and Brunches; Cakes, Cupcakes, and Cheesecakes; Chicken; Cookies and Biscotti; Cooking Basics; Fruit Desserts; Gifts from the Kitchen; Grilling;*

Healthy Cooking; Holiday Baking; Holiday Entertaining; Hors d'Oeuvres; Ice Cream and Sorbet; Kids Cooking; Mediterranean Cooking; Mexican Favorites; Muffins and Quick Breads; Outdoor Cooking; Pasta; Pasta Sauces; Pies and Tarts; Pizza; Pork and Lamb; Potatoes; Salads; Shellfish; Soups; Stews; Stir-Fry; Thanksgiving; Vegetarian; and Vegetables. **Time-Life.**

This extensive series, with Williams-Sonoma's founder, Chuck Williams, as general editor, and written by a solid list of (mostly West Coast) food professionals, is as classically stylish and solidly designed as the catalog's products. They're generously illustrated, too, with every recipe getting its own photo. A new series, Williams-Sonoma Lifestyle (same car, new hubcaps), has just been launched, while the Williams-Sonoma Outdoors series, with only two titles thus far (*Picnics and Tailgates* and *Cabin Cooking*), shows promise.

Index

423

INDEX

428

© Pat Roberts

© Adam Chinitz

About the Authors

SUSAN WYLER is the author of four cookbooks, most recently *Simply Stews*. After collaborating with many top food luminaries at *The Pleasures of Cooking* and *Cuisine*, she served for ten years as food editor of *Food & Wine* magazine, where she worked with the country's leading cookbook writers, cooking teachers, and chefs. Throughout her career, she has edited literally tens of thousands of recipes. Wyler resides in New York and rural Pennsylvania, where she houses her antique cookbook collection.

MICHAEL MCLAUGHLIN is the author or coauthor of twenty cookbooks, including *The Silver Palate Cookbook*, inducted in 1992 into the James Beard Foundation's Cookbook Hall of Fame. He is also the cooking and lifestyle book buyer for Cookworks, a gift and gourmet chain with stores in New Mexico, Florida, and Texas. He lives in Santa Fe.